english connection
Am Rainberg 7
5020 Salzburg
+43 662 876210
www.english-connection.at

PASS Cambridge
BEC Preliminary

Student's Book

Second Edition

Ian Wood, Anne Williams *with* Anna Cowper

MULTILINGUAL WORD LISTS ONLINE

Pass Cambridge BEC Preliminary Student's Book Second Edition
Ian Wood, Anne Williams *with* Anna Cowper

Publisher: Jason Mann

Senior Commissioning Editor: John Waterman

Editorial Project Manager: Karen White

Development Editor: Anna Cowper

Content Project Editor: Denise Power

Production Controller: Tom Relf

Marketing and Communications Manager: Michelle Cresswell

Head of Production and Manufacturing: Alissa McWhinnie

Compositor: MPS Limited, a Macmillan Company

Text Design: InPraxis

Cover Design: Maria Papageorgiou

© 2013, National Geographic Learning, a part of Cengage Learning

ALL RIGHTS RESERVED. No part of this work covered by the copyright herein may be reproduced, transmitted, stored or used in any form or by any means graphic, electronic, or mechanical, including but not limited to photocopying, recording, scanning, digitizing, taping, Web distribution, information networks, or information storage and retrieval systems, except as permitted under Section 107 or 108 of the 1976 United States Copyright Act, or applicable copyright law of another jurisdiction, without the prior written permission of the publisher.

> For permission to use material from this text or product, submit all requests online at **www.cengage.com/permissions**
>
> Further permissions questions can be emailed to **permissionrequest@cengage.com**

ISBN: 978-1-133-31320-5

Heinle, Cengage Learning EMEA
Cheriton House, North Way, Andover, Hampshire, SP10 5BE
United Kingdom

Cengage Learning is a leading provider of customised learning solutions with office locations around the globe, including Singapore, the United Kingdom, Australia, Mexico, Brazil and Japan. Locate our local office at **international.cengage.com/region**

Cengage Learning products are represented in Canada by Nelson Education Ltd.

Visit Heinle at **http://elt.heinle.com**
Visit our corporate website at **www.cengage.com**

Photo credits

Tony Watson/Alamy p21, Discpicture/Alamy p33(b), David J. Green – technology/Alamy p60(b), Islemount Images/Alamy p72(m), Jeffrey Blackler/Alamy p72(b), Golden Pixels LLC/Alamy p73(tr), mediacolor's/Alamy p73(br), John Miller/Alamy pp77 and 78, Charles Bowman/Alamy p81(m), Maurice Crooks/Alamy p81(b), allOver photography/Alamy p94(b), hans engbers/Alamy p96(r), Alexey Stiop/Alamy p116; David Lees/Getty p12(t), Fuse/Getty p12(b), Jose Luis Pelaez, Inc/Getty p17(r), AFP/Getty p20, Grant Faint/Getty p24, Terry Vine/Getty p33(t), Tetra Images/Getty p38, David Lees/Getty p53(l), Stockbyte/Gettyp57(bl), Ryan McVay/Getty p62(bm), altrendo travel/Getty p72(t), John Miller/Getty p77(b), DEX IMAGE/Getty p82, Erik Isakson/Getty p84, Sami Sarkis/Getty p94(tl), Plush Studios/DH Kong/Getty p102(r), IMAGEMORE Co.,Ltd./Getty p121, Comstock Images/Getty p132, Ed Pritchard/Getty p135; Jacob Wackerhausen/istockphoto p34(m), ALEAIMAGE/Istockphoto p34(r), Pali Rao/istockphoto p56, Elzbieta Sekowska/istockphoto p57(br), Michal Kram/istockphoto p60(t), Yvan Dubé/istockphoto p62(tl), LdF/istockphoto p62(tml), Ayaaz Rattansi/istockphoto p62(tmr), Skip ODonnell/istockphoto p62(tr), ryan burke/istockphoto p62(bl), Digital Paws Inc./istockphoto p62(bml), Hirlesteanu Constantin-Ciprian/istockphoto p62(br), John Pavel/istockphoto p73(l), Narvikk/istockphoto p78(bl), Lance Bellers/istockphoto p85(r), Muammer Mujdat Uzel/istockphoto p94(tr), Clerkenwell_Images/istockphoto pp104 and 106, Xin Zhu/istockphoto p134; Vladimir Pcholkin/Robert Harding p85(l); FreshPaint/Shutterstock p14(l), Paul Matthew Photography/Shutterstock p14(r), Diego Cervo/Shutterstock p17(l), Monkey Business Images/Shutterstock p34(l), Yuri Arcurs/Shutterstock p37, Tiggy Gallery!/Shutterstock p44(b), Tr3gin/Shutterstock p44(t), Vasiliy Koval/Shutterstock p53(r), Ruslan Ivantsov/Shutterstock p62(bmr), Kristina Postnikova/Shutterstock p73(mr), Fedor Selivanov/Shutterstock p78(bm), oksana.perkins/Shutterstock p81(t), osmera.com/Shutterstock p85(m), Omer N Raja/Shutterstock pp96(l) and 98, Goodluz/Shutterstock pp100 and 102(l), Voronin76/Shutterstock p134, MalDix/Shutterstock p134, Brazhnykov Andriy/Shutterstock p134, Andy Lidstone/Shutterstock p134, ssuaphotos/Shutterstock p136.

Printed in China by RR Donnelley
1 2 3 4 5 6 7 8 9 10 – 17 16 15 14 13 12

Introduction

The Cambridge BEC exam

The **Cambridge Business English Certificate (BEC)** is an international Business English examination which offers a language qualification for learners who use, or will need to use, English for their work. It is available at three levels:

Cambridge BEC Higher
Cambridge BEC Vantage
Cambridge BEC Preliminary

Cambridge BEC Preliminary is a practical examination that focuses on English in business-related situations. The major emphasis is on the development of language skills for work: reading, writing, listening and speaking.

Pass Cambridge BEC Preliminary

The book contains:

- **Introduction** — An introductory unit which gives you information about the examination.

- **Core units** — Twelve double units which cover a wide range of business-related topics.

- **Exam focus units** — Five units, each concentrating on a different aspect of the exam. They provide exam practice tests, plus tips and strategies to help you improve your exam technique.

- **Self-study** — A section in every core unit to provide consolidation coursework and examination practice. In order to prepare for the examination effectively, it is important also to spend study time outside your lessons.

- **Activity sheets** — Pairwork activities and games at the back of the book.

- **Audioscripts** — The content of the audio CDs.

- **Answer key** — Answers to **Self-study.**

- **Essential Vocabulary** — A list of the key vocabulary in each unit.

- **Irregular verb list** — A list of common irregular verbs.

Language development in *Pass Cambridge BEC Preliminary*

- **Grammar**

  Grammar is systematically reviewed throughout the book. However, the review is brief: look out for the **Don't forget!** sections in each unit. If you need to work on basic structures, you may need to supplement the material in this book.

  If you are not sure of basic verb forms, look at the **Irregular verb list** at the back of the book.

- **Functions**

  The book reviews and provides practice to activate basic functional language such as phrases for making requests, asking for permission, making suggestions and arranging an appointment. For Cambridge BEC Preliminary you also need to be able to express such functions in writing.

- **Vocabulary**

  Vocabulary is not tested separately in the examination but is very important. At the back of the book there is a list called **Essential vocabulary**, which lists the key vocabulary for each unit.

  You will probably meet words that you do not know in the Reading and Listening Tests so it is important to have strategies for dealing with difficult words. Unit 3, the **Exam focus: Vocabulary** unit, provides ideas on helping you to guess the meaning of words. It also provides ideas about storing and building your vocabulary.

  The exercises in the **Self-study** sections recycle vocabulary from the units.

- **Reading**

  The book contains a lot of reading practice, using authentic, semi-authentic and examination-style texts. Do not panic if you do not understand every word of a text; sometimes you only need to understand the general idea or one particular part.

  However, you need to read very carefully when answering examination questions; sometimes the most obvious answer on the first reading is not correct and you will change your mind if you read the text again.

- **Listening**

  Listening is also an important skill for the examination and most units contain listening activities. You can find the **Audioscripts** to the audio CDs at the back of the book.

- **Writing**

  In the examination you have to write short notes, emails and memos and also letters and longer memos. The examination expects you to pay attention to the task and the word limit. If you have good spoken English, it does not necessarily mean that you can write well. To be successful, you need training and practice.

- **Speaking**

  Unit 15 helps you to prepare for the Speaking Test. In addition, there are speaking activities in every unit.

Examination preparation in *Pass Cambridge BEC Preliminary*

- **Introduction**

    The **Introduction** presents the content of the examination and focuses on important examination dates. You will also do a quiz to get to know the book and start to think about how to study for the examination.

- **The core units**

    The core units contain general and examination-style activities. For example, multiple-choice and matching are both typical examination-style exercises.

- **Exam focus**

    Five **Exam focus** units in the book give you information about how to succeed in each of the examination tests. They are yellow to help you to identify them.

Unit 3	Exam focus:	Vocabulary	Unit 12	Exam focus:	Listening
Unit 6	Exam focus:	Reading	Unit 15	Exam focus:	Speaking
Unit 9	Exam focus:	Writing			

- **Exam practice**

    The final exercise in the Self-study section of each unit is **Exam practice**. As it is beige, you can see clearly that it is examination practice. The final unit of the book, Unit 18, provides four pages of examination practice.

Contents

Page	Unit	Language	Exam Skills
8	**Introduction**	Getting to know people	Introduction to the exam Studying for Cambridge BEC Preliminary
12	**1a Job descriptions**	Talking about jobs Present simple	Listening Speaking
16	**1b Working conditions**	Talking about working conditions Adverbs of frequency	Reading
20	**2a Company history**	Talking about company history and structure Past simple Prepositions of time	Reading
24	**2b Company activities**	Talking about company activities Connectors of addition and contrast Present continuous	Reading
28	**3 EXAM FOCUS: VOCABULARY**	Vocabulary practice	Successful guessing, storage and building of vocabulary
32	**4a Telephoning**	Telephoning Leaving and taking messages	Listening
36	**4b Internal communication**	Requests and obligation	Writing memos and emails
40	**5a Facts and figures**	Describing trends Adjectives and adverbs	Reading
44	**5b Performance**	Talking about company performance Present perfect and past simple Reasons and consequences	Listening
48	**6 EXAM FOCUS: READING**	Reading Test practice	How to succeed in the Reading Test
52	**7a Product description**	Describing products Dimensions, comparatives and superlatives Question formation	Listening
56	**7b Product development**	Talking about product development Sequencing words Present continuous and *going to*	Reading Listening Writing (describing a process)
60	**8a Business equipment**	Talking about business equipment Giving instructions	Reading Listening
64	**8b Correspondence**	Letter phrases	Letter writing Reading
68	**9 EXAM FOCUS: WRITING**	Writing Test practice	How to succeed in the Writing Test

Activity sheets 132 **Audioscripts** 141 **Answer key** 151

		Language	**Exam Skills**
72	**10a Business hotels**	Talking about hotel facilities Asking for and giving directions	Reading Listening
76	**10b Commuting**	Talking about traffic and transport Making predictions	Reading Listening
80	**11a Arranging a conference**	Talking about conference arrangement Checking and confirming	Reading Listening Letter writing
84	**11b At a conference**	Talking about a conference *before, after, when, until*, etc.	Reading Listening
88	**12 EXAM FOCUS: LISTENING**	Listening Test practice	How to succeed in the Listening Test
92	**13a Production**	Talking about production processes Passive	Listening
96	**13b Quality control**	Talking about quality control Conditional 1 (real) Making suggestions	Listening
100	**14a Direct service providers**	Talking about call centres, insurance and changes in working practices Future possibility/probability	Listening
104	**14b The banking sector**	Talking about banking *-ing*	Reading Listening
108	**15 EXAM FOCUS: SPEAKING**	Speaking Test practice	How to succeed in the Speaking Test
112	**16a Delivery services**	Talking about delivery services Prepositions of time	Reading
116	**16b Trading**	Talking about trading Tense review	Listening Reading Letter writing
120	**17a Recruiting staff**	Talking about recruitment Conditional 2 (hypothetical)	Reading Listening
124	**17b Applying for a job**	Talking about job applications Indirect questions	Reading Listening Letter writing
128	**18 EXAM PRACTICE**	Reading, Writing and Listening Test practice	

Essential vocabulary 158   **Irregular verbs** 162

Introduction

Cambridge Business English Certificate Preliminary

All Cambridge BEC Preliminary candidates receive a statement of results showing their overall grade (Pass with Merit, Pass, Narrow Fail or Fail) and their performance in each of the four papers. Look at the following extract from a sample statement.

Successful candidates also receive a certificate showing their overall grade. Each paper represents 25% of the total mark.

An overview

The following table gives an overview of the different parts of the examination, how long they take and what they involve.

	Test	Length	Contents
1	Reading & Writing	90 minutes	Reading: seven parts Writing: two parts (email, memo or note, formal letter)
2	Listening	40 minutes	four parts Approx. twelve minutes of listening material played twice plus time to transfer answers
3	Speaking	12 minutes	three parts (personal information, short talk and collaborative task) two examiners and two or three candidates

Important Cambridge BEC Preliminary dates

Your teacher will give you some important dates at the start of your course. Write these dates in the boxes below.

Cambridge BEC Preliminary examination

Your teacher will give you the dates of the written papers but can only give you the date of the Speaking Test after your entry has been confirmed by Cambridge.

- PAPER 1 Reading & Writing Test
- PAPER 2 Listening Test
- Speaking Test (to be confirmed)   Between _____ and _____

Entry date

This is the date by which the examination centre must receive your exam entry.

- Entries must be confirmed by

Grades and certificates

Cambridge sends out results approximately seven weeks after the examination. Successful candidates receive their certificates about four weeks after that.

- Results should be available by

Introductions

1 Introduce yourself to the people in your class. Find out the following information from them.

Name ....
Company ....
Position ....
Why is he/she doing Cambridge BEC? ....

Name ....
Company ....
Position ....
Why is he/she doing Cambridge BEC? ....

Name ....
Company ....
Position ....
Why is he/she doing Cambridge BEC? ....

Name ....
Company ....
Position ....
Why is he/she doing Cambridge BEC? ....

2 Now find someone in your class who ...

- has already taken an English examination.
- knows someone who has a Cambridge BEC Preliminary certificate.
- uses English regularly at work.
- has been to the UK or USA on business.
- has an English-speaking colleague.
- reads the same newspaper/magazine as you.
- has the same interests as you.

Studying for Cambridge BEC Preliminary

1 Work in pairs. Look at the diagram below and complete it with ideas for studying for Cambridge BEC Preliminary.

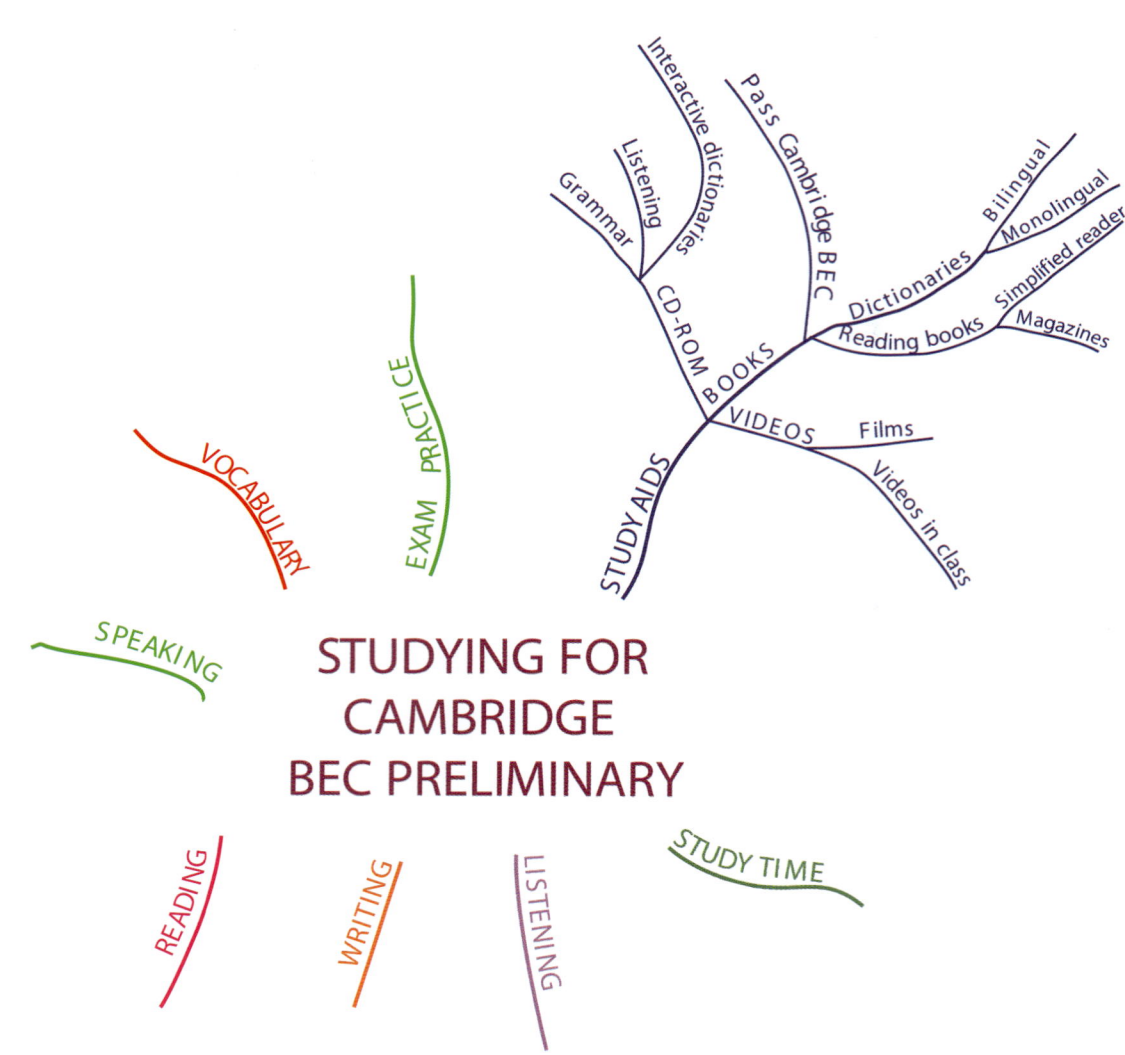

2 Work in pairs. How useful are the following?

		useless	useful	very useful
1	Using a bilingual dictionary	❑	❑	❑
2	Using an English-English dictionary	❑	❑	❑
3	Having the teacher correct all my mistakes	❑	❑	❑
4	Doing pairwork with other students	❑	❑	❑
5	Keeping vocabulary in a list	❑	❑	❑
6	Writing new words on cards	❑	❑	❑
7	Listening to a lot of CDs	❑	❑	❑
8	Reading audioscripts	❑	❑	❑
9	Recording myself to check pronunciation	❑	❑	❑
10	Doing a lot of grammar practice	❑	❑	❑
11	Doing a lot of examination practice	❑	❑	❑
12	Reading through class notes regularly	❑	❑	❑
13	Reading for pleasure	❑	❑	❑
14	Keeping a learner diary	❑	❑	❑

Quiz: Pass Cambridge BEC Preliminary

Where would you find the following in this book? Write the unit or page numbers.

1. Terms and conditions of employment
2. A picture of a very famous car
3. Information about the companies on this page
4. A game where you have to get to work before 9 am
5. Advice on how to write memos
6. Information about the use of the present perfect
7. A list of irregular verbs
8. Information about hotels in Hong Kong
9. A crossword
10. A job advertisement
11. An article about drug development
12. Useful tips for each of the Cambridge BEC Preliminary tests

Unit 1a Job descriptions

Duties

Listening 1 1 Business people from all over the world meet up at a global development seminar in Geneva. Listen to six conversations. Number the business cards in the order the people speak.
(1.01–1.06)

Eisenegger Foods International AG
Industriestrasse 47, PF 2673, 3028 Bern
Telephone: 00 41 (0)7965 7407
Fax: (00 41) 31 32726342
email: hans.kletter@eisenegger.com

HANS KLETTER
Production Manager

VACKPACK

Kurt Bjornson
Human Resources Manager

VACKPACK Sweden AB
Mariagatan 8
BOX 1441108 Göteborg, Sweden

Tel: (00 46) 3167 0409
Cell: (00 46) (0)7540 902 45
email: bjornson.kurt@vackpack.com

Phone: +90 0212 638 57 49
Cell: +90 (0)785619 0436
Fax: +90 0212 633 79 81
Sehit Muhtar Sokak
48/50, 34128 Istanbul
Türkiye
email: gureli@con-sys.com

con-sys
Information Technology CONSULTANCY

Elif Güreli
CONSULTANT

Vincenzi & Lang Financial Services FC
Alameda Santos, 1842 - Cerqueira César,
São Paulo, 01419-000, Brazil

Silvio Ruben
Sales Executive

Direct line: (55 11) 3086-2201
Cell: (55 11) 8562-2051
email: silvio.ruben@v&l.com.br

Lister-Marx Pharmaceuticals

Adrianna Marek
Marketing Manager

ul. Nowogrodzka 72
00-784 Warszawa
Tel: (48 22) 739 85 74
Fax: (48 22) 739 41 38
email: a.marek@lister-marx.pl

Unit 4, 36 Waterman Street
Shoreditch
London E2 8HT
Tel: 0207 445 3891
Mobile: 0777 5006262
email: sunita.nandi@quantum.com

Quantum Accounting Solutions
Sunita Nandi
Accountant

Listening 2 2 Adrianna Marek and Kurt Bjornson talk about their jobs. Before you listen, decide what you think their duties are. Then listen and check your answers.
(1.07–1.08)

3 Listen again and complete the notes below.

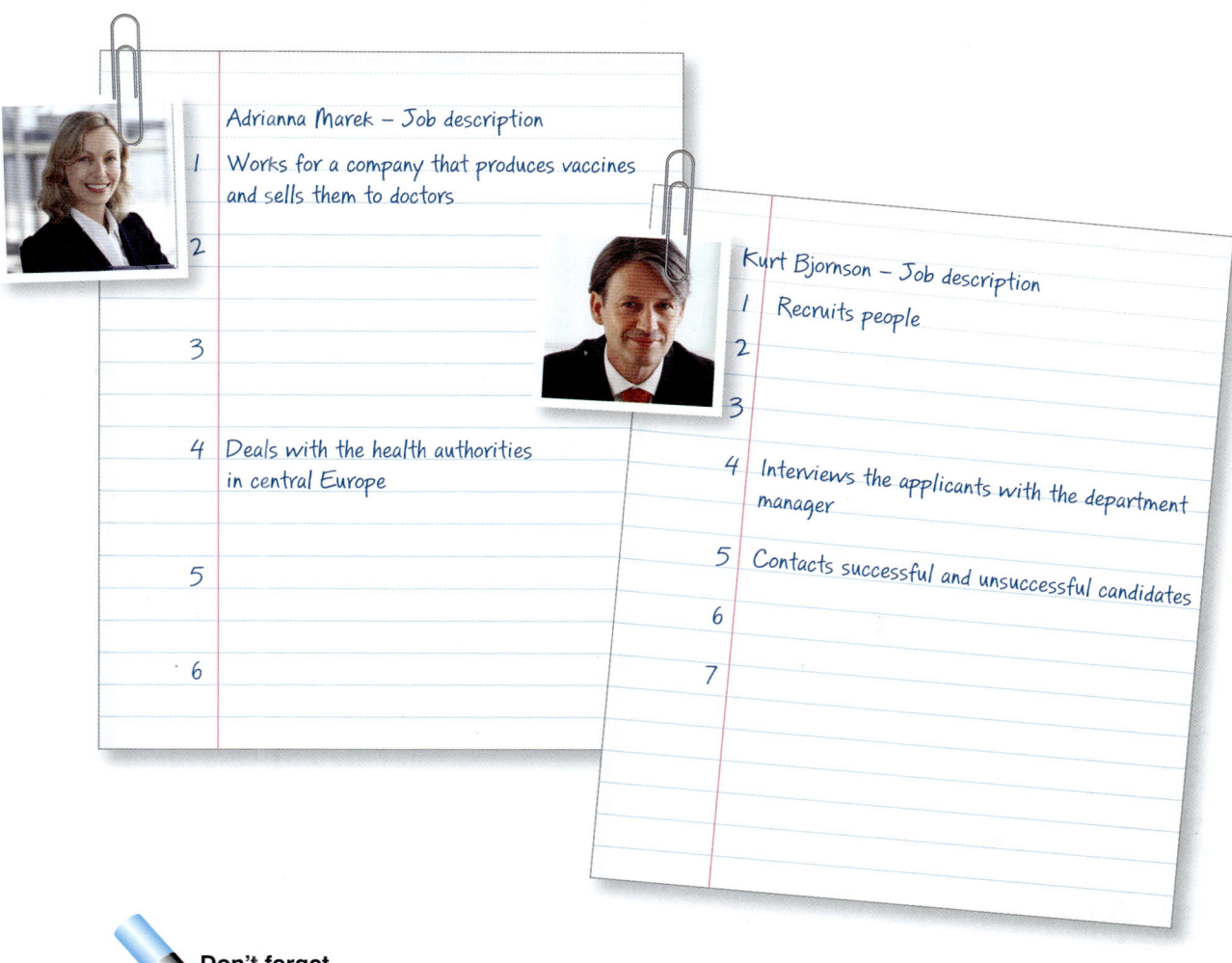

Adrianna Marek – Job description
1 Works for a company that produces vaccines and sells them to doctors
2
3
4 Deals with the health authorities in central Europe
5
6

Kurt Bjornson – Job description
1 Recruits people
2
3
4 Interviews the applicants with the department manager
5 Contacts successful and unsuccessful candidates
6
7

Don't forget

Present simple
- The third person singular form takes -s.
  She works in marketing.
- Negatives are formed with **don't** or **doesn't**.
  *I **don't** work with other people.*
  *He **doesn't** travel on business very often.*
- Questions are formed with **do** or **does**.
  ***Do** you work in an office?*
  ***Does** she work at head office?*

Reading

4 Look at the business cards again. Which person is each question for?

1 How many sales meetings do you attend each month?
2 What advertising do you want to organise for this product?
3 Why do we need to update our current network?
4 When do you want to discuss the balance sheet?
5 Could you give me some advice on investing money?
6 Do you want me to interview the short-listed candidates?
7 How do you plan to increase output at the factory?
8 What kind of after-sales service do you provide for this software?
9 When do you want the successful applicant to start?
10 Do I need to keep a record of the number of packs we produce a day?

Reading tip:
You do not need to know every word to understand the meaning of what you read. Concentrate on the words that you do know!

Speaking

5 Find out about people in your group. Find someone who ...
- organises things. What does he/she organise?
- attends meetings. What sort of meetings does he/she attend?
- deals with different nationalities. Which ones and why?
- provides a service. What service?
- travels a lot. Where to and why?

Talking about your job

Vocabulary

1 Match the sentence halves about Sunita Nandi.

1	I work as	questions people have about their accounts.
2	I'm responsible for	an accountant with Quantum.
3	My job also involves	produce financial reports.
4	I deal with	checking companies' accounts.
5	As part of my job I have to	Shoreditch in East London.
6	I am based in	giving financial advice.

Speaking

2 Work in pairs. You are going to write an article about your partner's job for a business review. Interview your partner about his/her job and take notes. Start your questions with the words below.

Do you ...?	Are you ...?	Where ...?	Who ...?
When ...?	What ...?	Why ...?	How often ...?

Self-study 1a

1 Match the verbs with the nouns. Then look back through the unit and check your answers.

1	give	a problem
2	provide	a record
3	interview	a conference
4	deal with	advice
5	attend	a service
6	keep	a meeting
7	organise	an applicant

(give — advice matched)

2 Think of another noun to go with each verb.

1 give ....
2 provide ....
3 interview ....
4 deal with ....
5 attend ....
6 keep ....
7 organise ....

3 Complete the table below.

Noun	Verb
discussion	discuss
product	....
sale	....
....	organise
interview	....
applicant	....
advertising	....

4 Now complete the following sentences with the correct form of the words from the table above.

1 We're going to _____ ten applicants for the position of accountant.
2 Could you _____ the room for the meeting tomorrow?
3 Are we going to _____ our new sports shoes on the radio or only on television?
4 There were forty _____ for the job but we short-listed only five of them.
5 My company sells financial _____.
6 We had a very interesting _____ about increasing output at the factory.
7 Peter works in the _____ department. His job involves a lot of travelling to visit clients.

5 Exam practice

- Read the profile below from a business networking site.
- Choose the correct word from A, B or C to fill each gap.
- For each question, mark the correct letter A, B or C.

Meet Silvio Ruben

Silvio Ruben works for Vicenzi and Lang Financial Services in São Paulo. He works (1) ..... a sales executive. He (2) ..... with a large number of small and medium-sized businesses in the São Paulo area. He (3) ..... them on the best financial products for their needs.

He is only in (4) ..... office in the morning when he discusses clients (5) ..... the Sales Manager. Then he travels around São Paulo to see his clients. He informs them (6) ..... new products on the market. He keeps a (7) ..... of any changes in the clients' information so that he can offer advice if necessary. He (8) ..... his paperwork and arranges (9) ..... from home or from his car between appointments.

If any members would like (10) ..... advice on insurance or any financial product, please do not (11) ..... to phone Silvio or one of his colleagues (12) ..... (55 11) 3086-2201. They will be happy to help you if they can!

	A	B	C
1	as	like	in
2	organises	provides	deals
3	advise	advises	advised
4	his	her	its
5	with	to	from
6	about	on	to
7	notice	record	reference
8	does	produces	deals
9	meets	meet	meetings
10	an	a	some
11	hesitate	stop	think
12	to	on	under

Unit 1a   15

Working conditions

Comments about work

Reading 1 The staff at Ideas One advertising agency have a comments box. Read the comments and answer the questions.

1. Why is one employee unhappy about taking calls?
2. What kind of supply problems does the office have?
3. What are the problems with pay?
4. What stops people from doing their job efficiently?
5. One person makes a suggestion as well as a comment. What is it?

Staff comments

I usually answer the phone when it rings in our department but the calls are rarely for me. It's really annoying.

Staff comments

We get our bonus annually. I'd prefer it monthly.

Staff comments

We frequently run out of stationery in our office. There doesn't seem to be a sensible sytem for ordering supplies.

Staff comments

We meet weekly to discuss sales performance – that is too often.

Staff comments

The equipment sometimes breaks down when I'm giving a presentation. It's always so embarrassing!

Staff comments

We often work late at the office but we never get overtime pay.

Vocabulary 2 Put the words into the correct order on the line below.

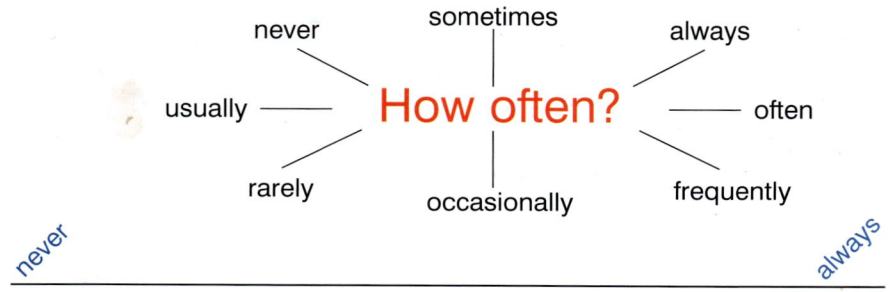

Work in pairs. Compare your order with your partner.

Grammar

3 Look at the comments on the previous page. What do you notice about the position of the adverb in each one? Complete the information below.

Don't forget

Adverbs of frequency: word order
- Words such as **always**, _____, _____, **frequently**, _____, **occasionally, rarely** and _____ usually come before the verb.
- However, these words come _____ the verb **to be**.
- Words such as **hourly, daily,** _____, _____ and _____ come after the verb, often at the end of the sentence.

Speaking

4 Work in pairs. Find something that you both do:

| frequently | occasionally | annually | weekly |

5 Work in pairs. Look at the comments again. How would you deal with them?

Terms and conditions of employment

Vocabulary

1 Match the following words with the correct meaning.

1	shift	work clothes that people wear to keep their own clothes clean
2	salary	rules people have to follow
3	to review	a period of work which starts when another one finishes
4	overalls	money a person receives for work
5	regulations	the person you are directly responsible to
6	overtime	holiday from work
7	leave	to look at something again in order to change it
8	line manager	to give somebody something he/she needs
9	break	extra hours a person works
10	to provide	time to have a rest and possibly something to eat or drink

Working conditions Unit 1b

Reading

2 Read this page of Arteco's conditions of employment. What type of work is it?

TERMS AND CONDITIONS OF EMPLOYMENT

These terms and conditions should be read before you sign your contract.

SALARY

Your starting salary is ...€18,500... This is reviewed annually.

HOURS

The normal hours of work are eight hours a day, Monday to Friday. A shift system is in operation. The shifts are:

A 06:00–14:00   B 14:00–22:00   C 22:00–6:00.

There are three shift groups and the following system is in operation.

Week one:	Group one	Shift A	Group two	Shift B	Group three	Shift C
Week two:	Group one	Shift B	Group two	Shift C	Group three	Shift A
Week three:	Group one	Shift C	Group two	Shift A	Group three	Shift B

For your first shift, week commencing ...08/06..., you will be in Group ...three... and Week ...three... will be in operation. On the first morning report to your line manager ...Karim Chami...

HEALTH AND SAFETY

Please read the safety regulations attached. If you have any questions, contact the Health and Safety Officer, whose name is at the top of the regulations sheet. If you have any health problems, please inform the Senior Nurse, ...Carmen Moratinos... If you cannot work because of illness, please telephone the factory before your shift is due to start.

ANNUAL LEAVE

During your first year of employment you are allowed twenty days' leave. This should be arranged with your line manager.

OVERTIME

If you work more than forty hours a week, you will be paid at the current overtime rate. Your line manager will keep a record of the overtime you work. If you work on public holidays, you will be paid at the current rates. If you prefer, time can be taken instead of extra pay for public holidays and overtime.

CLOTHING

The Supplies Department provides overalls. Inform Supplies of your size two days before you need them. You can also order any other special equipment you need for your job from Supplies.

Choose the correct option to complete the sentences.

1 This employee will start work at
   A 06.00.
   B 14.00.
   C 22.00.

2 Employees consult their line manager about
   A health problems.
   B their annual holidays.
   C a salary review.

3 If employees work on public holidays, the company will give them
   A only extra money.
   B only days off.
   C extra money or days off.

4 The company provides
   A special clothing.
   B no special clothing.
   C a uniform.

Speaking

3 Work in pairs. Discuss your conditions of employment. Use the ideas below.

| hours | overtime | leave | clothing | health and safety |

Which things are the same for you and your partner?

Self-study 1b

1 Write two things at work which:

- you can run out of.
  _____
- you discuss with your line manager.
  _____
- you keep a record of.
  _____
- you find really annoying.
  _____

2 Complete the sentences with the prepositions below. You can use the prepositions more than once.

about	at	in	with	of

1. You should arrange your holiday _____ the line manager.
2. I need to consult my boss _____ that.
3. If you work more than forty hours, you will be paid _____ the current overtime rate.
4. If you want, you can have time off instead _____ overtime pay.
5. We need to keep a record _____ the hours you work every month.
6. A shift system is _____ operation.
7. I don't work late _____ the office very often.
8. We have a lot of problems _____ pay.
9. Please write all meetings _____ the diary.
10. They are having a meeting next week _____ the new sales reps.

3 Choose three of these areas. Write about your own conditions of employment.

| hours | health and safety | |
| clothing | overtime | leave |

4 Exam practice

Questions 1–5

- Read the notice and email.
- Complete the form below.
- Write each word, phrase or number in CAPITAL LETTERS.

To All Line Managers
From Javier Caldera, Accounts

Overtime Payment

Please could you let me have any staff overtime details dating from 30 October to 29 November this quarter as soon as possible so that the salaries can be calculated. Please remember to state if the worker would prefer to be paid or have leave.

Thanks very much.

To: javier.caldera@arteco.com

From: karim.chami@arteco.com

Subject: Overtime payment

Mohammed Baddou, Quality Control Assistant in Production, has done thirty-two hours of overtime this month, i.e. four extra shifts. He would like to have time off.

OVER TIME PAYMENT

Worker's name : (1) ....
Hours worked : (2) ....
Period ending : (3) ....
Pay/Leave : (4) ....
Department : (5) ....

Unit 1b 19

Unit 2a Company history

The history of Volkswagen

Speaking

1 How much do you know about Volkswagen? Work in pairs and do the quiz below.

1 The company was first registered in
   A 1912.   B 1938.   C 1947.

2 The company produced its first car in
   A 1920.   B 1938.   C 1947.

3 The company exported the first Beetle to the USA in
   A 1949.   B 1957.   C 1976.

4 How many Beetles have been produced?
   A 3 million.   B about 12 million.   C over 20 million.

5 The company opened a Chinese joint venture in
   A 1977.   B 1982.   C 1994.

6 Volkswagen merged with Porsche in
   A 2007.   B 2009.   C 2011.

Reading

2 Read about the history of Volkswagen to find the answers to the quiz.

Volkswagen: a history

Ferdinand Porsche started work on the 'people's car' with money he received from the German government in 1934. First of all he travelled to America to learn about car production. Then in 1938 he returned to Germany, founded Volkswagen GmbH and started production with his new American machinery in Wolfsburg, Lower Saxony.

Commercial production stopped during the war and the factory and its 9,000 workers fell into British hands in 1945. After the war the British helped the local economy by ordering 20,000 cars but decided not to take over the company as they did not think it had a future. Instead, Heinrich Nordhoff took over as Managing Director and the Volkswagen success story began.

Within five years annual production went from 20,000 to 230,000 cars and the company founded its first South American subsidiary, Volkswagen do Brasíl SA. In 1949, the first exports to the USA arrived in New York, where they were described as 'beetle-like' and the VW Beetle legend was born. Thirty-two years later, the twenty-millionth Beetle rolled off a Volkswagen de Mexico production line. In 1960, Volkswagen became a public limited company valued at DM600m.

The company continued its globalisation by setting up its own production facilities in Australia (1957), Nigeria (1973) and Japan (1990) while expanding into the USA (1976) and Spain (1986) by buying car manufacturers. The company also set up a joint venture in China (1982). VW moved into central Europe at the end of 1989, where it soon began production in the former East Germany and expanded into the Czech Republic.

Volkswagen always had a close relationship with the Porsche, the sports car manufacturer, and, in 2011, the two companies merged to form one large car-manufacturing group. Today, the Volkswagen group is the biggest motor vehicle manufacturer in Europe and – after Toyota Group and General Motors (which are number one and number two respectively) – the third biggest car manufacturer in the world.

3 Choose the correct option to complete the sentences.

1 Porsche produced the first Volkswagen car
  A ten months after he received government money.
  B three years after he received government money.
  C four years after he received government money.

2 During the war the company
  A stopped producing cars completely.
  B stopped producing cars for sale to the public.
  C continued producing cars as before.

3 The British did not take over the company because
   A they did not think it would survive.
   B they did not have enough money.
   C Heinrich Nordhoff had already bought it.

4 Between 1945 and 1950 production increased
   A every year by 20,000.
   B from 20,000 to 230,000.
   C by 20,000 to 230,000.

5 Volkswagen expanded globally by buying other car companies
   A and forming partnerships.
   B and building its own car plants.
   C and also building new car plants and forming partnerships.

Vocabulary

4 Find words in the text which mean the same as the following.

1 buy more than 51% of a company
2 a company partly, or wholly, owned by another company
3 a company partly, or wholly, owned by shareholders
4 worldwide expansion
5 organising and building a factory
6 two or more companies joined together

Don't forget

Past simple
- All regular past simple verbs end in **-ed**.
  For a list of useful irregular verbs, see the back of this book (page 162).
- Negatives are formed with **didn't**.
  *The British **didn't** think Volkswagen would survive.*
- Questions are formed with **did**.
  *When **did** the company produce its first car?*

Speaking

5 Work in pairs. Find out five things about the history of your partner's company.

Company profile

Vocabulary

1 Match the company descriptions with the definitions.

1 A subsidiary   is owned by shareholders.
2 A public limited company   is at least 51% owned by another company.
3 A parent company   only administers other companies in a group.
4 A wholly-owned subsidiary   has a controlling stake in another company.
5 A holding company   is completely owned by another company.

Speaking

2 Work in pairs. Your teacher will give you some cards. Read about the eight companies in the MNE group and form an organigram of the group structure.

3 Work in pairs. Find out about your partner's company today. Use the ideas below.

| size | turnover | locations | products | markets | subsidiaries |

Self-study 2a

1 Complete the history of the clothing company Gap, Inc. Put the verbs in brackets into the correct past simple form.

It started in San Francisco in 1969 when Donald G. Fisher **(1)** _____ (*try*) to buy a pair of jeans. He **(2)** _____ (*visit*) store after store but only **(3)** _____ (*find*) jeans departments that **(4)** _____ (*be*) disorganised and difficult to shop in. So in August that year Fisher and his wife Doris **(5)** _____ (*decide*) to open a well-organised store that **(6)** _____ (*sell*) only jeans.

The company soon **(7)** _____ (*expand*) rapidly throughout the USA and in 1974, it **(8)** _____ (*begin*) selling its own-label products. Ten years later it **(9)** _____ (*had*) 550 stores and in 1983 it **(10)** _____ (*buy*) Banana Republic, a mail-order business. In 1985, Gap President Mickey Drexler **(11)** _____ (*have*) a bad experience buying clothes for his children so he **(12)** _____ (*set up*) GapKids in 1986. The following year the company **(13)** _____ (*go*) international with a store in London.

Gap grew fast throughout the 1990s and **(14)** _____ (*open*) new stores in Canada, France, Germany, Japan and the UK. The company had to close some stores during the economic crisis of 2008. However, it **(15)** _____ (*continue*) to expand into new markets, such as South America and China.

2 Write the following time expressions in the correct group below.

December	23 July
Friday	2011
10.30	summer
Christmas	Tuesday morning
the weekend	the 1990s

in	at	on
December		

3 Delete the verbs which do not go with the nouns.

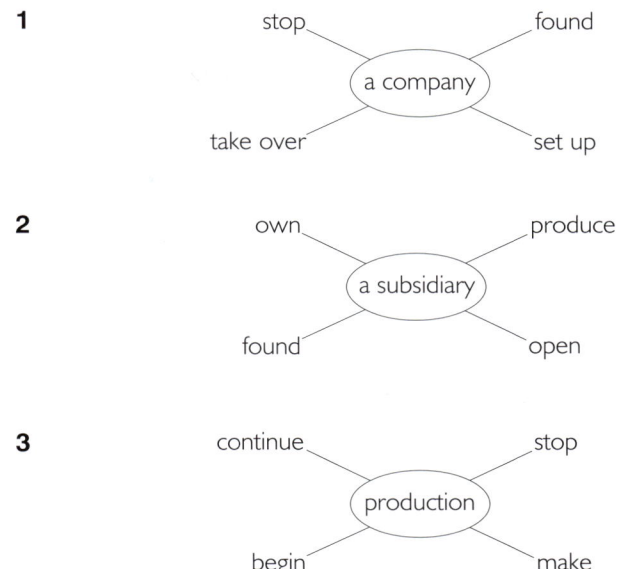

4 Exam practice
- Look at the list of industries A–H below.
- For questions 1–5, decide which industry A–H each person works in.
- For each question, mark the correct letter A–H.
- Do not use any letter more than once.

A	Financial services
B	Manufacturing
C	Telecommunications
D	Leisure
E	Retail
F	Construction
G	Pharmaceutical
H	Publishing

1 We have a chain of supermarkets all over Britain.
2 The company specialises in video-conferencing facilities.
3 We invest our clients' money on the stock market.
4 Our company is involved in major engineering projects.
5 I manage the local sports centre.

5 Exam practice
- Your company has just received new company brochures from the printers.
- Write a note to the Sales Manager:
  * telling her the brochures have arrived
  * saying which department they are in
  * asking her to collect her copies immediately.
- Write 30–40 words.

Unit 2b Company activities

Investing in China and India

Reading 1 Look at the information showing investment by multi-national companies in China. Answer the questions.

Microsoft
- to invest $1bn in research and development in China from 2011 onwards
- is expanding and opening branches in smaller cities, e.g. Jinan, Dalian

Starbucks
- first Starbucks coffee shop in Beijing in 1999
- to open 1,500 stores across China by 2015

Heinz
- to invest $165m by 2014
- is buying a Chinese soy sauce chain with headquarters in Guangzhou

Pepsi
- to invest $2.5bn over next four years
- is building 12–14 new plants in Fujian, Gansu, Henan, Yunnan

Adidas
- to open 500 new stores by 2011
- is expanding its distribution into 2,500 cities in China

Ford
- to invest $490 million on a new plant in Chongqing by 2012

1 Which company is spending money on research in China at the moment?
2 Which companies are opening new stores or outlets?
3 Which Chinese city is receiving lots of investment from a car manufacturer?
4 Which company is increasing its distribution?
5 Which companies are building new plants and production facilities in China?

Grammar **2** When do we use the present simple (*I work*) and present continuous (*I am working*)? Write each description in the correct group at the top of the opposite page.

| general facts | something happening now | routines |
| states | temporary situations | changing situations |

Present simple	Present continuous
general facts	

Don't forget

Stative verbs

We do not use the continuous form to express the following:

opinions (*think, believe*)

senses (*see, hear*)

emotions (*like, love*)

ownership (*own, have*)

! **I think** it's a good idea.   (opinion)
• **I'm thinking** of changing my job.   (process of thinking)

Speaking 3 Work in pairs. Why are companies investing so much in China? Do they invest in India for the same reasons? Which country do you think is more attractive to foreign investors?

The Dragon and the Tiger – China vs India

Reading 1 Put the five extracts below into the correct order to complete the newspaper article.

The Dragon and the Tiger – *China vs. India*

By Carla Umanova

Will the strongest economy of the future be the 'Chinese Dragon' or the 'Indian Tiger'? As China's and India's economies develop, they are attracting lots of foreign investment from around the world. They are *not only* a source of cheap labour and materials, *but also* big markets in themselves for goods and services.

1

It's not only China's manufacturing expertise that attracts many foreign investors to the country. In the cities, people are well educated and workers are generally well organised and efficient, so it's easy to employ local people. *In addition* to cheap labour and resources, China has good transport links, especially by sea. *Moreover*, the government wants to help foreign investors, so there aren't lots of laws that make it difficult for them to start a business.

In India, *however*, the legal system is more complicated and it's more difficult for foreigners to set up new businesses. *On the other hand*, labour is now generally cheaper in India than in China, where workers' wages are increasing as the economy develops. *Furthermore*, many people in India speak English (it's the second official language after Hindi), which makes communication easier.

So, where is the best place for modern companies to invest? *In spite of* the legal problems, some foreign investors find India easier to work in than China because Indian business culture is more like Western business culture. However, *although* capitalism is still quite a new concept for China's communist government, this doesn't seem to have stopped the Chinese from being very successful. Both the Dragon *and* the Tiger seem like excellent investments for the future.

As far as market size is concerned, China is larger than India. With its population of 1.35 billion people, China will soon be the largest market in the world for almost everything. By comparison, India's population is much smaller – only 1 billion. *However*, this is growing at a fast rate and the population is younger. India's economic strength is in service industries, especially IT, *but* China exports its manufactured goods to the whole world.

Company activities Unit 2b 25

2 **Say whether the following sentences are 'Right' or 'Wrong'. If there is not enough information to answer, choose 'Doesn't say'.**

1 Cheap labour is one reason foreign companies are investing in China and India.
   A Right   B Wrong   C Doesn't say

2 China is not an important market for foreign companies.
   A Right   B Wrong   C Doesn't say

3 Labour is more expensive in India - workers' wages are rising.
   A Right   B Wrong   C Doesn't say

4 The Chinese government wants to attract foreign investment.
   A Right   B Wrong   C Doesn't say

5 Communication is a problem for companies who want to invest in India.
   A Right   B Wrong   C Doesn't say

6 The Chinese economy is growing faster than the Indian economy.
   A Right   B Wrong   C Doesn't say

Vocabulary

3 **Look at the words and expressions in *italics* in the text. Write the words in the correct group below.**

Addition	Contrast
and	but

4 **Use appropriate words and expressions from Exercise 3 to connect the ideas below. There are often several possible answers.**

1 workers' pay is lower in India and China / not the only reason companies are investing there
   Workers' pay is lower in India and China, however, that's not the only reason companies are investing there.

2 transport links can be a problem for investors in India / many people speak English
   _____

3 India and China are attractive as new locations for production / they are important markets for services
   _____

4 India's legal system makes it difficult to set up new businesses / labour and materials are cheap
   _____

5 the unfamiliar culture can be a problem for foreign companies / the Chinese government want to encourage foreign investment
   _____

6 India is very strong in service industries, such as call centres / it is a world leader in software development
   _____

Speaking

5 **Work in pairs. Draw a map showing your company's markets. Explain to your partner what is happening in these places at the moment.**

Self-study 2b

1 Complete the sentences with the present continuous form of the verbs below.

| grow   invest   build   develop   earn   modernise |

1 Siemens _____ some new offices in London.
2 We _____ a new product at the moment.
3 Markets in China and India _____ rapidly and are now more attractive to large companies.
4 They _____ the offices this month so it's very hard to concentrate with all the noise.
5 The department _____ a lot of money in new computers at the moment.
6 Most workers _____ more money than before.

2 Put each verb in brackets into the present simple or continuous.

1 They _____ (work) a lot of overtime at the moment.
2 The company usually _____ (spend) a lot on foreign investment.
3 We _____ (think) about moving our IT services to the Philippines.
4 Normally, a software engineer in India _____ (not earn) as much as an IT professional in Europe or the US.
5 They _____ (build) a new car plant in Southern China this year.
6 At the present time, Volkswagen _____ (not develop) any new models for Europe.
7 Brazil is another country where the economy _____ (grow) fast at the moment.
8 Some economists _____ (believe) that the Chinese economy _____ (grow) too quickly.
9 The Indian government _____ (want) to attract new investment, so it _____ (offer) generous tax breaks at the moment.
10 Although wages _____ (increase) in China, it will be a long time before they reach Western levels.

3 Match the names, nationalities and activities. Then write complete sentences.

Aeroflot is a Russian airline.

1	Aeroflot	USA	chocolate manufacturer
2	Nokia	Switzerland	airline
3	Reuters	Russia	food group
4	Timberland	France	software distributor
5	ABN Amro	Finland	bank
6	Tata	Britain	communications company
7	Godiva	India	clothes manufacturer
8	Swatch	Netherlands	press agency
9	Softbank	Belgium	car manufacturer
10	Danone	Japan	watch manufacturer

4 Exam practice

- Read the newspaper article below about Japanese car companies.
- Choose the correct word from A, B or C to fill each gap.
- For each question, mark the correct letter A, B or C.

Japanese car-makers increase European production

Japan's third largest car manufacturer, Honda Motors, has announced plans to build a third model in China. The model, a small car to compete (**1**) ..... GM's Chevrolet Spark, will be produced at its Tianjin plant in northern China. The move will (**2**) ..... the Tianjin plant's output to 250,000 cars a year.

The expansion (**3**) ..... the decision in January by Nissan, Japan's second biggest car-maker, to start production on a new model at (**4**) ..... Zhengzhou plant in central China.

The car-makers' plans come (**5**) ..... a time when Japan's biggest car company, Toyota, is considering (**6**) ..... its third Indian model at a new plant in northern India (**7**) ..... than expanding its present production facilities in Bangalore. Toyota is already looking at a possible location in a (**8**) ..... near the Bangladesh border. The area has a very high rate of unemployment, so generous government (**9**) ..... would be available to the company to create new jobs.

Toyota's strategy is to try to (**10**) ..... it's market share in the Indian market, where sales for all Japanese car-makers have been falling due (**11**) ..... strong competition from local manufacturers, such as Tata and Mahindra. Toyota (**12**) ..... that the plans were still being studied and that a decision would be made early next year.

	A	B	C
1	for	to	with
2	rise	raise	build
3	results	follows	means
4	its	it's	his
5	on	at	in
6	building	build	built
7	other	instead	rather
8	country	land	region
9	grants	fund	profits
10	start	leave	increase
11	to	of	at
12	told	said	spoke

Unit 2b 27

Unit 3

Exam focus: Vocabulary

Vocabulary in the examination

You are not tested directly on vocabulary in the examination. However, you need to be able to deal with words you do not know in the Reading and Listening Tests. You also need to build your vocabulary so that you can read and listen successfully in the examination.

Understanding words

1 During the Cambridge BEC Preliminary examination you will have to guess the meaning of words from their type and the context. Match the following types of words with the examples.

1 verbs — sharp, interesting
2 nouns — buy, produce
3 prepositions   a, the
4 articles   which, that
5 connectors   industry, company
6 adjectives   on, with
7 adverbs   but, although
8 relative pronouns   slowly, soon

What type of word can fill each of the following gaps? Now complete the sentences.

1 There was a _____ rise in the number of unemployed.
2 I spoke to someone _____ the Marketing Department.
3 I expect the orders to arrive _____.
4 Here are the brochures _____ you asked for.
5 Barbara works for _____ same company as me.
6 I like the job _____ the money isn't very good.
7 The company invests a lot of money in _____.

2 Try to guess the meaning of the words in italics from the information in the rest of the sentence.

1 I would like to live in the city centre. Every day I have to *commute* to work and the train can be very slow!
2 The bank offers very cheap *mortgages* for people buying their first house.
3 We're going to *launch* the new product next week with TV advertisements.
4 Would you like me to *staple* all the pages together? Then if you drop them, it won't matter.
5 The company has cut jobs *despite* making large profits last year.
6 We've had a lot of telephone *enquiries* about the new product.
7 You don't need to worry about the expense of a taxi. The hotel has a *courtesy* bus which will take you to the airport whenever you want to go.

Storing new vocabulary

Speaking

1 As you learn new words on your course, it is important to store them effectively. You will need to find these words quickly, add to them and practise them. What are the advantages and disadvantages of storing new words in the following places?

- In your Student's Bookin the unit where you learn them
- On a separate sheet of paper
- In a separate vocabulary book in alphabetical order
- On cards
- On a computer

2 Look at the following ways of storing vocabulary. Which do you use?

Diagrams

Diagrams clearly show relationships that have some kind of hierarchy.

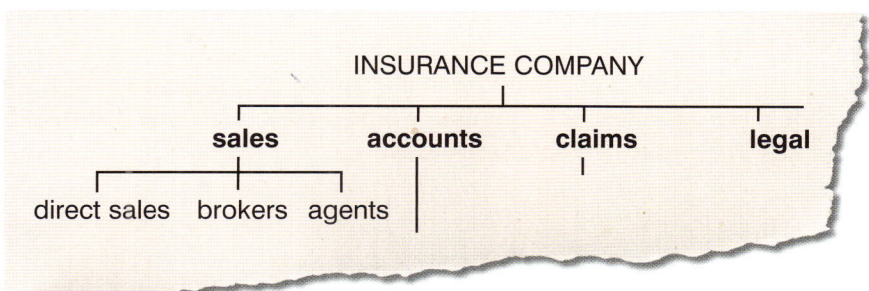

Tables

These are particularly good for showing how words are used together. By using tables, you learn vocabulary in groups rather than single words. Write example sentences to make the table even more effective.

	a meeting	a conference	a training session	an appointment
have	✔	✔	✔	✔
hold	✔	✔	✔	
attend	✔	✔	✔	
arrange	✔	✔	✔	✔

Keywords

You can show which words combine with a keyword. You also need to write example sentences.

Exam focus: Vocabulary — Unit 3

Scales

Groups of words that all measure the same thing can be stored together in order. The scale does not provide context so you need to write example sentences.

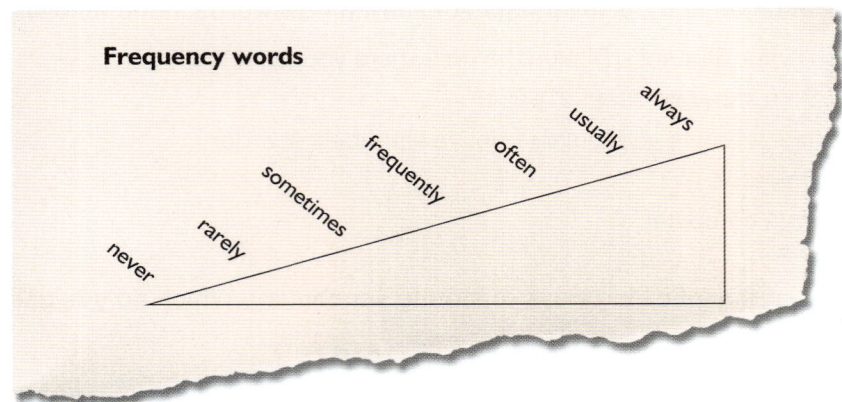

Word fields

If a group of words is connected with the same topic, store them in a word field. Decide what the topic word is and place the other words around it. It does not matter what type of word they are. Then write example sentences.

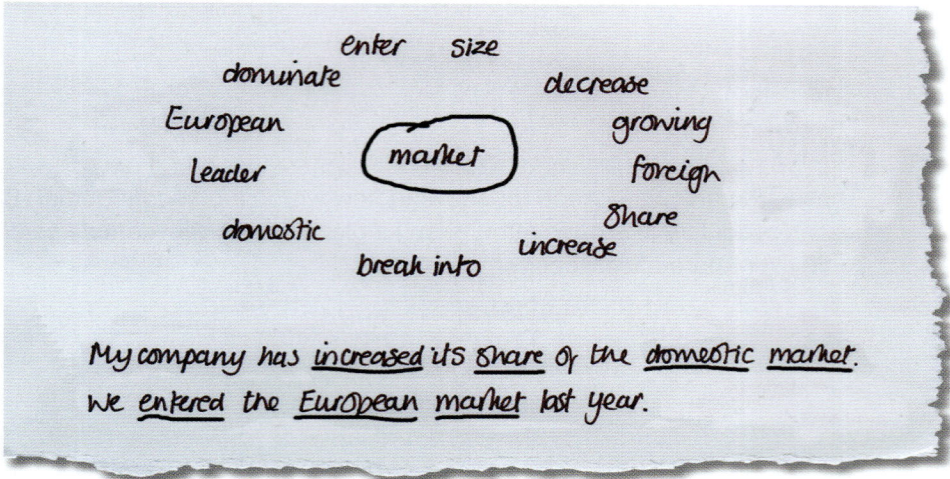

3 Work in pairs. Now look at the groups of words below. What is the best way of storing them?

1 slightly, steadily, sharply, dramatically
2 commission, contract, target, results, figures, executive
3 send a package, send documents, send a shipment, send a letter, post documents, post a letter
4 group, holding company, division, subsidiaries, offices
5 pension, salary, leave, hours, duties
6 a long time ago, recently, currently, in the near future, long term
7 chairman, sales director, regional sales managers, sales executives, agents, head of production, production manager, shift managers
8 merchant bank, bank loan, bank transfer, bank manager, investment bank

Vocabulary cards

1 Cards can be an effective and flexible way of learning vocabulary. You can read them on the way to work if you travel by bus or train. Look at the example below and make cards for the following words. Use a dictionary to help you.

| equipment | steady | available | receipt |

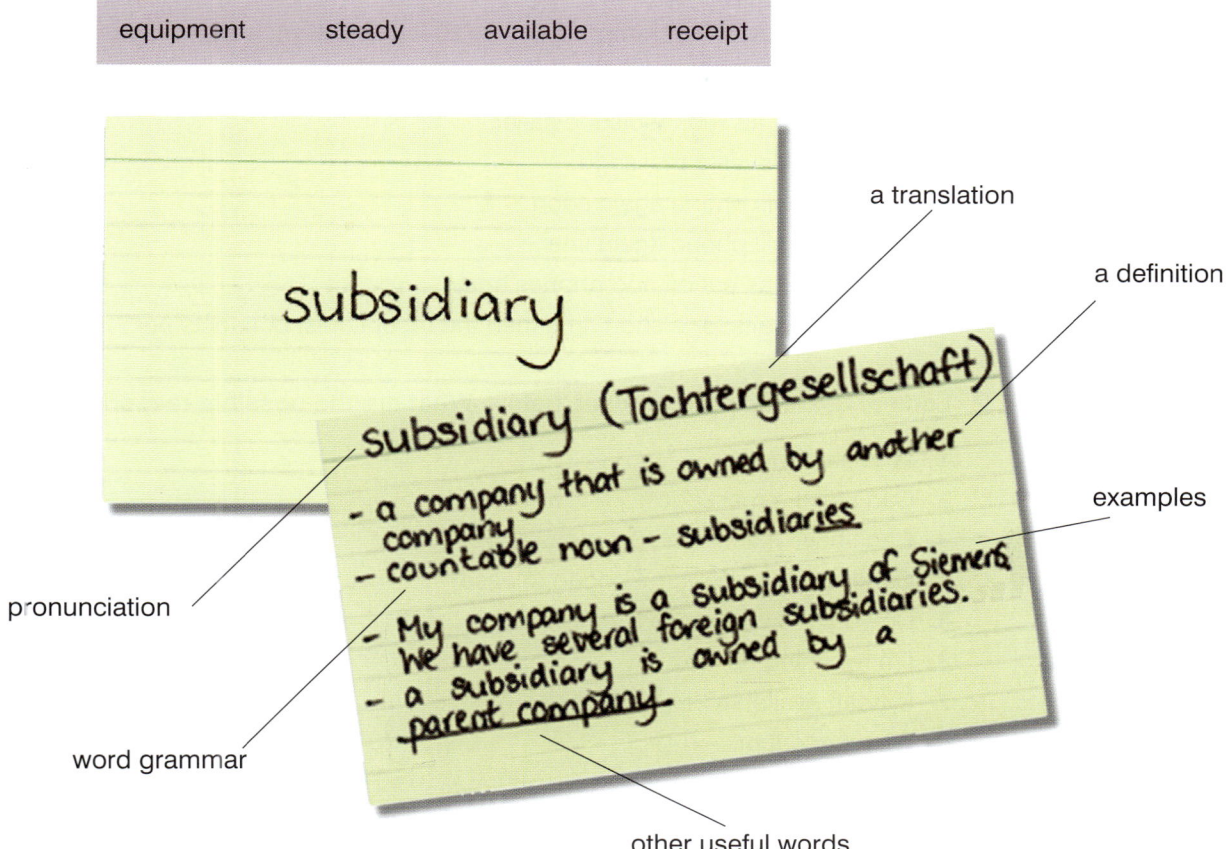

Building your vocabulary

1 Many words have several forms (*produce, production, producer, productive* and *productively*). Look at the following ways of changing the forms of words.

Change	Add	Example
Noun to verb	-ise	globali**se**, standardi**se**
Verb to noun	-tion/sion/ment	confirma**tion**, employ**ment**
Verb to person/company/machine	-er/or	manufactur**er**, invest**or**
Adjective to noun	-ity/ty	probabil**ity**, loyal**ty**
Adjective to adverb	-ly/ily	normal**ly**, stead**ily**
Adjective to its opposite	un-/im/in	**un**interesting, **im**probable
To add the meaning "do again"	re-	**re**launch, **re**write

2 Work in pairs. How many different forms of the words below can you think of? Use a dictionary to check your answers.

| possible | develop | operate | safe |
| general | organise | private | employ |

Now write example sentences for two forms of five of the words.

Exam focus: Vocabulary   Unit 3   31

Telephoning

Getting through

Listening 1  1 Clare MacPherson is a receptionist for Baker and Kerr, a manufacturer of cosmetic products. Clare takes six calls. Listen and number the descriptions of the calls.

    A The receptionist connects the caller.
    B The caller leaves a message.
    C The caller will phone again soon.   1
    D The caller will phone again later.
    E The caller was cut off and phones again.
    F The caller waits for a short time then the receptionist connects her.

2 Look at the telephone phrases below. What are the possible responses?

1 Who's calling?
2 Can I take a message?
3 Can I have extension 184, please?
4 Can I speak to William Grogan, please?
5 Do you know when he'll be free?
6 I'm returning her call.
7 Is Keith available?
8 We were cut off.

Now listen to the conversations again. How do the speakers respond?

Don't forget

Immediate decisions with *will*

We use **will** to express an immediate decision, offer or promise.
(In spoken English **will** becomes 'll.)
I'll call back in about ten minutes.
I'll put you through.

3 Match the telephone phrases below with the responses.

1 I'm afraid the line's busy.   It's OK. I'll phone back later.
2 Can I have extension 236, please?   It's OK. I'll hold.
3 I'm afraid he isn't in the office.   Sorry, I'll try to reconnect you.
4 Could you tell Sarah that I called?   I'll put you through.
5 It's Dave Rogers again for Joe West. We were cut off.   OK. I'll give her your message.

Reading

4 Work in pairs. Look at the maze below. Use the language in the squares to make a telephone conversation. To start, find the correct square. Then follow the conversation to the end (the highlighted green square). Move in any direction except up.

Good morning. Anna Jones speaking.	Good morning. Davis and Sons. Can I help you?	Hello. My name's Pete Brown. Can you put me through to Craig Wilson, please?	Good morning. Walton's. Can I help you?	Yes. Can you put me through to Ellen Symes, please?
Extension 471, please.	Hello Anna. It's Marion again. We were cut off.	I'm afraid he's in a meeting. Can I take a message?	Do you know when he'll be free?	Who's calling, please?
I'm sorry. Could you repeat that?	I'm calling about a problem with the delivery dates.	Could you repeat the name of the company, please?	Alan Murphy from RSL Finance.	He should be available in about an hour.
Hold the line, please. I'll put you through to Sales.	RSL.	The line's busy at the moment. Would you like to hold?	Right. I'll call back later. Thank you.	Did you say 'F' for Freddie or 'S' for Sugar?
Yes, I'll tell him that. Shall I ask him to call you back?	I'm sorry. He won't be free until this afternoon.	OK.	I'm afraid I can't hold. Could you take a message, please?	It's 'S' for Sugar.
Yes, please. I'll be in the office all afternoon.	I'm sorry, the line's still busy. Can I take a message?	Yes, please. Could you tell Ms Symes I'll have to cancel our meeting on Thursday?	Could you repeat your name, please?	Alan Murphy.
Fine. I'll tell her that. Thank you. Bye.	Thank you for your help.	I'll ask her to call you as soon as possible.	**Fine, Mr Murphy. I'll give her your message.**	Yes, I'll tell Ms Lewis it's urgent. Thank you. Bye.

Speaking   5 Work in pairs. Choose two squares from the maze. Make them into a conversation.

Reasons for calling

Listening 2   1 Clare takes another call. Listen and complete the message.

Telephone Message

To: Sharon Thomson
Name of caller: ....
Company: ....

MESSAGE

....
....
....
....
....
....

2 Listen again. Write the phrases that the speakers use …

- to ask for spelling   _____
- to give the reason for calling   _____
- to check what the other speaker said   _____

Speaking   3 Work in pairs. Student A: Look at the Activity sheet on page 132. Student B: Look at the Activity sheet on page 136.

34

Self-study 4a

1. **Look at the telephone conversation below. Put the conversation into the correct order.**

   Receptionist
   - ☐ Thank you, Mr Abraham. I'll give Mr Green the message.
   - ☐ I'm afraid the line's busy. Can I take a message?
   - ☐ You're welcome. Bye.
   - ☐ Good morning, Priory Hotel.
   - ☐ And what's the message, please?
   - ☐ Could you spell your surname, please?
   - ☐ Did you say 7.15 or 7.50?

   Caller
   - ☐ Yes, please. Could you tell him Alan Abraham called?
   - ☐ Thank you very much.
   - ☐ Could you tell him I've booked a table at Marcel's restaurant for 7.15 this evening and I'll meet him there?
   - ☐ A-B-R-A-H-A-M.
   - ☐ Hello, could you put me through to Mr Green in room 105, please?
   - ☐ 7.15. Quarter past seven.

2. **Robin Hobson applies for a job at Baker and Kerr. He telephones to arrange an interview. Read the conversation and complete the gaps.**

Clare	Baker and Kerr. Can I help you?
Caller	Hello. I'd like to speak to Louise Sanderson, please.
Clare	I'm afraid she's out of the office this morning. (1) _____?
Caller	Yes, please. My name's Vic Hobson.
Clare	(2) _____?
Caller	H-O-B-S-O-N.
Clare	(3) _____ B-S or P-S?
Caller	B for book - S. (4) _____ the position as sales executive.
Clare	Yes?
Caller	Ms Sanderson left a message on my voicemail asking if I could come for an interview at 2 pm on 16 May. (5) _____ that I'll be able to come then?
Clare	So, that's 2 o'clock on 16 May.
Caller	That's right.
Clare	Fine. (6) _____.
Caller	Thank you. Bye.

3. **Exam practice**
   - Look at questions 1–5.
   - In each question, which phrase or sentence is correct?
   - For each question, mark the correct answer A, B or C.

   1.
   > Sally phoned. She said your email was deleted by accident. Could you send it again?

   The email
   A did not arrive.
   B was sent to the wrong address.
   C was destroyed.

   2.
   > Ms Haan called. Our order's been delayed due to problems with a supplier.

   The order has
   A arrived late.
   B not arrived yet.
   C been cancelled.

   3.
   > Tuesday, 6 pm
   >
   > Alex
   >
   > Sebastian Pave returned your call from yesterday. He'll try again in the morning.

   Sebastian Pave is going to
   A call Alex tomorrow.
   B wait for Alex to call back later.
   C call Alex again later today.

   4.
   > ParcelExpress CH called to say they'll collect the parcel at 3 o'clock this afternoon.

   The delivery service
   A will pick the parcel up today.
   B intends to deliver the parcel at 3 pm.
   C came for the parcel at 3 pm.

   5.
   > Chris
   >
   > Call Annette Pohl. She's on her way to a meeting so try her mobile on 0486 366 57.

   Annette Pohl is in
   A her office.
   B a meeting.
   C her car.

Unit 4b Internal communication

Memos, notes and notices

Reading 1 Danos is a manufacturer of office furniture and supplies. Look at the examples of the company's internal communication below and find the following information:

- the company's markets
- some of the company's activities
- where it is based.

MEMO

To: All National Sales Managers
From: Henry Wallace
 Sales Director
Date: 10 July 2011

INTERNATIONAL SALES CONFERENCE

Our International Sales Conference will take place from 30 October to 1 November in Rome. I will send details of the hotel later. Please go ahead and book your flight to Rome now. Please note that you need to arrive in Rome by 15.00 on the Friday and stay until 16.30 on the Sunday. It is essential that everybody books an APEX flight or equivalent. Please contact me in case of any difficulty.

Henry
Meeting with Veronique Leboeuf cancelled. Could we meet anyway?
Paula

SALESPERSON OF THE YEAR

The decision for Salesperson of the Year has been almost impossible as there have been so many excellent performances. However, because of her work in turning round a long-term fall in sales, the prize goes to:

Paula Viadotti
(Madrid office)

Congratulations to Paula, who wins a holiday in Florida.

Sue,
Can't find name or tel no. of customer who phoned about new seating range. If you've got it, could you give it to me ASAP?

Thanks
Mike

From: Sarah Longman
To: Managers
Subject: Cost Sheets
Sent: 15 May 2011 | 15:22

All managers must send their cost sheets for the third quarter to Accounts by the following dates:

For August: Thursday 23 July
For September: Thursday 21 August
For October: Tuesday 23 September

NB It is ESSENTIAL that you meet these deadlines.

Sarah Longman
Accounts Manager

2 Answer the questions below.

1 When is the next International Sales Conference?
2 What is the prize for Salesperson of the Year?
3 When do cost sheets for August have to arrive at Accounts?
4 Who is the Head of the Sales Department?
5 Who is meeting on 14 July?
6 What has Mike lost?

3 Read the communications on the opposite page again. What are the differences between memos, notes and notices?

Functions

4 Look at the communications again. Find phrases to express requests and obligation/necessity. Put them in the groups below.

Requests	Obligation/necessity
please (send ...)	*you need to (arrive ...)*

Speaking

5 Work in pairs. How many emails does your partner receive on average per day? How much time does he/she spend writing and answering emails?

Writing memos

Listening 1   1.13

1 Sarah Longman calls Henry Wallace to talk about expenses. Listen and take notes.

Don't forget

> **Writing memos**
>
> It is not necessary to use very formal language when writing memos. We often make requests with simple forms such as **Please ...** and **Could you ...?**
>
> **Please** *inform*   *the secretary by 24 November.*
> **Could you** *please inform?*

Writing

2 Now use your notes to write the email Henry needs to send his salespeople.

Writing emails

Speaking 1 Work in pairs. Say the email and website addresses below. Use the following words to help you.

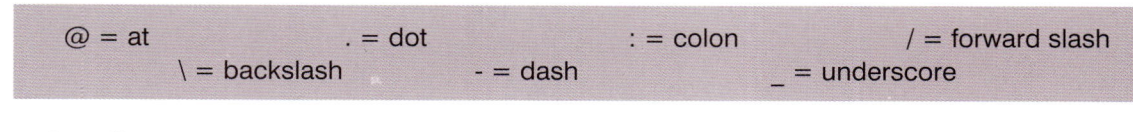

| @ = at | . = dot | : = colon | / = forward slash |
| \ = backslash | - = dash | _ = underscore | |

1 http://www.ikea.com
2 morgan_i_t@zig-zag.de
3 www.thebritishmuseum.ac.uk/
4 c_jones\71@dfe.org.nz

2 Now take turns in saying and writing down other email and website addresses.

Writing 3 Emails are often quite short and contain contractions and other characteristics of spoken English. Look at the email and Henry's note below and use them to write an email from Henry to Sue. Write 30–40 words.

Writing tip: When you write emails always think about your relationship with the person you are writing to.

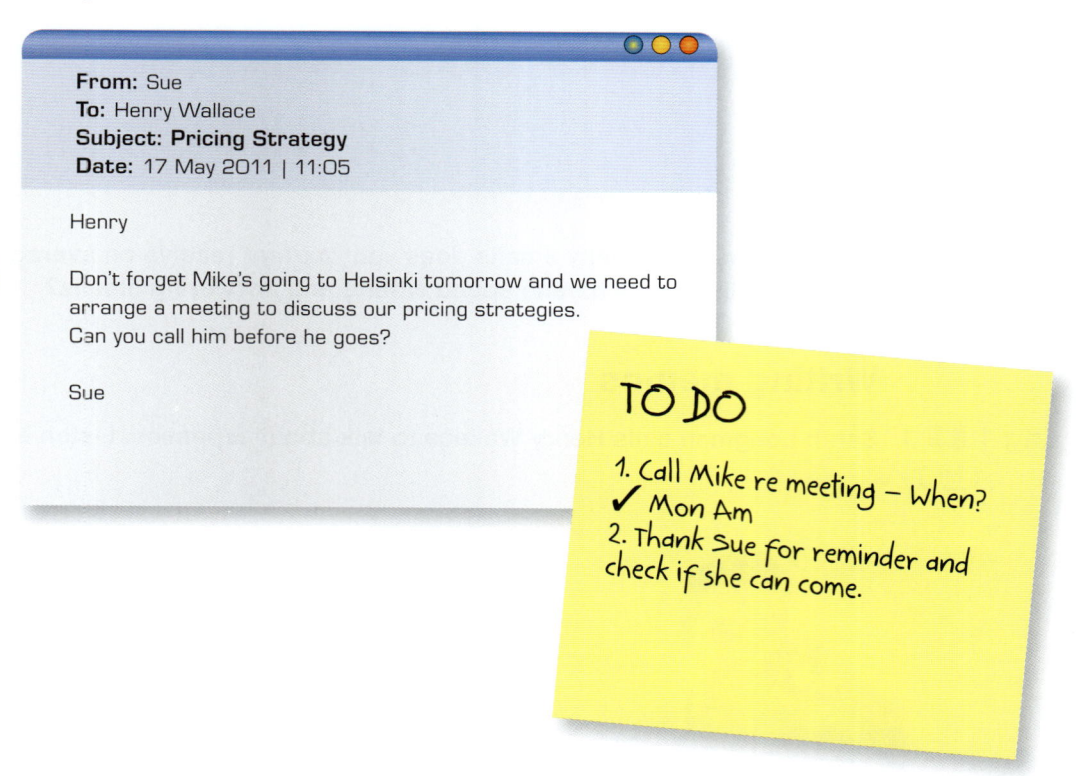

From: Sue
To: Henry Wallace
Subject: Pricing Strategy
Date: 17 May 2011 | 11:05

Henry

Don't forget Mike's going to Helsinki tomorrow and we need to arrange a meeting to discuss our pricing strategies.
Can you call him before he goes?

Sue

TO DO
1. Call Mike re meeting – When? ✓ Mon Am
2. Thank Sue for reminder and check if she can come.

Listening 2 1.7 4 Monica Sanchez receives a phone call from Evan Chang, the Head of Human Resources. Listen and take notes. Then write an email for Monica to send to Steve Cooper.

Self-study 4b

1. **Look at the memo below from Evan Chang to all Training Officers. Rewrite the information as an email from Evan to Monica Sanchez. Write 30–40 words.**

To:	All Training Officers
From:	Evan Chang Human Resources Manager
Date:	14 January 2012

   There will be a meeting on Tuesday 21 January to discuss the training schedule. Please prepare your proposals by 18 January and make sure that everyone has a copy in advance.

   Thank you

To:	m.sanchez@danos.com
From:	e.chang@danos.com
Subject:	Training schedule

   Dear Monica

   _____
   _____
   _____
   _____
   _____

   Eva

2. **Use the note and diary page below to write a memo for the staff noticeboard in the Marketing Department. Write 30–40 words.**

   Alex

   Could you organise a meeting on Tuesday with all the Marketing Department to discuss our new brochure and then send a memo to inform them about it?

   Look at my desk diary for the best time. We'll hold the meeting in the boardroom and I think it'll take about an hour.

   Thanks

   Tuesday 8 June
   09.00 Meeting with Paul Rossi
         9.30–10.30
   10.00 _____
   11.00 _____
   12.00 Lunch with Dieter Lang
         12–1.30
   13.00 _____

   MEMO

   To: Marketing Dept
   From:

   _____
   _____
   _____
   _____
   _____
   _____
   _____

3. **Exam practice**

   - Elizabeth Sharp is going to be the new Human Resources Manager at your company.
   - She is going to visit your office to learn more about the company.
   - Write an email to all staff:
     * explaining who she is
     * saying when she will be in the office
     * asking staff to introduce themselves to her.
   - Write 30–40 words.

   To: All staff
   From:

Unit 4b 39

Unit 5a — Facts and figures

An annual report

Reading 1 Look at the extracts from the Annual Report of UK-based video-games developers Kobra Arts. Are the sentences on the opposite page 'Right' or 'Wrong'? If there is not enough information to answer, choose 'Doesn't say'.

Chairman's Statement

Last year saw both the continued development of trends within the industry and some unexpected results. Domestic sales in the UK continued to grow, but could be overtaken by USA sales next year. As in 2009, sales in the USA rose sharply with the successful release of American versions of best-selling games like *Virtual Ninja* and *Law and Order* for PlayStation 3 and Xbox 360. However, the European market fell slightly at the beginning of the year due to the global economic crisis, but then remained steady.

Sports titles increased their domination of sales of new games in 2010 with the football game *Football Maniacs* selling over 800,000 units in World Cup year. We plan to further develop our range of sports simulation games over the next five years.

The company also enjoyed a sharp rise in sales of educational products. Our new range of interactive multimedia products, *SupaSchool*, launched in late 2009, is now a top-selling brand. Further *SupaSchool* titles to be launched this year should ensure continued growth in this market.

Sales figures for 2010 show very clearly the changing face of the company's activities. 70% of Kobra's revenue now comes from action and simulation games developed primarily for portable games consoles. In order to maintain our profile in this highly competitive market, the company will have to expand by increasing its range of new games and reducing its development times.

Moreover, the company faces new challenges in distribution. Online superstores now account for almost 40% of the sales of our computer games. They offer a narrow product range, based on top-selling titles, at extremely competitive prices which eat into profit margins. There is also a strong second-hand market. Gamers are buying and selling their old games online and this may be affecting sales of our most established games.

David Matthews

David Matthews, Chairman

Annual Report 2010

2010 distribution

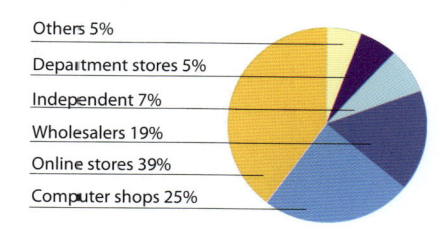

- Others 5%
- Department stores 5%
- Independent 7%
- Wholesalers 19%
- Online stores 39%
- Computer shops 25%

Top selling Kobra Arts titles 2010

Title	Units
Football Maniacs	850,000
Sports Pro 500	796,000
Golf Go!	460,000
Law & Order II	348,000
Virtual Ninja	239,000
Hero City	122,000

Sales per platform as %

- PlayStation 3 — 42%
- Xbox 360 — 28%
- PCs — 24%
- Sega Genesis — 6%

1   Online superstores sell more Kobra products than computer shops.
    A Right   B Wrong   C Doesn't say
2   PCs are the most widely-used platform for Kobra games.
    A Right   B Wrong   C Doesn't say
3   Sales increased sharply in the company's home market last year.
    A Right   B Wrong   C Doesn't say
4   *Football Maniacs* sold more copies in South Africa than Britain.
    A Right   B Wrong   C Doesn't say
5   The company is developing its range of multimedia educational software.
    A Right   B Wrong   C Doesn't say
6   In future the company will have to produce new games more quickly.
    A Right   B Wrong   C Doesn't say
7   Online superstores sell a wide range of computer games.
    A Right   B Wrong   C Doesn't say

Speaking 2 Work in pairs. What will be in the Chairman's Statement in the next Annual Report of your partner's company?

Describing graphs

Reading 1 Read the sentences below about Kobra's performance. Write a letter from the diagrams next to each sentence.

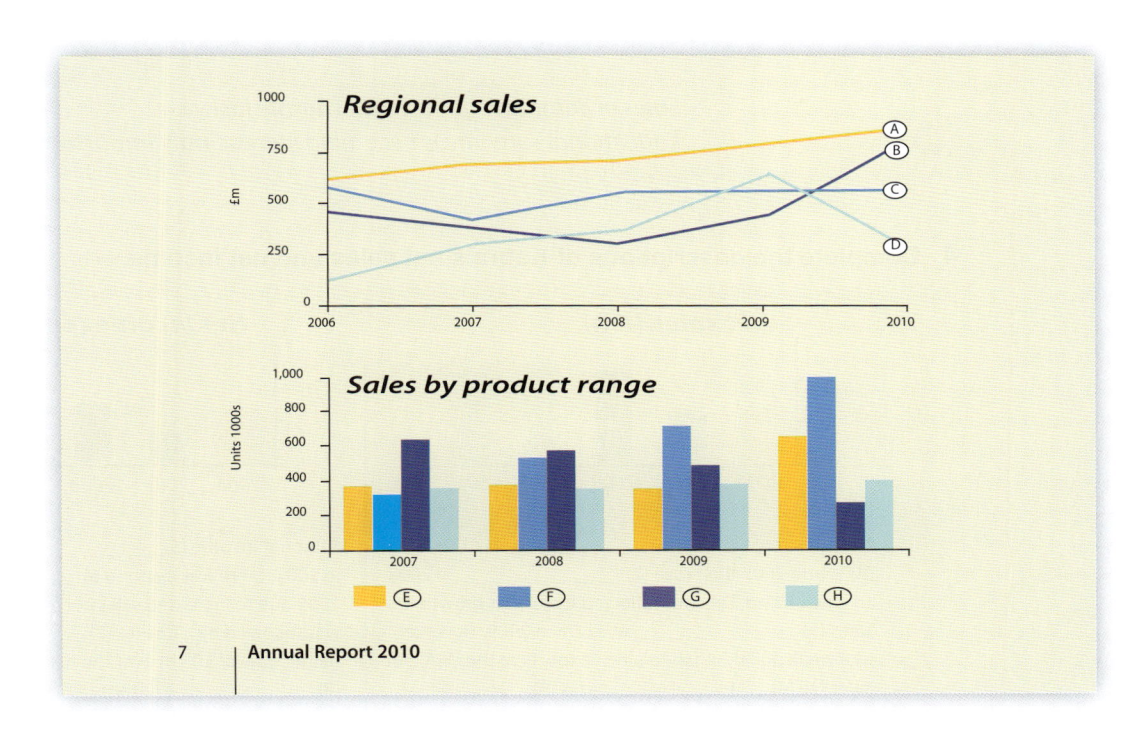

1 After a fall in 2007, sales in Asia recovered and then levelled off.   C
2 There was very strong growth in sales of computer games from 2007 to 2010.
3 Sales in Britain improved steadily throughout the period from 2005 to 2008.
4 Sales in the USA fell slightly in 2007 and 2008 before a strong recovery in 2009, followed by a sharp rise in 2010.
5 Sales of educational software remained steady until 2009 but increased sharply in 2010.
6 There was a steady decrease in sales of office software from 2007 to 2010.
7 Sales in continental Europe grew from 2006, peaked in 2009 and then dropped sharply.
8 Sales of communications software remained steady throughout the period.

Vocabulary

2 Complete the table below.

Verb		Noun
Infinitive	Past simple	
fall	fell	a fall
drop	....	....
....	....	a decrease
increase	....	....
rise	....	....
....	....	growth
improve	....	....
....	recovered	....
peak	....	....

Grammar

3 Look back at the adjectives and adverbs in the unit. Complete the information below.

Don't forget

Adjectives and adverbs
- Adjectives give information about _____.
  *There was a **sharp rise** in sales of computer games.*
- Adverbs give information about _____ or _____.
  *Sales of computer games **rose sharply** last year.*
  *Educational software is becoming **increasingly important**.*

4 Complete the descriptions of Kobra's net sales and net income.

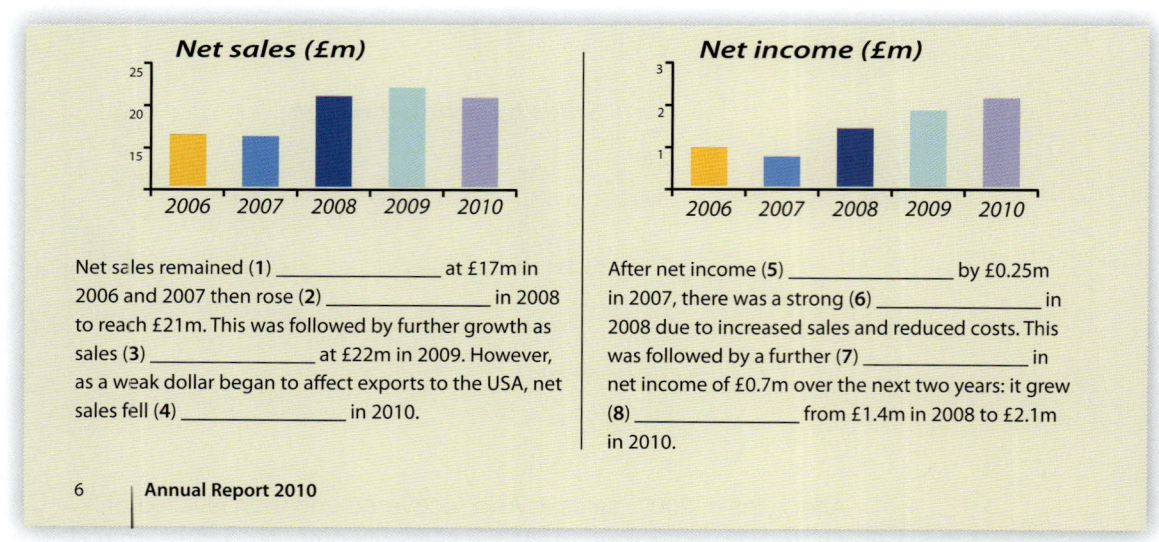

Net sales (£m)

Net income (£m)

Net sales remained (1) _____ at £17m in 2006 and 2007 then rose (2) _____ in 2008 to reach £21m. This was followed by further growth as sales (3) _____ at £22m in 2009. However, as a weak dollar began to affect exports to the USA, net sales fell (4) _____ in 2010.

After net income (5) _____ by £0.25m in 2007, there was a strong (6) _____ in 2008 due to increased sales and reduced costs. This was followed by a further (7) _____ in net income of £0.7m over the next two years: it grew (8) _____ from £1.4m in 2008 to £2.1m in 2010.

6 | Annual Report 2010

5 Underline the prepositions in Exercise 4. Then complete the following sentences.

Operating costs
£12m
£10m

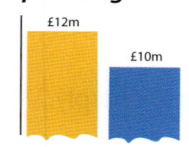

1 There was a fall _____ operating costs.
2 Operating costs fell _____ £12m _____ £10m.
3 Operating costs fell _____ £2m.
4 There was a fall _____ £2m.

Speaking

6 Work in pairs. Student A: Look at the Activity sheets on pages 132–133. Student B: Look at the Activity sheets on pages 136–137.

Self-study 5a

1 **Use the words below to label the diagrams.**

| peak | remain steady | fall |
| rise | level off | recover |

A — (falling)
B — (fall then rise)
C — (rise)
D — (steady)
E — (steady then fall)
F — (rise then fall)

2 **Complete the sentences with one of the following prepositions.**

| in | at | by | from | of |

1 Last year there was a drop _____ net sales _____ 9%.
2 Market share increased _____ 3%, up to 8%.
3 Net sales peaked _____ £22m in 2007.
4 European sales went _____ £4.2m to £3.0m.
5 Sales levelled off _____ £5m in 2008.
6 Costs rose _____ £3.3m. This was a rise _____ 10%.
7 Office software sales fell _____ 10% in 2007.
8 A strong pound meant a fall _____ exports in 2008.

3 **Match the following words.**

1 retail   brand
2 product   chain
3 net   income
4 top-selling   report
5 annual   launch

4 **Write a short description of the graph below.**

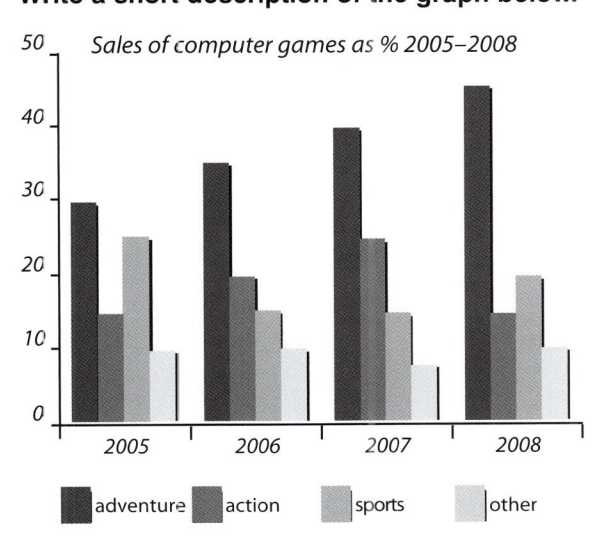

Sales of computer games as % 2005–2008

(bar chart: adventure, action, sports, other; years 2005, 2006, 2007, 2008)

5 **Exam practice**

- Look at the charts below. They show the orders for eight different companies over three years.
- Which company does each sentence 1–5 describe?
- For each sentence mark the correct letter A–H.
- Do not use any letter more than once.

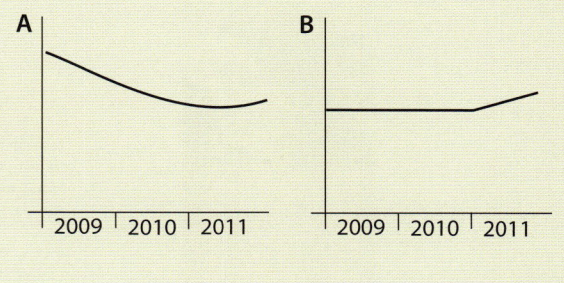

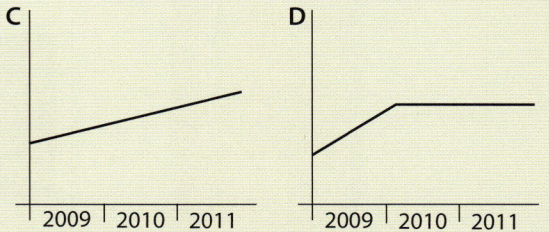

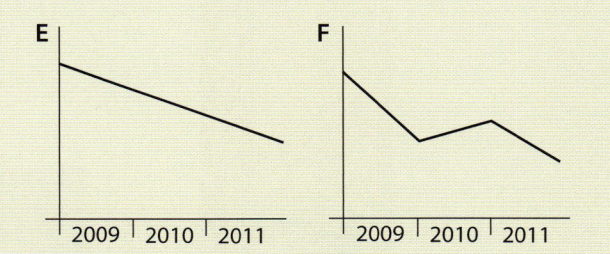

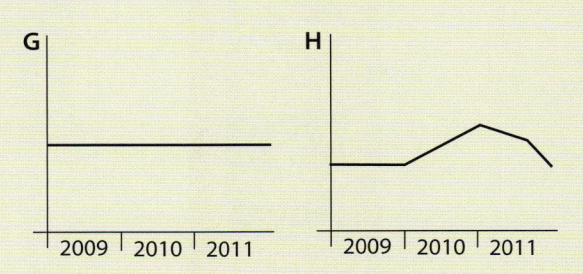

(Charts A–H with years 2009, 2010, 2011)

1 After a sharp drop in 2009, orders recovered for twelve months and then fell again in 2011.
2 Orders rose sharply in 2010 but peaked at the end of the year and then fell back to their 2009 levels.
3 Orders remained steady between 2009 and 2011.
4 The order books showed strong growth throughout the three year period.
5 After decreasing steadily for two years, orders finally levelled off and began a recovery in 2011.

Unit 5a 43

Unit 5b

Performance

Measuring performance

Listening 1 1.18

1 Railwork West is one of twenty-eight private rail companies operating in Britain. The company's Communications Manager, Shelley Cohen, makes a presentation to possible investors. Listen and complete the information below.

> "Transcons is transforming the Railwork West network and bringing it into the 21st century."
>
> Shelley Cohen
> Communications Manager

Transcon bought Railwork West in 2007 after a difficult period for the company, following its privatisation ten years earlier. However, after a period of investment and rationalization, the figures below show changes in the performance of Railwork West over the last four years.

Fig 3. Annual growth in passenger revenue

Fig 4. Reliability and punctuality

Railwork West   page 8

2 Listen again and answer the questions.

1. When did Railwork West become a private company?
2. What is the name of its parent company?
3. How did the company increase revenues in 2008/09?
4. Why have some rail companies been in the newspapers recently?
5. Why has Shelley not given the punctuality figure for 2010?

Grammar

3 Look at the audioscript on page 142. Find an example of each of the following:

- an action at an unfinished or indefinite time

  _____

- a situation that started in the past and is still continuing

  _____

- an action that happened at a definite time in the past

  _____

- a change that affects the present situation

  _____

Now write descriptions in the correct groups below.

Present perfect	Past simple
unfinished or indefinite time	

Don't forget

For and *since*
- **For** is used with periods of time such as days, months and years.
  *I've worked here **for** three months now.*
- **Since** is used with points in time such as **Monday, July, 2009**.
  *We've lived here **since** 2007.*

4 Match the sentence halves about Railwork West.

1 Railwork West has been a private company — the last two years.
2 The Conaxus Group had — since 1997.
3 Transcon bought the company — so far this year.
4 Reliability improved steadily — lots of problems.
5 Revenue has increased sharply over — between 2006 and 2008.
6 The company has not published any figures — in 2007.

Speaking

5 Find people in your group who have done the things below.
Then ask three follow-up questions. Find someone who has ...

- been to a conference this year.
- changed jobs this year.
- worked in a foreign country.
- done some kind of training this year.
- been promoted in the last five years.

Speaking tip:
To keep a conversation going, follow up all yes/no questions with more open questions (when? why? how? etc.).

Explaining results

Listening 2 1 Shelley Cohen finishes her presentation and the investors ask her questions. Listen and complete the notes below.
[1.19]

> **Railwork West**
>
> Punctuality in 2009?
>
> Investment plans?
>
> Profits in the future?

2 Listen again and choose the correct option to complete the sentences.

1 The railway track that Railwork West uses belongs to
   A the company.
   B another private company.
   C the Government.

2 The company is spending £9m in order to
   A improve the condition of the track.
   B build new stations and improve punctuality.
   C improve customer service and reliability.

3 The company's biggest costs are paying
   A other companies for the track and trains.
   B the Government so it can operate services.
   C for new stations and facilities.

> **Don't forget**
>
> **Reasons and consequences**
> - We can talk about reasons with the following:
>   Reliability fell **because of/due to** problems with the track.
>   **That's why** we're improving our service.
> - We can talk about consequences with the following:
>   Our costs are fixed **so** we have to increase passenger volumes.
>   There will be less financial support. **Therefore**, we have to increase revenue.
>   The investment will **lead to/result in** better customer service.

Speaking 3 Work in pairs. Write five results or consequences that have happened in your company on a piece of paper. Give the paper to your partner. Find out the reasons for the results and changes.

Self-study 5b

1 **Re-arrange the words to make presentation phrases.**

1 you'll / the / notice
   You'll notice the ...

2 I'd / at / with / a / like / begin / look / to
   _____

3 can / as / see / you
   _____

4 the / clearly / shows / graph
   _____

5 I'd / at / like / to / you / look
   _____

6 I'd / to / your / like / to / draw / attention
   _____

2 **Complete the presentation. Put the verbs in brackets into the present perfect or past simple.**

Good afternoon everyone. Welcome to the presentation of the company's half year sales results. As you can see, this year (1) _____ (*be*) very successful so far and the company (2) _____ (*already/achieve*) many of its targets for the year. Our sales people (3) _____ (*work*) very hard and the department (4) _____ (*perform*) very well. The success is especially pleasing when you think back to the problems we (5) _____ (*have*) last summer. Sales (6) _____ (*be*) down by 10% and things (7) _____ (*not/look*) good at all. We (8) _____ (*make*) some difficult decisions last year, which a lot of people (9) _____ (*not/be*) happy with. However, since then we're happy to say that performance (10) _____ (*improve*) sharply.

3 **Write sentences linking the following ideas.**

1 the £9m investment → better customer service
   The £9m investment led to better customer service.

2 new trains → more reliable service
   _____

3 the number of delays increased → track problems
   _____

4 we can't raise prices → we have to increase volumes
   _____

5 customer satisfaction has improved → better facilities
   _____

6 reduced ticket prices → an increase in passenger volumes
   _____

4 **Exam practice**

- Look at the graphs below. They show a comparison of the quarterly sales figures for 2009 and 2010 for eight different companies A–H.
- Which company does each sentence 1–5 describe?
- For each sentence, mark the correct letter A–H.
- Do not use any letter more than once.

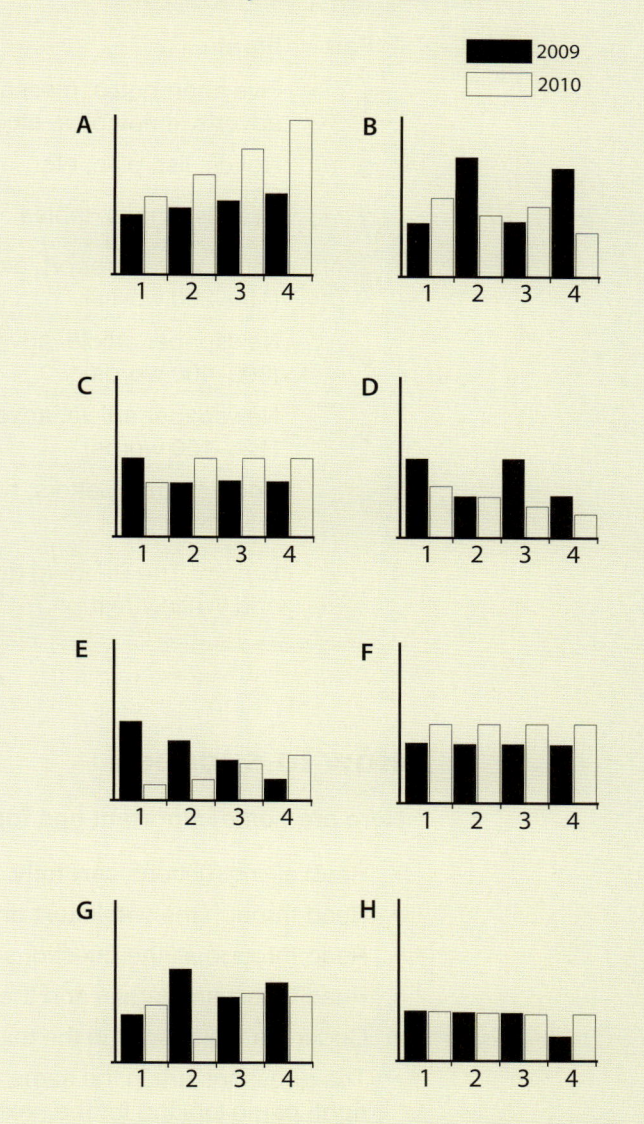

1 Sales fluctuated dramatically in 2009, whereas 2010 saw a steady decline in sales.

2 Sales rose steadily throughout the two-year period, but the increase was more dramatic in 2010.

3 Although sales in 2009 reached a peak in the second quarter, this was the worst period for sales in 2010.

4 Sales remained steady for most of the two-year period despite a sudden fall at the end of 2009.

5 Sales started slowly in 2010, before recovering in the third quarter, in contrast to the previous year when sales declined steadily.

Unit 6 — Exam focus: Reading

The Reading Test

The Cambridge BEC Preliminary Reading Test has seven questions. Questions 1–5 test general comprehension. Question 6 specifically tests your knowledge of grammar and vocabulary. Question 7 tests your ability to process information accurately.

Part	Input	Task
1	Five short notes, messages, adverts, timetables, etc.	Multiple-choice
2	Notice, list, plan, etc.	Matching
3	Graphs, charts, tables	Matching
4	Letter, advert, report, etc. (150–200 words)	Right, Wrong, Doesn't say
5	Newspaper article, advert, etc. (300–400 words)	Multiple-choice
6	Newspaper article, advert, etc. (125–150 words)	Multiple-choice gap-filling
7	Short memos, letters, notices, adverts, etc.	Form-filling, note completion

Length: The Reading questions should take about 60 minutes of the Reading and Writing Test.

How to succeed

Here are some important tips for doing the Reading Test.

- Read all instructions **carefully.**
- Read through the whole text once before looking at the questions.
- Read through all the questions before answering Question 1.
- Read Question 1 again and then look quickly through the text for the answer.
- Underline the answer in the text – it will make checking quicker.
- The questions are in the same order as the answers. If you are confident that an answer is right, begin looking for the next answer from that point in the text, not from the beginning.
- Leave difficult questions and return to them later if you have time.
- Only write **one** answer for each question.
- **Never** leave a question unanswered. If you are running out of time or have no idea, guess.
- Use any time you have left to check your answers.

Exam practice

PART ONE

Reading tips
1 Read all three options before answering.
2 Be careful of negative forms.

Questions 1–5

- Look at questions 1–5.
- In each question, which phrase or sentence is correct?
- For each question, mark the correct letter A, B or C.

1
> I am sorry but the parts will not be available until 25 January.

The parts can be delivered
A immediately.
B before 25 January.
C after 25 January.

2
> Mr Ranson called while you were on the phone – he'll try again this afternoon.

Mr Ranson
A promised to call back.
B left a message.
C was put through.

3
> Congratulations to Vanessa Clark on her promotion to Brand Manager.

Vanessa Clark works in
A production.
B marketing.
C finance.

4
> Sales were good but distribution problems led to a slight drop in profits.

The company had problems with
A producing enough goods.
B delivering enough goods.
C selling enough goods.

5
> ❑ Tick if you wish to make an immediate purchase

You have to tell the company if you want
A to buy the product.
B more information.
C a product demonstration.

PART TWO

Reading tips
1 Read **all** the information before answering.
2 Do the easy questions quickly and then see which possible answers are left.

Questions 6–10

- Look at the list below. It shows the contents of a company's Annual Report.
- Decide in which part of the report (A–H) you would find the information (6–10).
- For each question, mark the correct letter (A–H).

Stella Group Plc

Annual Report

A Chairman's Statement
B National Sales Reports
C Review of Subsidiaries
D Changes in Key Personnel
E Group Organigram
F Auditor's Report
G Profit and Loss Account
H Balance Sheet

---

6 A statement of the company's income and expenses.

7 The names of new executives and board members.

8 A look at the performance of smaller companies that Stella owns.

9 A list of what the company owns and owes.

10 A statement by the company that checked the financial reports.

Exam practice

PART THREE

Reading tips
1 Look at the graphs and try to predict vocabulary describing direction (*rise*, *fall*) and the strength of movement (*steadily*, *sharply*).
2 Read **all** the sentences before answering.
3 Be careful of words such as *but*, *despite*, etc.

Questions 11–15

- Look at the graphs below. They show unemployment in eight different regions compared to the national average.
- Which region does each sentence 11–15 describe?
- For each sentence mark the correct letter A–H.
- Do not use any letter more than once.

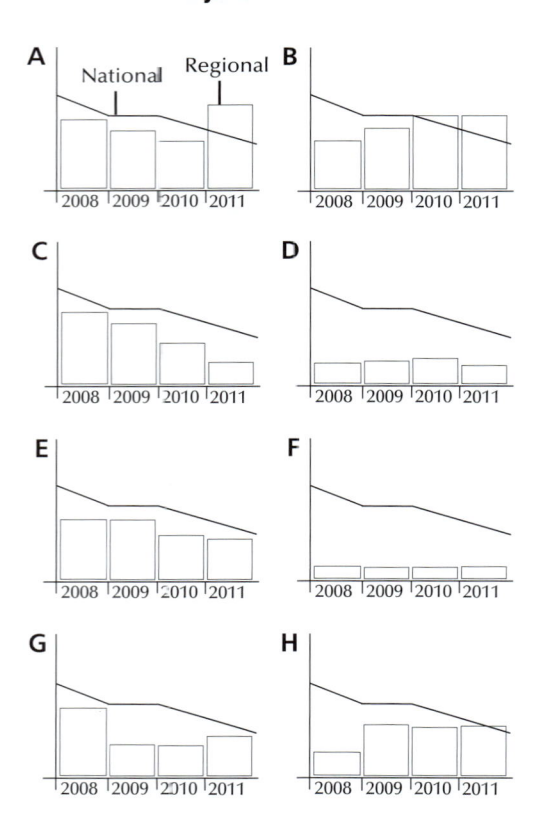

A (National, Regional) 2008 2009 2010 2011
B 2008 2009 2010 2011
C 2008 2009 2010 2011
D 2008 2009 2010 2011
E 2008 2009 2010 2011
F 2008 2009 2010 2011
G 2008 2009 2010 2011
H 2008 2009 2010 2011

11 After an initial fall, unemployment figures remained steady before showing a slight increase, in contrast to the national situation.
12 Unemployment fell steadily throughout the period and remained below the national average.
13 Despite a drop in the national average, the rate of unemployment remained steady for two years before falling in 2010.
14 Although there was a fall in the national average, unemployment in this region rose sharply at the end of the period.
15 After rising steadily, unemployment finally began to reflect the national situation and decreased.

PART FIVE

Reading tips
1 Read through **all** the text first.
2 Read **all** questions before answering.
3 Begin with question **16** and work through the text.
4 **Never** leave a question unanswered.
5 When you have finished, check **all** your answers.

Questions 16–21

- Read the Chairman's Statement below and answer questions 16–21 on the opposite page.

Chairman's Statement

Despite the appearance of a new competitor on the market the company continued to grow and increase its market share throughout 2010. Partly in response to this new threat but, more importantly, as part of a strategy for growth, several key decisions were taken this year. The most significant new developments included a range of vitamin rich children's drinks and low calorie diet drinks, which both proved very popular.

The company is still best known for its range of refreshing fruit drinks and, not surprisingly, these were our biggest sellers once more. There were two new additions to the range last year, *Squish!* and *Liquid Sunshine*, both of which have a distinctive Caribbean flavour. The first sales figures suggest that our expensive TV advertising campaign was very successful and that these products will soon be as popular as the rest of the fruit drinks range.

Growth in the keep-fit and health markets meant our energy drinks did well in 2010. Sales of one brand, *Booster!*, were second only to fruit drinks in April. The strength of this particular market also explains the success of our new diet drinks.

There were, however, big differences in the performance of our older products. The company's oldest product, mineral water, continued to enjoy a healthy share of a very profitable mass market. It seems our customers are still happy to stay with the brand despite the increasing number of competitors' products. Unfortunately, the same cannot be said of our *Ice-T* and *Chocomania* drinks. Sales showed an initial increase in the summer after both products were launched but customers soon bought other brands and total annual sales for both product ranges were disappointing.

The company also said goodbye to its own brand of cola, launched in 2008. After two unsuccessful years of trying to break into the huge cola market, 2010 looked like being another poor year. The company finally accepted that it had made a wrong decision and stopped production in September of that year.

Exam practice

Questions 16–21

- **For questions 16–21, choose the correct answer.**
- **For each question, mark the correct letter A, B or C.**

16 What was the main reason the company decided to launch its new product ranges?
 A It faced increased competition.
 B It wanted to enter new markets.
 C It initiated a policy of expansion.

17 The new fruit drinks cost a lot of money to
 A develop.
 B produce.
 C launch.

18 The best selling drinks in April were
 A energy drinks.
 B fruit drinks.
 C diet drinks.

19 The company's brand of mineral water has a
 A small share of a small market.
 B large share of a small market.
 C large share of a large market.

20 Sales for *Ice-T* and *Chocomania*
 A rose and then fell again.
 B increased steadily.
 C were disappointing all year.

21 When did the company stop producing its own brand cola?
 A 1998.
 B 2000.
 C 2002.

PART SIX

Reading tips

1 Read through all the text first.
2 What type of word could fill each gap?
3 Write possible answers in the gaps in pencil on the exam paper. Then look to see if these words are among the answers.
4 Look again at the gaps you are not happy with.
5 **Never** leave a gap unanswered.
6 When you have finished, **read** the complete text.

Questions 22–33

- **Read the newspaper article below about a new alliance in the packaging industry.**
- **Choose the correct word from A, B or C below.**
- **For each question, mark the correct letter A, B or C.**

The Big Number

The country's demand for mobile phones and on-line communication is growing at an increasingly fast rate. In fact, it is growing (22) ..... quickly that our telephone numbering system needs re-organising (23) ..... some major changes will have to (24) ..... made.

These changes, (25) ....., will make the system simpler and easier to use. It is (26) ..... an important task that all the UK telecoms companies are working together to make (27) ..... changes. The changes will (28) ..... only make hundreds of millions of new numbers, but they will (29) ..... bring order and flexibility to the system for years to come.

(30) ..... main changes are due to happen (31) ..... now and the year 2014, which will give you (32) ..... of time to prepare. You will find details of the number changes on our website, (33) ..... you can visit any time at www.numberchange.org or call our freephone helpline on 0808 224 2000.

22	A so	B that	C too
23	A and	B with	C before
24	A been	B be	C being
25	A despite	B however	C although
26	A much	B such	C so
27	A this	B there	C these
28	A if	B not	C but
29	A furthermore	B additionally	C also
30	A The	B Those	C Their
31	A from	B between	C until
32	A plenty	B many	C lot
33	A when	B who	C which

Unit 7a

Product description

Presenting a product

Listening 1 🎧 **1** Robert Saunders, the Sales Manager at Columbine Games, talks about two new
1.20 products. Listen to his presentation. Which products does he talk about? How much do they cost?

2 Listen to the presentation again. The speaker refers to the following things. What is he talking about?

1 General knowledge

2 Size, weight and cost

3 Wood

4 23 × 23 cm

5 300 grammes

6 €14.99

Grammar

3 Write questions for the answers in Exercise 2.

1 What type of game is Mindtwist?
2 _____
3 _____
4 _____
5 _____
6 _____

Speaking

4 Work in pairs. Describe a board game that you like.

Describing a product

Listening 2

1 Robert Saunders talks to Sophie Pwell, a retailer, about some of Columbine's products. Which games is Sophie interested in?

- *Mindtwist*
- *Mindtwist Travel*
- *Collect*

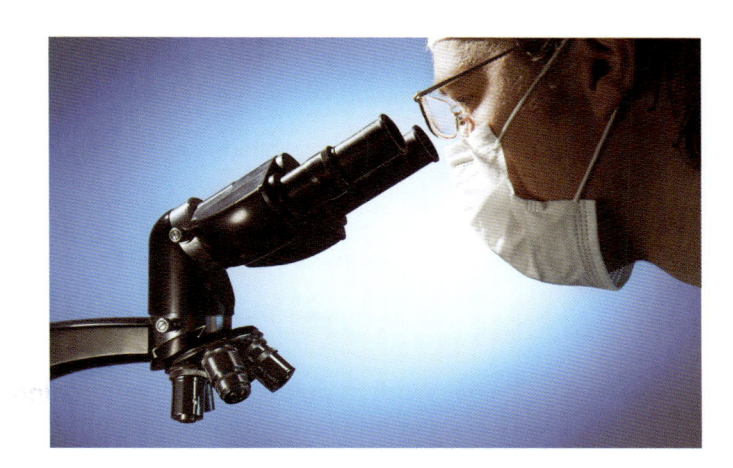

2 Listen again. Answer the questions below.

1 Why is Sophie interested in board games?
2 What is special about *Mindtwist*?
3 How many travel size general knowledge games does Sophie stock?
4 What does Sophie not like about some of Columbine's board games?
5 Why is Sophie not interested in *Collect*?
6 What does Sophie think about the price of *Mindtwist Travel*?
7 How can Sophie get a discount on *Mindtwist*?

Don't forget

Comparison

- The comparative is formed by adding **-er** to short words and **more/less** to longer words.
  This game is smaller than the other games on the market.
  Mindtwist is more interesting than the other games.

- We use **as ... as** with two things that are the same and also with negatives.
  Collect is as new as Mindtwist.
  It isn't as big as the other game.

- The superlative of short words is formed with **-est**. With longer words we add **the most/the least**.

  These games are the latest in Columbine's range.
  This is the least interesting of the games.

  ! good – better – the best
    bad – worse – the worst

3 Correct the information about Columbine games in the sentences below.

1 Sophie is selling ~~fewer~~ *more* board games than before.
2 *Mindtwist Travel* is ~~heavier than~~ *not as heavy as* the standard game.
3 The instructions on Columbine games have become more difficult than before.
4 *Collect* is the biggest of the products that Robert shows Sophie.
5 Sophie's customers will be more interested in *Collect* than *Mindtwist*.
6 *Mindtwist Travel* costs the same as the standard version.

Speaking

4 Work in pairs. Think of something you have both bought. Make a list of the points you considered when you bought it. Discuss the importance of the points and put them in order. Then prepare to report back to the rest of the group.

Product name ....

Points considered	Me	My partner
price		

Self-study 7a

1 Complete the groups of words below. Then use one word from each group to form a question.

1 weight — *heavy* / light

How heavy is the travel version of the game?

2 length — long / ....

3 cost — expensive / ....

4 .... — big / small

5 difficulty — difficult / ....

2 Look at the catalogue information comparing three display panels and complete the sentences below.

Portable Folding Display Panels

Product name	Number of panels	Weight	Dimensions	Price
Standard	4 panels	10 kilos	1.8 × 1.2m	$498.00
Super	6 panels	15 kilos	1.8 × 1.6m	$545.00
Extra	8 panels	17 kilos	1.8 × 2.4m	$660.00

1 The Extra has more *panels than the Super.*

2 The Extra is two kilos _____

3 The Extra is more _____

4 The Super is not as _____

5 The Standard is the least _____

6 The Standard is the _____

3 Write about a product you have recently bought.
- Where was it made?
- What is it made of?
- Why did you buy it instead of a similar product?

4 Exam practice
- Read the text below about a smartphone.
- Choose the correct word from A, B or C to fill each gap.

The Lotus Century X Smartphone

The new Lotus Century X is the (1) ….. addition to our extensive (2) ….. of mobile technology devices. It is probably the (3) ….. advanced smartphone on the market today. The wide range of cutting-edge (4) ….. includes a four-inch AMOLED display screen, HD video recording, camera phone and many apps. Improved technology means that the screen is now 20% brighter, the colours are 20% (5) ….. and the screen is 80% (6) ….. responsive to the touch. (7) ….. the 1GHZ processor uses (8) ….. power than many other models; as a result the Lotus Century X is one of the (9) ….. smartphones to use. The five megapixel camera is also an HD video recorder and Lotus DNA convergence technology (10) ….. you to take videos and send them to a compatible TV. (11) ….., the Lotus Century X hub technology puts all your social media contacts, such as Facebook, Twitter or LinkedIn into one place, so it really does make your life (12) ….. , both at work and at home.

	A	B	C
1	later	latest	late
2	variety	spread	range
3	most	more	much
4	things	features	characters
5	clear	clearest	clearer
6	many	more	most
7	Furthermore	Extra	Addition
8	least	less	lesser
9	cheaper	cheapest	cheap
10	allows	gives	has
11	However	Finally	Last
12	easier	easy	easiest

Unit 7b Product development

Product testing

Speaking

1 How much do you know about the development of drugs in the pharmaceutical industry in the USA? Work in pairs and do the quiz below.

1. How many years of testing are there before a drug reaches the market?
   A 6–8   B 10–12   C 12–15

2. About how much does it cost to develop a new drug in the USA?
   A less than $4m   B at least $5m   C $11bn

3. What percentage of drugs tested on humans reaches the market?
   A 20%   B 40%   C 60%

4. How many stages of testing on humans are there in the USA?
   A three   B four   C nine

5. How many people, on average, take part in testing drugs?
   A 1,000–5,000   B 5,000–10,000   C 10,000–15,000

6. How long do the authorities take to approve a New Drug Application?
   A six months   B two and a half years   C five years

7. What percentage of turnover do companies invest in research?
   A 15%   B 18%   C 22%

Reading 2

Read the article below to find the answers to the quiz.

Drug development in the USA

The development of new drugs is essential if we are to stop the spread of diseases. However, it takes an average of twelve to fifteen years to develop a drug and it costs a company from $500m to over $1bn. Only five out of every 5,000 drugs that start the testing process are tested on humans. Only one in five of those actually reaches the market.

There are four stages of testing a new drug. First of all, a company carries out tests for about two and a half years in the laboratory and on animals. This is to show how the drug works against a particular disease and to show its level of safety. Then testing on humans can begin.

The first stage of human testing tests the safety of the drug on fewer than one hundred healthy people and lasts about a year. After that, the drug is tested for about two years on 100–300 people who suffer from the disease to see how well the drug works. The final stage lasts about three years: the drug is usually tested on 1,000–3,000 patients in hospitals and clinics. While they are carrying out these tests, doctors monitor the patient closely and keep a record of the success of the drug and any side-effects.

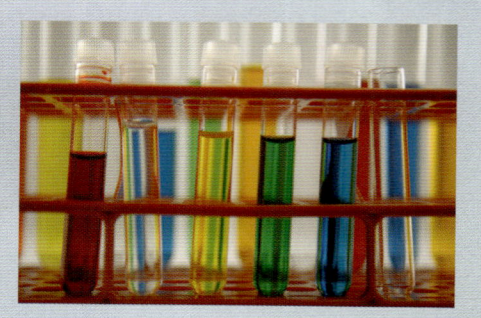

Science Now

Science Now, March 2001   Issue no.1

When a company has completed the three stages of tests on humans, the company makes a New Drug Application to the FDA (Food and Drug Agency), which is often 1,000 pages or more.

How long the FDA takes to review a New Drug Application depends on many things. Sometimes, important new discoveries are 'fast-tracked'; the average review time is 29.9 months.

When the FDA has approved the New Drug Application, doctors can finally give it to their patients. The company still keeps a quality control record of the drug, including any side-effects.

Discovering and developing safe and successful new drugs is a long, difficult and expensive process. America's pharmaceutical companies spent $65bn last year on developing new drugs. Companies invest up to 18% of their sales on research and the high investment is likely to continue.

3 Read the article again and complete the table below.

	Laboratory	People		
		Stage 1	Stage 2	Stage 3
Test period:				
Tested on:				
Reason for testing:				

Vocabulary

4 Underline the sequencing words and phrases in the text.

> **Don't forget**
>
> **Sequencing**
>
> When we are describing a sequence or process, it is important to be clear about the order.
>
> - We can talk about the stages involved:
>   *There are four stages of testing a new drug.*
>   *The first/second/third/final stage is ...*
> - We can also use simple sequencing words:
>   first/first of all   when
>   then/next/after that   while
>   finally

Writing

5 Work in pairs or groups. Your teacher will give you some cards describing drug development. Put the stages in order. Then write a description of the process.

Speaking

6 Work in pairs. Talk about the development of one of your company's products or services.

Product development   Unit 7b

Marketing a product

Listening 🎧 1.22

1 A medical journalist asks a marketing manager about a new drug for arthritis. Listen and answer the questions.

1. What is the drug called?
2. Who is the drug for?
3. Where will patients be able to get the drug?
4. What are the possible side effects?
5. How will patients get information about the drug?

2 Listen again and note down any dates you hear. Then put the actions below into the correct order.

- ❏ give general information posters to doctors
- ❏ visit doctors to talk about the product
- ❏ launch the drug
- ❏ give information leaflets to patients
- ❏ send information packs to doctors   (end of April)

> **Don't forget**
>
> **Future arrangements and intentions**
> - We use **the present continuous** (often with a time phrase) to talk about arrangements in the future.
>   *We're visiting* doctors at the beginning of May.
>   When *are* you *launching* the new product?
> - We can use *going to* to talk about our intentions.
>   We *are going to work* closely with doctors.
>   We *aren't going to* have any direct contact with patients.

Speaking

3 Work in pairs. Find out if your partner's company has plans for any of the following.

| a new product launch | a new advertising campaign |
| new training courses | new projects |

4 Work in pairs. Your teacher will give you some cards. Ask your partner questions about his/her plans for the future.

Self-study 7b

1 Complete the text below with sequencing words.

The process for testing new drugs involves many stages. **(1)** _First of all,_ they are tested in a laboratory and on animals. **(2)** _____ the company applies to the authorities to start tests on people. There are three stages of testing on humans. The company completes the third stage of tests on humans and **(3)** _____ it applies to the authorities for a licence to start using the drug. **(4)** _____ the company has its licence, it supplies doctors and hospitals with the new drug. The company continues monitoring the drug **(5)** _____ patients are using it.

2 Complete the conversation below about the launch of a new product. Put each verb into the correct form (present continuous or _going to_).

Felipe	Have you heard about the new product in our range?
Su Lin	Yes. When **(1)** _are you launching_ (you/launch) it?
Felipe	On 14 September.
Su Lin	How much advertising **(2)** _____ (you/do) before then?
Felipe	Oh, quite a lot. First, we **(3)** _____ (start) an advertising campaign on television on 10 September. Then we **(4)** _____ (use) newspaper advertisements the following week.
Su Lin	**(5)** _____ (you/use) the internet?
Felipe	Of course, we have a strong online presence.

3 Complete the sentences with the correct word.

1 Our company is _____ a new product in spring.
  A launching B bringing C giving

2 It _____ several years to develop one of our products.
  A lasts B needs C takes

3 I'm afraid that product isn't _____ until next week.
  A free B available C public

4 We'll have to _____ sales of this new product for several months.
  A monitor B look C see

5 What _____ do you need?
  A informers B information C informs

4 Exam practice

- Look at questions 1–5.
- In each question, which phrase or sentence is correct?
- For each question, mark the correct letter A, B or C.

1
> While we are developing the product, we will write regular reports to ensure that you are informed of its progress.

A We're going to write reports before we develop the product.
B We're going to write reports at the same time as we develop the product.
C We're going to write reports after we develop the product.

2
> To: Peter
> From: Alessia
> The new marketing website won't go live until Friday 11 July.

A We might have a new marketing website.
B We won't have a new marketing website.
C We are sure to have a new marketing website.

3
> **Launch schedule**
> 24/5 – Press conference.
> 31/5 – TV advertising starts. Email posters.
> 7/6 – Social media advertising starts. Internet advertising starts.
> 14/6 – Free competition starts on the radio.

How many written forms of publicity are there?

A two
B three
C four

4
> We are carrying out market research in northern Europe from 22nd–26th.

A We have done the research in northern Europe.
B We haven't done the research in northern Europe yet.
C We have decided not to do research in northern Europe.

5
> Carmen
> Still waiting for approval from the New York office. Hope to get it next week so that we can finalise the launch date.
> Pete

A They have finalised a date for the launch.
B They hope to launch the product next week.
C They cannot yet finalise a date for the launch.

Unit 7b 59

Unit 8a Business equipment

Office equipment

Vocabulary 1 Put the following words into the groups below.

| laptop | shredder | envelopes | whiteboard | fax machine |
| pencils | scissors | photocopier | printer | stapler |

essential for you at work	necessary but you don't use every day	not important

Reading 2 Look quickly at the two advertisements for photocopiers.

- Which machine has more special features?
- Which advertisement includes a special offer?
- How long is the offer available for?

The New Xanda Pro 220X

To manage high volumes of work in a fast, competitive environment, you need a photocopier you can trust. The Xanda Pro 220X offers you advanced printing technology which is fast and reliable. It is internet-ready, so you can connect with your office network quickly and easily. Programming jobs is also very easy, thanks to the large colour interface showing all available functions and modes. The wide range of document reproduction features ensures that every job is produced on time, every time.

Key Details
- **Technology** – 2 × 4-way laser diode array & electro-photographic printing
- **Paper input capacity** – Standard 2 × 1,000-sheet paper trays / 2 × 500-sheet paper trays / Maximum 3,000 sheets
- **Print speed** – 95 pages per minute
- **Warm-up time** – 360 seconds or less
- **First print speed** – Less than 4.3 seconds
- **Memory** – Standard 512 MB, 1 GB / Hard Disk Drive 160 GB

THE BEST COPIER DEALS FROM ZENLYS

The i-ZENLYS60 is the perfect high-performance copier for the small or home office. This laser all-in-one colour copier provides professional laser printing, copying, faxing and scanning on your desktop. It's network-ready and no accessories are required so you benefit from complete colour productivity from one machine and can save on office space as well as investment in office equipment.
Print Resolution – 2400 × 600dpi **Paper-Capacity** – 250 Sheet **Memory** – 384MB
Print speed – 20 pages per minute black-and-white, five pages per minute colour. Included with this product is the three-year Express Exchange Warranty unique to ZENLYS.
Purchase now and receive the NEW ZENLYS Colour Laser Printer, The DocuPrint XU40 (RRP €198 including VAT), absolutely free.
Offer available only until 31.03.12

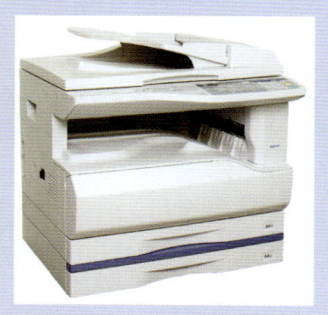

3 Read the advertisements again and look at the sentences below. Choose 'Right', 'Wrong' or 'Doesn't say' for each sentence.

1 The Xanda Pro 220X makes both black-and-white and colour photocopies.
   A Right   B Wrong   C Doesn't say

2 The i-ZENLYS60 has more programs than the Xanda Pro 220X.
   A Right   B Wrong   C Doesn't say

3   The Xanda Pro 220X can also function as a fax machine.
    A Right   B Wrong   C Doesn't say

4   If the customer buys the i-ZENLYS60, the printer only costs €198.
    A Right   B Wrong   C Doesn't say

5   The Xanda Pro 220X is a faster copier than the i-ZENLYS60.
    A Right   B Wrong   C Doesn't say

6   The i-ZENLYS60 has a five-year guarantee.
    A Right   B Wrong   C Doesn't say

7   The Xanda Pro 220X has two paper trays.
    A Right   B Wrong   C Doesn't say

8   Both photocopiers are network-ready.
    A Right   B Wrong   C Doesn't say

Speaking

4 Work in pairs. The following people want to buy a photocopier immediately. Which of the two photocopiers should each person buy?

1 **Carl Jacobsen** is a self-employed architect who works from home. He has one employee: a part-time secretary. He mainly needs to copy contracts before sending them to clients.

2 **Monica Szabo** is the Head of the Marketing Department at Pyramid, a large graphic design and publishing company. Her department makes heavy use of photocopiers for publicity materials and work samples.

3 **Jaswinder Singh** works as an account manager for Global Insurance. Although he sometimes works in the office, most of the time he visits clients or works from home. He does not have a photocopier at home at the moment but would like to be able to use one occasionally.

Reading

5 Carl Jacobsen decides to get more information about the i-ZENLYS60 photocopier. Complete the online information request form below for him.

For further information about products featured in this catalogue, please complete the address panel and put a tick in the relevant boxes below.

Name: _____   Company name: _Jacobsen Design_____
Job title: _____   Tel: _+45 3322 7442_   Email: _jacobsen.design@woco.dk_
Address: _Fredensgade 7B, DK-1176, Copenhagen V, DENMARK_____

1 ❑ Xanda Pro 220X photocopier   5 ❑ Canon Personal Copiers   9 ❑ Xanda Vision-X Scanner
2 ❑ Brit Vic Vending Machines   6 ❑ Hewlett Packard Laserjet 4000   10 ❑ Philips Speechmike
3 ❑ BT Video Conferencing System   7 ❑ Hewlett Packard Scanjet 6100C   11 ❑ Sharp Notevision Projector
4 ❑ Canon BJC-4200 & Powershot 350   8 ❑ Lotus Intranet Software   12 ❑ i-ZENLYS60 photocopier

How many employees are there in your company?   1–25 ❑   26–50 ❑   51–100 ❑   101–200 ❑   Over 200 ❑

Company activity:
❑ AGRICULTURE   ❑ HOTELS AND CATERING
❑ BANKING/FINANCE/INSURANCE   ❑ LEGAL/ACCOUNTING
❑ BUSINESS AND PROFESSIONAL SERVICES ❑ MANUFACTURING
❑ CENTRAL AND LOCAL GOVERNMENT   ❑ REAL ESTATE
❑ CONSTRUCTION   ❑ RESEARCH AND DEVELOPMENT
❑ EDUCATION AND TRAINING   ❑ OTHER

Tick if you require this information for an immediate purchase ❑
Or for a purchase within 3–6 months ❑   6–9 months ❑   9–12 months ❑   12+ months ❑

Giving instructions

Listening

1 The Accounts Department at Pyramid has bought a new shredder. The secretary, Anna, has a problem. She telephones Zoltan in the Purchasing Department. What is the problem? Listen to their conversation. What do they do about it?

2 Listen again and take notes. Then complete Anna's notice.

Instructions for use of shredder

How to use
- To switch on, press the green button.
- Put the paper in.
- To switch off, press the red button.

Possible problems   **What to do**
- The machine jams
- The motor overheats

Caution!
-
-

Call the Services Department on 7653 if there are any other problems

Don't forget

Giving instructions
- The easiest way to give instructions in English is to use the imperative.
  Switch on the machine.
- Sometimes you need to give negative instructions.
  Never insert your fingers into the shredder.
  Don't use the machine without reading the instructions first.

Speaking

3 Look at The Business Equipment Game on page 134. Your teacher will give you instructions.

4 Work in pairs. Student A: Choose one of the pictures below. Give instructions. Student B: What piece of equipment is it?

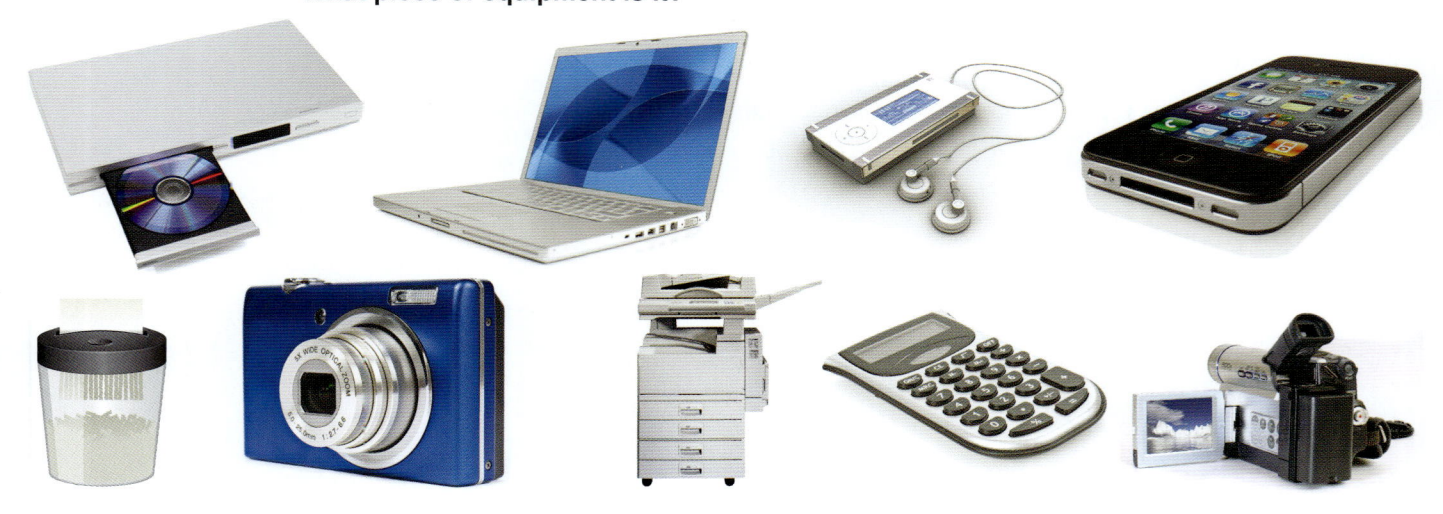

Self-study 8a

1 Put the following verbs into the groups below. You can use some verbs more than once.

dial	jam	enlarge	reduce	press	print
insert	shred	switch on	overheat	send	copy

fax machine	printer	photocopier	shredder
dial			

2 Complete the table below.

Noun	Verb
enlargement	enlarge
insertion	....
operation	....
....	reduce
copy	....
printer	....
removal	....

3 Read the problems below. What instructions would you give each person? Write your answers.

1 I can't send this email; it keeps coming back.
   Check the email address. Perhaps it's not correct.

2 The photocopier has run out of paper.
   _____

3 The cutter on the shredder has jammed.
   _____

4 Some paper is jammed in the photocopier.
   _____

5 The photocopier is overheating.
   _____

6 The stapler on the photocopier isn't working.
   _____

4 Write operating instructions for one of the pieces of equipment in Exercise 4 on page 62.

5 In each question, which piece of equipment does the sentence refer to? For each question, mark the correct letter A, B or C.

1 Always test the sound equipment to make sure it works.
   A printer   B shredder
   C video-conferencing system

2 The cutter will jam if you insert too much paper.
   A shredder   B photocopier   C printer

3 If you reduce the size of the article, you can use A4.
   A shredder   B smartphone   C photocopier

4 You can use it for organising contacts, dates and personal information.
   A photocopier   B shredder   C smartphone

5 I'll send you the podcast so you can listen to it later.
   A shredder   B printer   C laptop

6 Remove the paper from the feeder and put it on the glass – it might work then.
   A shredder   B photocopier   C printer

6 Exam practice

- Look at the graph below. It shows the number of photocopies made by a company over eight months, and the proportions of recycled and new paper used.
- Which month does each sentence 1–5 describe?
- For each sentence mark the correct letter A–H.
- Do not use any letter more than once.

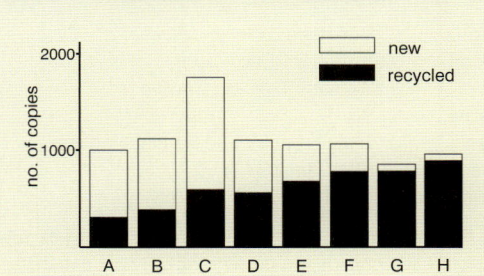

1 After a sharp rise in demand, the company was forced to use a larger proportion of new paper.

2 For the first time there was a higher proportion of recycled paper in use.

3 In this month a balance was achieved between the use of new and recycled paper.

4 This month saw the lowest number of copies made on recycled paper.

5 Whereas demand for recycled paper remained high, the overall number of copies made fell.

Unit 8b

Correspondence

Sending a quotation

Reading 1 Beto Delgado works for Complete Career, an international recruitment company. He contacts three training providers to ask for quotations for a management training course. Look at the replies and say who:

- has already organised courses for Complete Career
- has not worked with Complete Career before
- is a personal friend of Beto's.

From: j.zwick@ATC-consulting.com
To: beto.delgado@completecareer.com
Subject: Business excellence seminar
Date: 16 April 2011

Dear Beto
Many thanks for the enquiry about a one-day Business Excellence Seminar. Here's the information you requested and a quotation.

Date:	14 May
Time:	10.00am–4.00pm
Location:	ATC Consulting
No of people:	6
Price:	$650 per person

As before, this price includes VAT and a small, buffet-style lunch. I've attached a copy of the seminar content but please don't hesitate to get back to me if you need more details. Once again, thanks for the enquiry.

Best regards
Julian
Julian Zwick
Customer Contact Manager

From: scialdoni.rebecca@synergy.com
To: beto.delgado@completecareer.com
Subject: Training Course Booking
Date: 17 April 2011

Dear Mr Delgado

Thank you for your enquiry of 16 April regarding Business Excellence training courses. We are able to offer the following one-day seminars for the week commencing 14 May:

Training	Business Excellence Level 3
Duration:	1 day, 9.30am–5pm
Venue:	Synergy Training Centre
Delegates:	Six
Included:	Training pack and seminar notes
Cost per head:	$680 (incl VAT)
Available dates:	14, 15, 16, 17 or 18 May

Please find enclosed a copy of the seminar schedule. Should you have any further questions, please do not hesitate to contact me on 415 862 1730 ext 204.

Yours sincerely
Rebecca Scialdoni
Seminar Sales

> -----Original Message-----
> From: dwbowes@enterprisesolutions.com
> To: beto.delgado@completecareer.com
> Subject: Business Excellence Programme

> Beto
> Thanks for your call yesterday. Here's the quote you wanted for our Business Excellence programme:
> Date: 14 May
> Time: 09.30–16.30
> Place: Here at Enterprise Solutions or in-company
> No. of people: 6
> Included: Training pack & lunch
> Cost: $799 (excl VAT) per person.
> If you have any questions, give me a call. I've attached a PDF file with the course schedule –
> hope you can open it OK.
> Best wishes

> Dave

2 Answer the following questions.

1 Which is the longest seminar?
2 Which company's offer includes a training pack and food?
3 Which of the quotations is the cheapest?
4 Which company offers more than one possible date?
5 Which of the companies is prepared to travel to give the seminar?

Speaking **3** What differences are there in the style and register of the three emails? Which are the most and least formal?

Emails of acceptance

Reading **1** Beto decides to accept the Synergy offer and writes an email to Rebecca Scialdoni. Put the paragraphs of his email into the correct order.

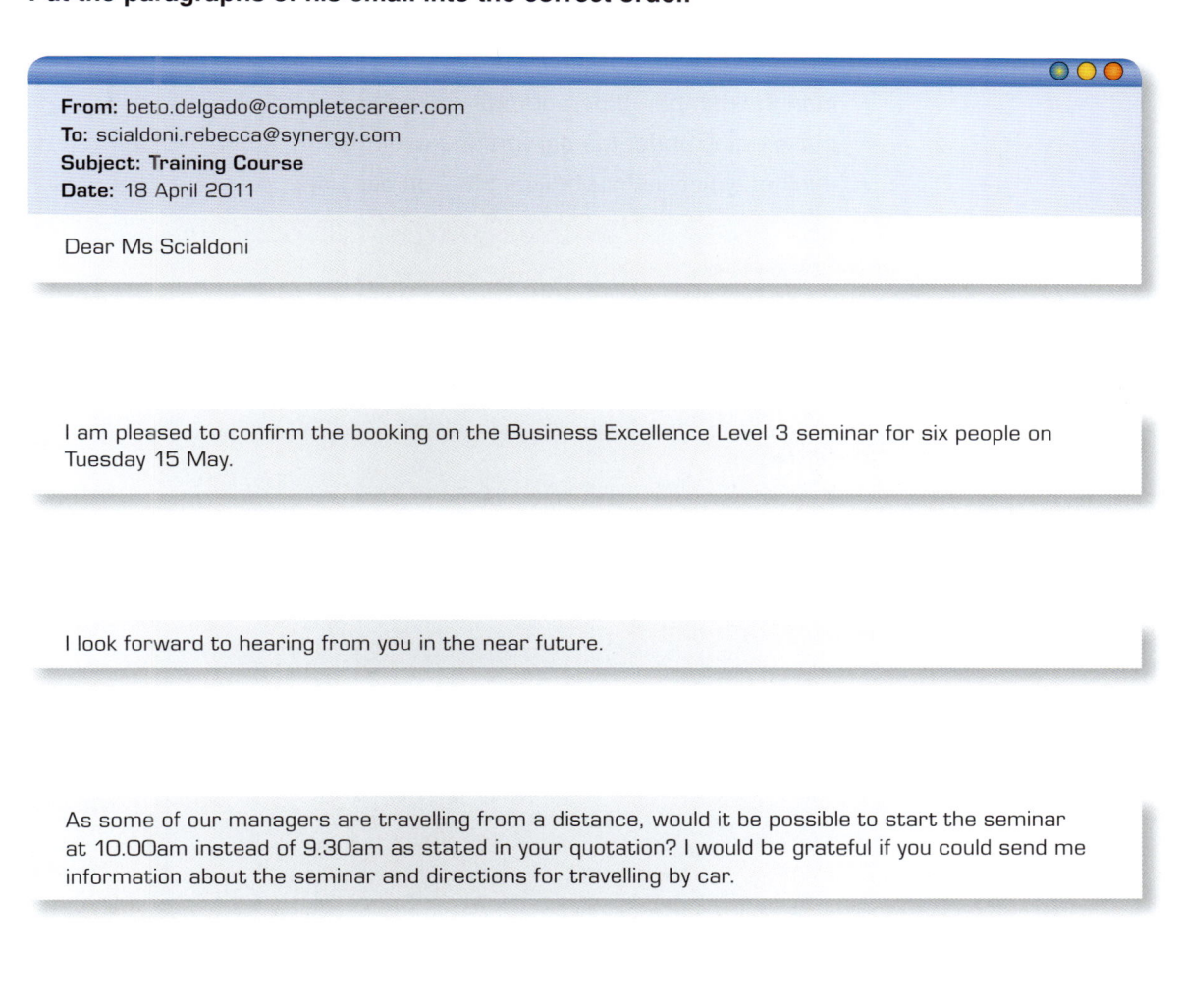

From: beto.delgado@completecareer.com
To: scialdoni.rebecca@synergy.com
Subject: Training Course
Date: 18 April 2011

Dear Ms Scialdoni

I am pleased to confirm the booking on the Business Excellence Level 3 seminar for six people on Tuesday 15 May.

I look forward to hearing from you in the near future.

As some of our managers are travelling from a distance, would it be possible to start the seminar at 10.00am instead of 9.30am as stated in your quotation? I would be grateful if you could send me information about the seminar and directions for travelling by car.

I am writing with reference to your quotation of 17 April regarding the one-day Business Excellence seminar at your premises in downtown San Francisco.

---

2 Match the functions with the paragraphs above. Underline the phrases that helped you.

| making a request | making reference |
| giving the reason for writing | signalling the end of an email |

Correspondence **Unit 8b** 65

Vocabulary

3 Match the functions with the phrases.

1	Making reference	I am afraid that ...
2	Giving the reason for writing	With reference to your letter of ...
3	Giving good news	We would be grateful if you could ...
4	Giving bad news	I look forward to receiving your reply.
5	Making a request	I am pleased to ...
6	Enclosing something	I am writing to ...
7	Offering assistance	I enclose ...
8	Referring to future contact	If you require any further information, please do not hesitate to contact us.

(1 is matched to "With reference to your letter of ...")

Writing

4 Beto Delgado receives the invoice from Synergy after the training course. There are some items which he thinks are wrong. Use the invoice and his handwritten notes to write a reply to Synergy.

Before you write:

- plan the number of paragraphs you need
- make notes under the paragraph headings
- think of typical letter phrases that you can use.

From: scialdoni.rebecca@synergy.com
To: beto.delgado@careercomplete.com
Subject: Training course invoice
Date: 25 May 2011

Dear Mr Delgado

Thank you for your letter of 17 May. I am very pleased that you enjoyed the course and found it useful for your managers.

I attach the invoice which you requested in your email.

A 2% reduction is offered on payments within ten days.

I would like to thank you for booking your training course with our organisation and we look forward to seeing you again in the future.

Yours sincerely

Rebecca Scialdoni
Seminar Sales

---

820 Market Street #704
San Francisco, CA 94104-5102
Tel: 415 862 1730
Email info@synergy.com

Synergy
Management Consultants

Mr Beto Delgado
Complete Career
300 E Santa Cruz Street,
San Jose 9511

INVOICE

Invoice date: 24 MAY
Invoice number: 1948

TRAINING COURSE 14 MAY 2001

COURSE:	1 day business excellence Level 3
DELEGATES	8 @ $680 per person
EXTRAS:	Training Packs @ $4.50 per person

Total Cost: $5,476 (incl VAT)

offered on payments

Bankers:	Bank of America, 1347 Fell Street, San Francisco, CA 95233
Account number:	00086954
Bank sort code:	ABA 756934533
Registered office:	Synergy Management Consultants, 820 Market Street # 704 San Francisco, CA 94104-5102
Registered number:	768462

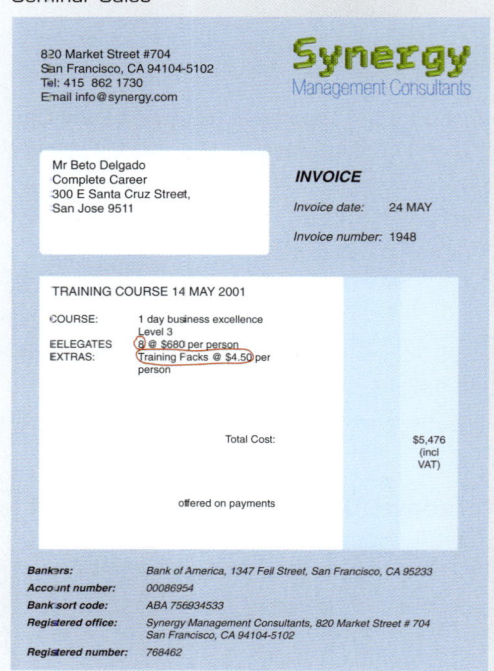

*Maria,
Could you contact Rebecca Scialdoni and question the things I've circled on her invoice?*

Thanks

Self-study 8b

1 What do the following abbreviations mean?

1. ASAP — as soon as possible
2. enc _____
3. Dept _____
4. NB _____
5. re _____
6. wk _____
7. excl _____
8. incl _____
9. ext _____

2 Match the following opening and closing phrases.

1. Dear Ms Garcia   Regards
2. Dear Paul   Yours truly
3. Dear Sir/Madam   Yours sincerely
4. Gentlemen   Yours faithfully

3 Are the following usually spoken (S) or written (W)?

1. A We got the goods yesterday.
   B We received the goods yesterday.
2. A I want to ask about your new product.
   B I would like to enquire about your new product.
3. A We're sorry that the order was late.
   B We are afraid that the order was delayed.
4. A Could you please confirm the date?
   B Let me know if the date is OK.
5. A If you require any further assistance, ...
   B If you need any more help, ...
6. A I can't wait to see you.
   B I look forward to seeing you.

4 A colleague has written a formal email and asked you to check it. There are no grammatical mistakes in the email but some of the style is not formal enough. Find and change the informal phrases.

Dear Ms Daley

I am writing because we want some information about your latest photocopiers. We are renting a photocopier from you but now we want to buy one.

I'd be really happy if you sent us a brochure and some product literature. Please send us a price list as well.

Thanks a lot. We can't wait to hear from you.

Regards

Marco Francone

---

5 Exam practice

Read the email in Exercise 4 again.

- Write a reply to Marco Francone:
  * thanking him for his enquiry
  * attaching a brochure and price list
  * telling him about a new special offer
  * asking him to contact you if he has any questions.
- Write 60–80 words.

Dear Mr Francone

_____
_____
_____
_____
_____
_____
_____
_____
_____
_____
_____
_____

Yours sincerely

6 Exam practice

Simon Howe is leaving the company next week. You decide to have a farewell party for him.

- Write an email to all your colleagues:
  * informing them about the party
  * saying when and where the party is
  * inviting them to the party.
- Write 30–40 words.

_____
_____
_____
_____
_____
_____

Unit 9 Exam focus: Writing

The Writing Test

The Cambridge BEC Preliminary Writing Test has two questions.

Part	Input	Task
1	Instructions only	Write an email or note (30–40 words)
2	Letter, notice or advertisement	Write a letter (60–80 words)

Length: About 30 minutes of the Reading and Writing Test should be used for Writing.

How to succeed

Your ability to complete the task successfully is just as important as the accuracy of your grammar and vocabulary.

Task

- Successful task completion means following **all instructions**.
- Pay attention to the word limit. If you do not write enough words, you have probably not completed the task fully. If you write too many, you have probably included unnecessary information.
- You will lose marks if your piece of writing includes facts or information that are not relevant to the task.
- Even if you write a grammatically perfect answer, it may still get low marks if you do not include all the necessary information.

Language

- Task completion is so important that you can still get top marks even with small grammar and spelling mistakes.
- However, accuracy is important so use language that you feel confident about.
- Try not to repeat the same words. Show a range of vocabulary.
- Organise your ideas clearly
  - addition (*also, as well, furthermore* etc.)
  - contrast (*but, although, however* etc.)
  - sequence (*first of all, then, after that* etc.).
- Make sure the language is appropriate to the type of writing. (Short forms, e.g. *I'm*, are acceptable in notes but not in formal letters.)
- Check your writing when you have finished.

Part One Writing Task: Emails and notes

1 Read the examination tips on the opposite page and look at the Part One task below. Underline the task and language errors. Then put them in order from best to worst.

> **Question 46**
> - You are attending a conference on 14–18 May in Budapest. You need to make your travel arrangements.
> - Write an email to Jessica Carston, your secretary:
>   - giving her the dates
>   - saying when you want to fly
>   - asking her to book a flight.
> - Write 30–40 words.

Candidate A

> I have to go to a conference in Budapest. Could you book a flight for me please? I want to go on the 14th May and come back on the 18th. Thank you.

Candidate B

> I am attending a conference on 14-18 May in Budapest. I need you to make travel arrangements. Please you book for me a flight.

Candidate C

> I am very sorry to trouble you Jessica but you know that I am assisting a conference in Budapest and I am needing you to book me a fly in the morning early. Could you please do it for me? I am very gratefull for your help.

Candidate D

> Could you please book me a return flight for the conference in Budapest? I would like to arrive in Budapest before lunch 14th May and leaving 18th May after 6pm. Thank you.

2 Read these tips and do the exam question below.

1. Read all the instructions carefully. Do you need to write a note or an email?
2. Think about what you need to say and who you are addressing. What register of language should you use?
3. Check you have completed all three parts of the task. Use the instructions as a checklist.
4. Check the length of your first draft and edit if necessary.
5. Think about ways of making your message short and clear. Which words can you leave out?
6. Proof-read your answer before transferring it. Check grammar, vocabulary and style.

> **Question 46**
> - Your department has just received several large new orders. The company has decided to ask everyone in the department to work five extra hours per week.
> - Write an email to all staff in the department:
>   * explaining the situation
>   * saying when overtime will begin
>   * asking the staff to work overtime.
> - Write 30–40 words.

Part Two Writing Task: Longer emails and letters

1 Read the Part Two task and follow the instructions below.

Question 47

- Read this email from Marta Abram, the Sales Manager at one of your suppliers.

> **To:** fabio.ramos@aleco.com
> **From:** marta.abram@expo_tech.co.pl
> **Subject:** Our new brochure
>
> Dear Mr Ramos
>
> As part of our customer service, we are pleased to attach our latest brochure, showing our exciting new products and unbelievable prices.
>
> We would like the opportunity to visit your company in order to inform you personally of the latest product developments and discuss ways of making our service even more suited to your needs.
>
> If you would like to take advantage of a visit from a member of our sales team, could you please inform us of a suitable date and time? Could you also tell us which products would be of particular interest to you?
>
> Yours sincerely
>
> **Marta Abram**
> Sales Manager

- **Write a reply to Ms Abram:**
  * **thanking her for the brochure**
  * **accepting the offer of a visit from a salesperson**
  * **suggesting a date and time for the visit**
  * **saying which products you would be interested in.**
- **Write 60–80 words.**

1 Plan the structure of your answer. How many paragraphs will there be? What is their purpose?
2 Think of phrases and key vocabulary to put in the paragraphs.
3 Check that your plan fully completes all four parts of the task. Then write a first draft.
4 Check the first draft:
  – Does it fully complete the task?
  – Is the information clearly organised?
  – Is there any unnecessary information?
  – How many words are there?
5 Make changes to the first draft.
6 Check the final version:
  – Does it fully complete the task?
  – Are the grammar, spelling, punctuation and style correct?

Exam practice

PART ONE

- You have been waiting all morning for Mr Jablonski, an important client, to return a phone call. Now you have a meeting with a supplier.
- Leave a note for your colleague Luisa Blanco:
  * saying where you are
  * saying when you will be back
  * telling her what to say if Mr Jablonski calls.
- Write 30–40 words.

PART TWO

- Read this message from a salesperson enquiring about the transport and accommodation arrangements for a conference you have organised.

> I am writing to confirm my attendance at this year's sales conference from 24 to 27 October.
>
> I will be arriving on Wednesday 24 and would like to stay until Sunday 28 so that I can do some sightseeing. Could you possibly reserve me an extra night in the same hotel? I would also be very grateful if you could recommend some places for me to visit in my free time.
>
> I look forward to hearing from you.

- Write an email in reply:
  * agreeing to make the hotel booking
  * explaining that she will have to pay for the extra night
  * asking her for her flight details
  * suggesting places for her to visit.
- Write 60–80 words.

PART ONE

- You are going to be out of the office.
- Write an email to a customer:
  * reminding them that you are out of the office
  * saying when you will be back in the office
  * suggesting who should be contacted for urgent questions.
- Write 30–40 words.

PART TWO

- Your department needs a new photocopier and you have seen this advertisement in a magazine.

TX2000 OfficePro
Three machines in one!

The new **TX2000 OfficePro** is all you need to print, copy or scan all your colour office documents. With the **OfficePro** you can print up to four high quality colour pages a minute, copy up to five near-photo quality A4 images a minute and scan full colour A4 documents.

Easy to use and compact, the new **OfficePro** is the ideal solution for the small office that needs to produce high quality documents.

- Write an email to your boss:
  * mentioning the advertisement
  * describing some features of the TX2000
  * saying why the department should buy it
  * giving the price and delivery time.
- Write 60–80 words.

Unit 9   71

Unit 10a Business hotels

Hotel facilities

Reading   **1** Which of the three hotels should the people below stay at and why?

Grosvenor Square London Royal Hotel ★★★★★

Centrally located, the elegant London Royal is in Mayfair, near shops, parks, theatres and other attractions. The hotel has express check-in, 204 standard rooms and fully-equipped business centre and conference facilities. The hotel also has a large lounge, health club and well-equipped fitness centre.

Standard double room £285 per night

The Strand St Steven's Hotel ★★★

In the heart of theatreland, close to Covent Garden and only metres from Charing Cross, St Steven's is the ideal place for a London break. The hotel offers comfortable, well-equipped rooms and an efficient and friendly service. There is a restaurant, bar and free swimming pool access. The price includes a buffet breakfast.

Price per person per night £80
Midweek single supplement £80

Portman Square Hyde Park Gardens Hotel ★★★★

A quiet hotel a short walk from Oxford Street and West End theatres, the Hyde Park Gardens has the famous Maritime Restaurant, an informal dining room and a full fitness centre. It also offers a large buffet breakfast, afternoon tea in the lobby and a Sunday Jazz Brunch.

Price per person per night £120
Midweek single supplement £120

LONDON

Marco and Francesca Bianchi
Marco is the Managing Director of a large Italian company. He has a meeting with an important supplier in London. His wife is coming to London with him.

Maurice Breton
Maurice is an advertising executive attending an international advertising conference in London. He wants to stay for just one night. He needs to email a report back to his company before he leaves London.

Linda de Hamm
Linda has an interview on Friday for a job as a PA in London. She wants to stay for the weekend and do some shopping while she is in the city.

Speaking   **2** Work in pairs. Which of the three hotels would your partner choose. Why?

The business traveller

Listening 1

1 Kara Franklin, the Deputy Manager of the Docklands Barclay Business Hotel in London, talks about what is important for the business traveller. Before you listen, decide which five things below are most important. Then listen and compare your answers.

sauna	Wi-Fi access	bar	good room lighting
pool	secretarial service	fax	video conferencing
TV	quick check-in	room service	distance from airport

2 Listen again and choose the correct option to complete the sentences.

1 Many guests like to eat in their rooms
   A so they can watch TV while they eat.
   B because it is cheaper than the restaurant.
   C so they can do more work.

2 Good lighting means
   A low lighting so guests can relax.
   B bright desk lighting so guests can work.
   C bright lighting for the whole room.

3 The business centre at the hotel
   A is a self-service facility for copying and faxing.
   B organises the food during a conference.
   C recruits temporary secretaries during conferences.

4 The hotel provides
   A a free taxi service to the centre of London.
   B a cheap bus service to the centre of London.
   C a free bus service to the centre of London.

5 Corporate guests
   A do not usually exercise during their stay.
   B like to go swimming during their stay.
   C like to use the fitness room during their stay.

Grammar

3 Look at the audioscript on pages 143–144. Find examples of verbs and adjectives followed by the infinitive. Write them below.

Verb + infinitive	Adjective + infinitive
want to	

Speaking

4 Work in pairs. Ask your partner about the best hotel he/she has stayed in. Would your partner recommend it to a business traveller? Why/Why not?

Business hotels Unit 10a 73

Asking the way

Listening 2

1.25

1 Montse Garcerón is staying at the Docklands Barclay Business Hotel. She asks about travelling into central London. Listen and complete her notes.

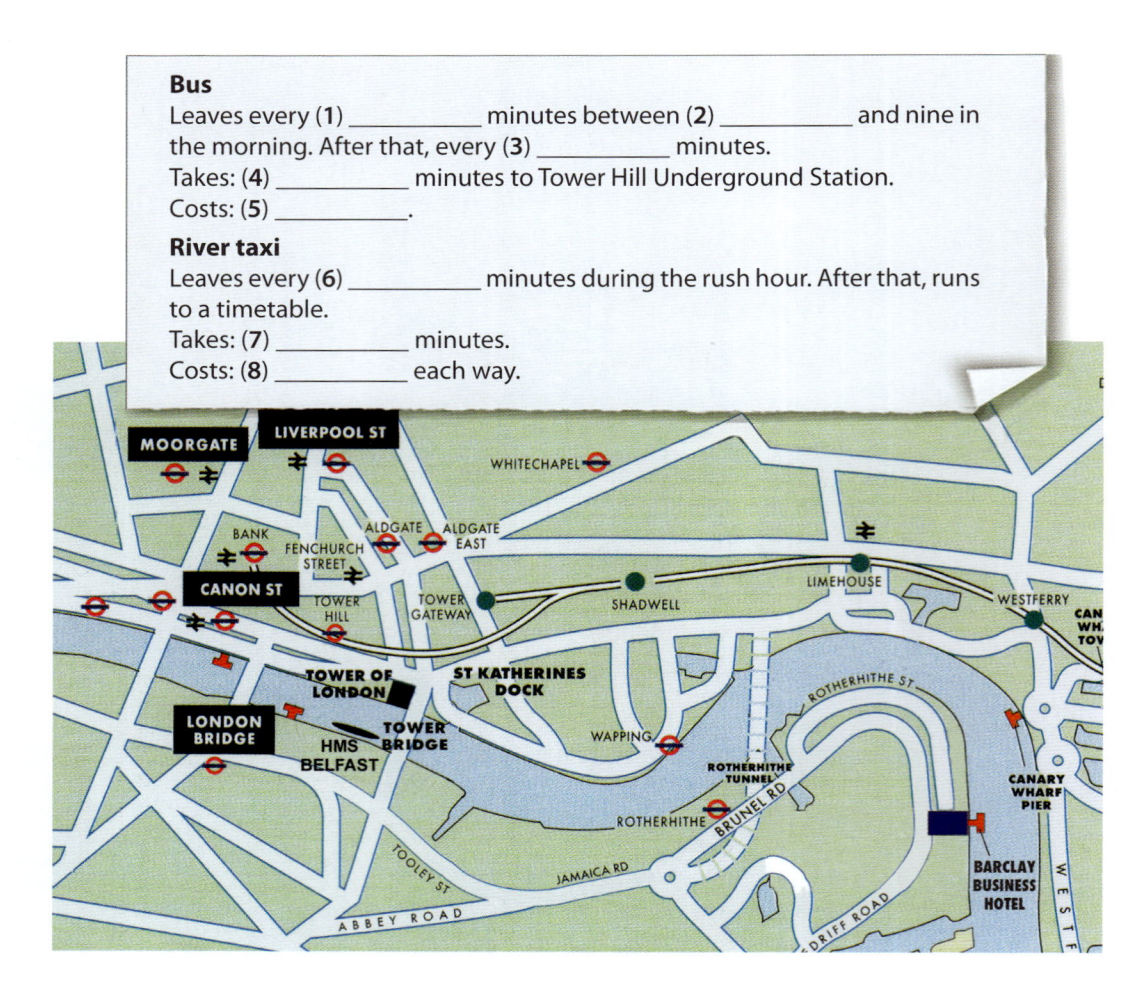

Bus
Leaves every (1) _____ minutes between (2) _____ and nine in the morning. After that, every (3) _____ minutes.
Takes: (4) _____ minutes to Tower Hill Underground Station.
Costs: (5) _____.

River taxi
Leaves every (6) _____ minutes during the rush hour. After that, runs to a timetable.
Takes: (7) _____ minutes.
Costs: (8) _____ each way.

2 Listen again and draw the routes for the bus and the river taxi on the map.

Writing

3 You are the receptionist at the Docklands Barclay Business Hotel. Write quick directions for the following guests.

- Mr Kiriakov wants to visit HMS Belfast. It is 9.30 am.
- Mrs Sanz wants to visit Canary Wharf Tower and then the Tower of London. It is 8.30 am.

Speaking

4 Work in pairs. Your teacher will give you some cards. Look at the map of London on page 140 and give your partner directions to the places on the cards. You both start from HMS Belfast. Use the words below.

Take the	first left/right.	Go	straight on ...	It's	next to ...
	bus to ...		past ...		near to ...
	train to ...		along ... Street.		opposite ...
Turn left /right at ...					on the left / right of ...

74

Self-study 10a

1 Complete the diagrams with adjectives from the advertisements on page 72.

- rooms: large, ___, ___
- service: ___, ___, ___
- hotel: ___, ___, ___

2 Match the words below.

1. room — service
2. Wi-Fi — access
3. fitness — centre
4. courtesy — bus
5. single — supplement
6. express — check-in
7. rush — hour
8. health — club

3 Complete the diagram with vocabulary from the unit.

- parts of a hotel: reception, ...
- facilities in the rooms: TV, ...

4 Exam practice

- You work for the Park Hotel in New York.
- Read this email from a company enquiring about room vacancies.

> **To:** reservations@parkhotel.com
> **From:** chung.charles@KLComputers.com
> **Subject:** Reserving four rooms
>
> Dear Sir/Madam
>
> I am writing to enquire about room vacancies for myself and three of my colleagues from KL Computers for 9–11 July. We would need four double rooms, preferably with Wi-Fi access.
>
> I would be very grateful if you could send me a quotation for the above rooms with information about the business facilities that the hotel offers. Is it possible to hire meeting rooms with audio-visual presentation equipment?
>
> Yours faithfully
>
> Charles Chung
> Personal Assistant to Kim Lee
> CEO, KL Computers

- Write a reply to Mr Chung:
  * confirming the availability of the rooms
  * confirming the dates
  * quoting the price
  * giving information about business facilities.
- Write 60–80 words.

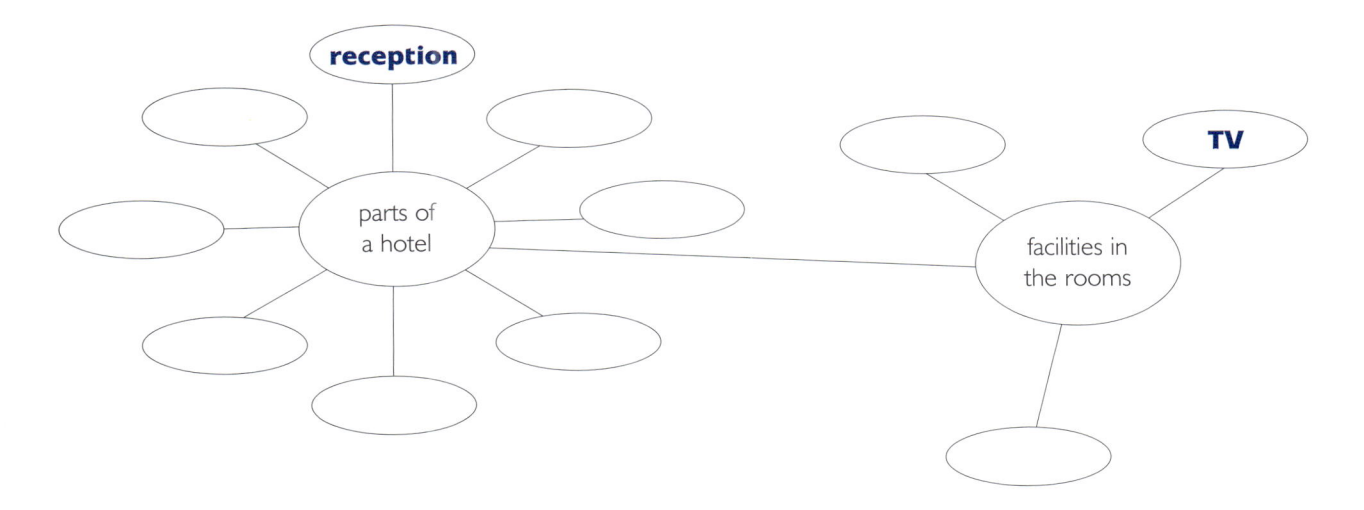

Unit 10b Commuting

Reducing traffic

Listening 🔘 **1** Six people talk about the topics in the newspaper headlines below. Listen to the
1.26–1.31 speakers and number the headlines.

Green tax could push up fuel prices by up to 60%

Edinburgh launches new pay-as-you-drive scheme

Government to tax parking at work
By Jan Suttie

European cities reduce city centre traffic with pedestrian zones

New smart card makes buses and trains cheaper

German city centres to get fast lane for people sharing cars
By Ian Robinson

New bus lanes for motorways

2 Listen again. Does each speaker agree or disagree with the particular transport scheme? Why?

	Agrees/disagrees	Reason
Speaker 1	Disagrees	Traffic will be twice as bad, more accidents, people will be stuck in traffic jams, late for work
Speaker 2		
Speaker 3		
Speaker 4		
Speaker 5		
Speaker 6		

Speaking

3 Work in pairs. Look at the newspaper headlines on the opposite page. Which are the two best schemes? Why?

Transport policy

Reading

1 Read the newspaper article about Government transport policy and complete the table.

THE GAZETTE

How much are we prepared to pay for our cars?

Bridget Connolly reports on the search for an effective *and* popular transport policy.

Everyone agrees that there are simply too many cars on the road but who will be the first to stop using theirs? Although everyone hates being stuck in traffic, no-one sees their car as part of the growing problem. However, with traffic growth of up to eighty-four per cent expected by 2031 and the ever-increasing cost of accidents and delays already at $160bn in Europe, there is a growing need to change our 'car culture' and develop alternative forms of transport as quickly as possible.

One answer is to make cars more expensive by increasing taxes on petrol. However, tax increases will affect the people who live in the country more than city drivers and do little to reduce inner city traffic. The Government is also looking at pay-as-you-drive schemes on motorways but this will push cars on to smaller 'free' roads, which will make the problem worse.

A successful transport policy is not just a question of making the car too expensive but of offering car drivers a real alternative. Many motorists dislike driving to work but say public transport services are too slow, offer poor quality and are far too expensive. If new transport policies are to succeed, public transport needs to be quick, reliable and affordable.

Transport planners are also developing ways of managing the existing road network more efficiently. New technology such as smart cards and electronic monitoring of roads will lead to a more efficient use of transport systems. However, technology will not reduce the number of cars on the road or solve the real problem of how to persuade car drivers to leave their beloved car at home more often.

Changes in travel in Britain 1965–2005

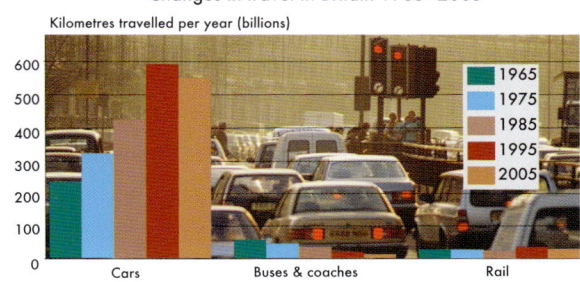

Kilometres travelled per year (billions)

Transport schemes	Effects
Increase tax on petrol	

2 Are the sentences below 'Right' or 'Wrong'? If there is not enough information to answer, choose 'Doesn't say'.

1 Cars are the only form of transport that has grown since 1985.
   A Right   B Wrong   C Doesn't say

2 Delays and accidents will cost Europe $160bn in 2031.
   A Right   B Wrong   C Doesn't say

3 The Government is going to double the tax on petrol.
   A Right   B Wrong   C Doesn't say

4 Pay-as-you-drive schemes will reduce the amount of traffic on motorways.
   A Right   B Wrong   C Doesn't say

5 The Government is planning to build more roads in the future.
   A Right   B Wrong   C Doesn't say

6 The use of new technology will reduce the amount of traffic.
   A Right   B Wrong   C Doesn't say

Don't forget

Making predictions

We can use both **going to** and **will** to make predictions about the future.

- We make spoken predictions with **going to** or **'ll**.
  Petrol prices **aren't going to make** any difference.
  The traffic **'ll be** twice as bad.
- **Will** is used in newspaper articles, formal letters and formal speeches.
  The Government **will increase** tax on petrol next year.
  The meeting **will take place** on Tuesday 2 May.

Speaking

3 Work in pairs. How will transport change in your country in the future? Think about the following issues.

| the use of company cars | the cost of public transport | the cost of driving |
| the quality of public transport | the use of alternative transport |

4 Look at the Commuter Game on page 135. Your teacher will give you instructions on how to play the game.

Self-study 10b

1 Complete the crossword.

Across
1. Someone who travels into a city or town to work.
4. The opposite of early.
6. Put your car in a place where it can stay.
7. All cars and buses on the roads.
8. In Britain you drive in the left one.
9. Money you have to give to the Government.

Down
2. A fast road with three lanes in each direction.
3. The long piece of hard ground you drive on.
5. Something that happens when one car hits another.
6. Fuel for cars.

2 Complete the following sentences by adding the word *traffic* or *transport* in the correct place.

1. Every set of lights was on red this morning. *traffic*
2. Public is very good in the city where I live.
3. The Government's new policy won't change anything.
4. Sorry I'm late. I was stuck in for hours.
5. There's always a jam on the motorway in the morning.
6. City centre was reduced by the park-and-ride scheme.
7. There isn't any alternative where I live.
8. With growth of over 2% a year, we need more roads.

3 Write about transport in your city. What are the problems? How is the Government dealing with these problems?

4 Exam practice

- Look at the newspaper headlines in questions 1–5.
- In each question, which phrase or sentence is correct?
- For each question, mark the correct letter A, B or C.

1 Motorway technology improves flow of rush hour traffic

A There are fewer accidents during rush hour.
B There is less traffic during rush hour.
C There are fewer traffic jams during rush hour.

2 Delays expected on commuter train services

A People travelling to work by train may be late.
B There are problems with high speed trains.
C Due to problems, all trains will be late.

3 Public transport fares to increase

A There will be more bus and train services.
B It will be more expensive to travel by bus and train.
C Customer service will improve on buses and trains.

4 Punctuality improves on bus services

A The quality of service is improving on buses.
B More buses are now running on time.
C Buses are becoming cheaper to use.

5 Pedestrian zones reduce city centre pollution

A Traffic reductions have improved city centre air quality.
B Larger roads have reduced city centre traffic jams.
C Cycle areas have improved the flow of city centre traffic.

Unit 11a   Arranging a conference

An enquiry

Vocabulary

1 Work in pairs. Your teacher will give you some cards about organising a conference. Put them in order.

Listening 1 1 32

2 Daniel Black calls Jessica Yeung at Events Asia to discuss a conference. Listen to their conversation. Are the following sentences true or false?

1 Daniel is calling to confirm arrangements for a conference.
2 The company has made a final decision on the location.
3 The company wants to have the conference in autumn.
4 The delegates will have two nights at the hotel.
5 Jessica is going to ring Daniel back with a proposal.

3 Listen again and complete the form below.

Briefing Form

Company name

Contact name
Daniel Black
Company address
152 Jalan Pemimpin #02-08
Singapore

Postcode   *6553 6839*

Telephone number

Number of delegates

Location

Budget

Date

Duration

Room requirements

Speaking

4 Work in pairs. What do you think Jessica's job involves?

Reading

5 Read the information below about conference packages. Which hotel:

- offers easy access to Hong Kong airport?
- employs somebody to help arrange meetings and conferences?
- has business facilities which are available throughout the day?
- is suitable for smaller conferences with fewer than 30 people?
- has its conference facilities in a separate part of the building?
- charges for the use of business equipment?
- do you think is the best choice?

Events Asia

The Regal Pacific Hotel, Hong Kong (Min. 40 delegates)

With its quiet West Central waterfront location, the Regal Pacific offers high-tech rooms with first-class facilities. The transport links to the airport are excellent and the central business area and Hong Kong Convention and Exhibition Centre are only twenty minutes away. Our excellent conference facilities include two large conference rooms and four smaller seminar rooms, a business centre, a rest area and a small restaurant.

The Renaissance Hotel, Hong Kong (Max. 45 delegates)

This elegant hotel on Hong Kong Island offers easy access to the mainland and also to popular tourist destinations on the island. Our chic modern rooms all have Wi-Fi access and an iPod docking station, and there are personal computers available to rent in our business centre. We offer a choice of meeting and conference facilities for a range of events and have a professional organiser to assist with your requirements.

The Central Hotel, Hong Kong (Min. 20 delegates)

This hotel is a favourite with both business travellers and tourists because of its central location close to Hong Kong's major shopping and sightseeing hot-spots, including the Man Mo Temple, Times Square and Stanley Market. All rooms benefit from free high-speed Wi-Fi access and our business centre is open twenty-four hours. The fully-equipped conference centre occupies the top floor of the hotel and offers excellent facilities.

We are pleased to quote as follows:

	The Regal Pacific	The Renaissance Hotel	The Central Hotel
Single room inc breakfast	HK$1,550	HK$1,780	HK$2,200
Conference room (per day)	HK$2,300	HK$2,700 HK$1,800 (smaller – max 20)	HK$5,700
Seminar room (per day)	HK$1,380 HK$1,010 (smaller – max 10)	HK$1,475	HK$1,500
Technical equipment (per day)	HK$1,550	HK$2,600	Included in price
Lunch per person	HK$155	HK$165	HK$178
Dinner per person	HK$195	HK$200	HK$230

Speaking

6 Work in pairs. Which hotel would be the cheapest for Daniel Black's conference? Would you choose this hotel for him?

Confirming arrangements

Listening 2 **1** Jessica telephones Daniel to check some details about the conference. Listen to their conversation and take notes.

Amtech - Phone Daniel Black to confirm Hong Kong conference details

- September _____

- _____ delegates

- Accommodation for _____

- One conference room and _____

- Delegates pay for _____

- Drinks _____

- Events Asia to confirm _____

Events Asia

Don't forget

Checking and confirming
- We often have to check information on the telephone.
  I'd like to check some details.
  So, ... Is that correct?
  Sorry, did you say ...?
- We often confirm arrangements with a letter or fax.
  I am writing to confirm ...
  We are happy to confirm ...

Speaking **2** Work in pairs. Student A: Look at the Activity sheet on page 133. Student B: Look at the Activity sheet on page 137. Complete the conference programme.

Writing **3** Work in pairs. Write Jessica's letter to Daniel to confirm the conference booking. Enclose the conference programme from Exercise 2. Plan the letter before you begin to write.

- What information do you need to include?
- How many paragraphs do you need?
- What information will you write in each paragraph?
- What phrases will you use in each paragraph?

Self-study 11a

1 Match each verb with a noun.

1. arrange — a quotation
2. decide on — a conference
3. ask for — delegates
4. make — a budget
5. invite — details
6. finalise — a proposal

(arrange — a conference is shown linked)

2 Complete the sentences with the correct form of the words below.

| quote require locate arrange propose confirm |

1. When I have all the details of your requirements, I'll make a _____ in writing.
2. The conference is in a quiet _____.
3. Jessica Leung is _____ a conference for us in Hong Kong in October.
4. Please let me know if any delegates have any special food _____, for example, if they are vegetarians.
5. They have given us a _____ of HKD223,000 (about 29,000 US dollars) for the organisation of our sales conference.
6. I'll send you a letter of _____ next week.

3 You are a conference organiser. A client wants to organise a conference. Write questions to ask the client about the following.

1. delegates — *How many delegates will there be?*
2. location
3. budget
4. time of year
5. duration
6. rooms

4 Look back through the unit (including the audioscripts). How many words connected with *conference* can you find? Now write words which go before and after *conference*.

to arrange _____   _____ *room*

_____   _____

_____ (a) conference _____

_____

_____

_____

5 You are Jessica Leung. Make your letter to Daniel Black more concise. Write only the essential information. Write 60–80 words.

6 Exam practice

- You are Daniel Black. You have organised a marketing conference for your company at the The Central Hotel, Hong Kong.
- Write an email to the delegates:
  * saying where the conference will be
  * saying when the conference will be
  * asking everyone to confirm if they can attend.
- Write 30–40 words.

From: Daniel Black
To: Marketing Personnel

Unit 11a 83

Unit 11b — At a conference

Welcome to the conference

Listening 1

1.34

1 Didier Legrand, the Sales Director of Vitesse Sportswear, makes the opening speech at the company's Annual Sales Conference. Listen and complete the programme.

Vitesse Sportswear
Annual Sales Conference 2011

Programme

Saturday 16 June

Time	
10.00	Arrival
10.15	Opening speech
10.30	**(1)** _____
12.30	Lunch
14.00	**(2)** _____
15.30	Coffee
16.00	Guest speaker:
	(3) _____ (Allman & Partners)
(4) ____	Sessions end
19.00	**(5)** _____
20.00	Dinner

Sunday 17 June

Time	
(6) ____	Workshop: **(7)** _____
10.30	Coffee
11.00	**(8)** _____
12.00	Farewell lunch

2 Listen again and answer the questions.

1. How many annual sales conferences has the company already had?
2. How many days do Vitesse conferences normally last?
3. Why are all the delegates together at the first session?
4. What is the guest speaker going to talk about?
5. How far away is the restaurant?
6. Where is Jodie Cox based?

Grammar

3 Read the audioscript on page 145 and underline the verb forms that follow *as soon as*, *after*, *when*, *until* and *before*. Then complete the information on the opposite page.

Don't forget

Time clauses
- When we express time in the future, **before**, **after**, **when**, **as soon as** and **[Check font]** are followed by the _____ or _____ .
*We'll start the session **as soon as** he arrives.*
*We can go for lunch **after** she's finished her presentation.*

Speaking

4 Work in pairs. Your teacher will give you some cards. Use the information on the cards, the agenda and the words below to form complete sentences.

| before | after | when | as soon as | until |

5 Work in pairs. A company is organising a weekend conference in your city. The delegates are arriving at 6 pm on Friday and leaving at 8 pm on Sunday. Four hours of sightseeing is on the programme. What would you show them and at what time?

The conference report

Reading

1 Two weeks after the conference Vitesse produces a report summarising the conference sessions. Match the extracts from the report with the sessions on the programme.

A   An extremely useful presentation that gave us all something to think about. I'm sure everyone will benefit from the helpful tips for dealing with customer calls. We are planning a training pack to improve the way the group deals with incoming calls.

B   A highly productive workshop session that resulted in some intelligent ideas for promoting the company's latest product. The launch will mean that we all have an exciting and busy twelve months ahead of us.

C   As always, it was interesting to see how the whole company has performed over the last twelve months. All the presentations were brief, professional and extremely well-prepared. The positive figures were certainly a great start to the conference.

D   This workshop session gave people the opportunity to discuss the company's sales objectives and strategies. This was a hard but rewarding session with serious and occasionally heated discussion on a range of issues.

At a conference   **Unit 11b**   85

2 Answer the questions.

1 What is Vitesse going to do as a result of the guest speaker's session?
2 In which session did the speakers make short presentations?
3 How has the company performed over the last twelve months?
4 What did the delegates find difficult to agree on?

Vocabulary

3 Read the extracts from the report again and underline all the adjectives describing the sessions. What are the opposites of the adjectives?

Listening 2

1.35

4 All the Vitesse delegates have to fill in a feedback form. Listen to Jodie Cox talk to a colleague about the conference and fill in the form for her.

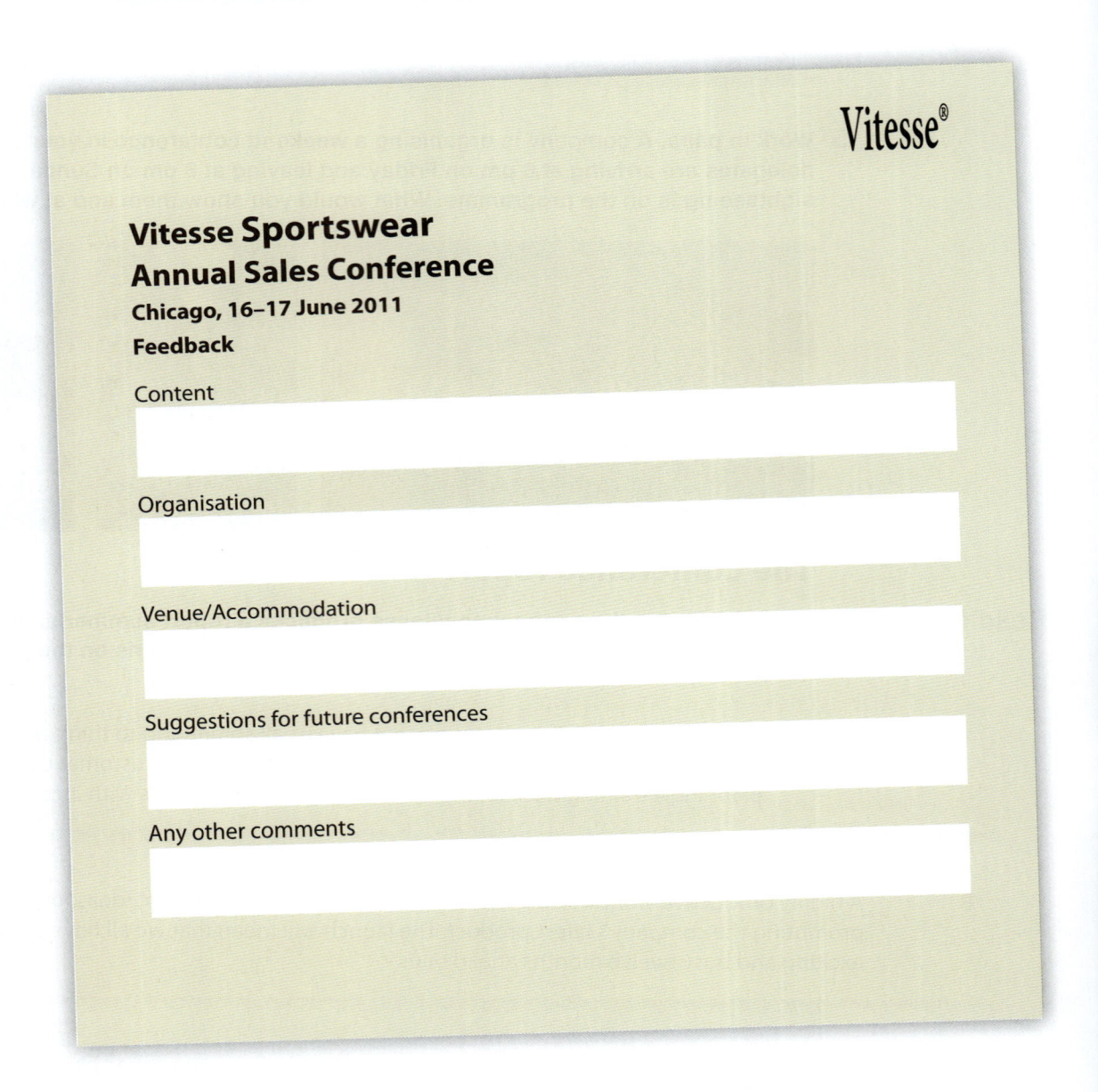

Vitesse®

Vitesse Sportswear
Annual Sales Conference
Chicago, 16–17 June 2011
Feedback

Content

Organisation

Venue/Accommodation

Suggestions for future conferences

Any other comments

Speaking

5 Work in pairs. What makes a good conference?

86

Self-study 11b

1 **Complete the following sentences in your own words.**

1 We'll send everyone a memo as soon as ...
   we make the final arrangements.

2 We can't book the rooms until ...

3 I'll give you the programme before ...

4 The conference will finish after ...

5 We'll start the session as soon as ...

6 I'll copy the report for you when ...

2 **Look at the adjectives below. Write the opposite adjective next to it.**

1 helpful .... *unhelpful* ....
2 well-prepared ....
3 positive ....
4 useful ....
5 productive ....
6 exciting ....
7 rewarding ....

3 **Write the opposites of the sentences below.**

1 She sent me a *long* conference report.
   She sent me a short conference report.

2 The conference was *hard* to organise.

3 She gave a *long* sales presentation.

4 Some of the sessions were too *long*.

5 The hotel beds were very *hard*.

6 The journey to the restaurant was *long*.

7 The speaker was *hard* to understand.

4 **Exam practice**

- Look at questions 1–5.
- In each question, which sentence is correct?
- For each question, mark the correct letter A, B or C.

1
> Due to circumstances beyond our control, the conference will be postponed.

A The conference will take place as planned.
B The conference will not take place.
C The conference will take place at a later date.

2
> Delegates are asked to check out by 10.30 am.

The delegates should leave their rooms

A before half past ten.
B at ten thirty.
C earlier than half past eleven.

3
> Could all speakers please produce summaries of the sessions they gave.

The speakers should write

A full details of what is in their session.
B a brief report about their session.
C a proposal for their session.

4
> **WORKSHOPS**
> Improving margins — Wagner suite
> Selling on the telephone — Schumann suite
> Marketing new products — Bach suite

The workshop on increasing profits will be in the

A Wagner suite.
B Schumann suite.
C Bach suite.

5
> Mr Sylvester is used to giving presentations to large audiences.

Mr Sylvester

A doesn't give presentations to large groups any more.
B often gave presentations to large groups in the past.
C often gives presentations to large groups.

Unit 11b   87

Unit 12 — Exam focus: Listening

The Listening Test

The Cambridge BEC Preliminary Listening Test has four parts.

Part	Input	Task
1	Short conversations	Multiple-choice
2	Short telephone conversation or monologue	Note completion (numbers and one spelling)
3	Monologue	Note completion (words and one date)
4	A longer conversation or monologue (3–4 mins)	Multiple-choice

Length: A total of 12 minutes of listening material played twice, plus 10 minutes at the end to transfer answers to the Answer Sheet.

Before listening

1 It is important that you use your time well even before you listen. Here are some tips.

- Always read the instructions very carefully before you listen.
- Check the type of answer you need to give. Is it a letter, numbers or words?
- Check the number of words you should write for each answer.
- You will always be given time to read through the questions before you listen. Use this time well. Try to predict words you might hear and what the answer might be.

2 Work in pairs. Look at the Listening Test below. Predict words that you might hear in the recordings.

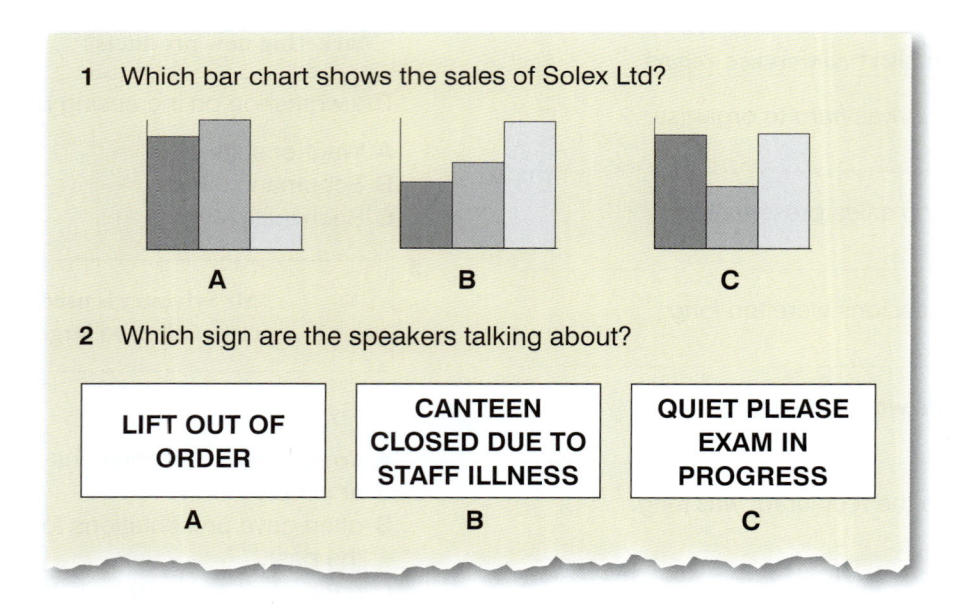

1 Which bar chart shows the sales of Solex Ltd?

A   B   C

2 Which sign are the speakers talking about?

LIFT OUT OF ORDER	CANTEEN CLOSED DUE TO STAFF ILLNESS	QUIET PLEASE EXAM IN PROGRESS
A	B	C

While listening

You will hear every part of the Listening Test twice.

First listening
Try to get an idea of the general context and answer as many of the questions as possible. However, do not worry if you do not understand every word. Also, do not worry if you do not know all the answers yet. The second listening will give you a second chance.

Second listening
Do not stop listening if you think you know the answer: with multiple-choice questions the recordings often include words from the incorrect options. Listen for negatives and words such as *but* or *instead of*.

After listening

1 **In order to obtain a high mark, you need to check your answers carefully. Here are some tips.**
   - Make sure that you give only **one** answer for each question.
   - Make sure that you answer **every** question.
   - Check your answers **after** transferring them on to the Answer Sheet.

   Find the candidates' mistakes on the question papers below.

Questions 16–22
- Look at the notes below.
- Some information is missing.
- You will hear part of a presentation by a Human Resources manager.
- For each question, fill in the missing information in the numbered space using one or two words.

Department: (16) ....
Vacancy: (17) *New department Secreta* ....

Questions 23–30
- Listen to two managers discussing the price of a product.
- For each question **23–30**, mark the correct letter **A**, **B** or **C**.
- You will hear the conversation twice.

23 The managers want to raise the price because
   - (A) materials have become more expensive.
   - B   the product is selling very well.
   - (C) of a pay rise for the workers.

Exam practice

PART ONE

Listening tips

1 Read the instructions carefully.
2 Read the information before you listen.
3 Listen to the end of each extract before you choose your answer.
4 Use the second listening to check your answers.
5 Transfer your answers carefully to the Answer Sheet.

Questions 1–8

- For questions 1–8, you will hear eight short recordings. (2.01)
- For each question, mark one letter A, B or C.
- You will hear each recording twice.

1 What is Maria's job title?

   A Sales Executive
   B Marketing Manager
   C Managing Director

2 Where are they going to take the visitors?

The Italian Experience	The Thai House	The Potato House
A	B	C

3 What was the final decision about the meeting?

   A It will take place as arranged.
   B It will take place at a later date.
   C It will not take place.

4 Which part of the job offer was George unhappy about?

   A The amount of pay.
   B The number of hours.
   C The number of holidays.

5 Which graph is the Head of Department talking about?

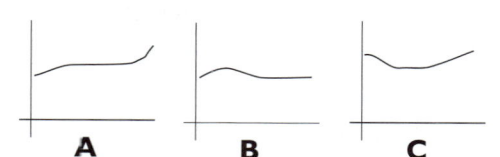

   A   B   C

6 When are the visitors arriving?

   A Ten o'clock.
   B Half past ten.
   C Eleven o'clock.

7 Which photocopier do they decide to buy?

   A The X40.
   B The BT100.
   C The RX200.

8 Which part of the factory does Alan want to change?

   A The packing hall.
   B The warehouse.
   C The production line.

PART TWO

Listening tips

1 Read the instructions carefully.
2 Read the information before you listen.
3 Use the second listening to check your answers.
4 Transfer your answers carefully to the Answer Sheet.

Questions 9–15

- Look at the notes below.
- Some information is missing.
- You will hear two people discussing an invoice. (2.02)
- For each question, fill in the missing information in the numbered space using a word, numbers or letters.
- You will hear the conversation twice.

Premium Office Supplies

Invoice number:	(9) ....
Invoice date:	(10) .... February 2011
Photocopy paper:	(11) .... boxes @ €14.99
V.A.T. @	(12) .... %
Total to pay:	(13) € ....
To reach us by:	17th March 2011
Contact name:	(14) Natalia ....
Telephone no.:	(15) 0176 ....

90

Exam practice

PART THREE

Listening tips
1 Read the instructions carefully.
2 Read the information before you listen.
3 Think what kind of information the answer might be: a name, address, number, etc.
4 Use the second listening to check your answers.
5 Transfer your answers carefully to the Answer Sheet.

Questions 16–22

- Look at the notes.
- Some information is missing.
- 🎧 2.03 You will hear a woman talking to some journalists about a new product range.
- For each question, fill in the missing information in the numbered space using one or two words.
- You will hear the presentation twice.

NatureSoft Skincare

Head Office:	(16) ....
Core market:	(17) ....
New range:	(18) .... cosmetic range
Target market:	(19) .... women
Selling point:	(20) ....
Public launch date:	(21) ....
Advertising slogan:	(22) ....

PART FOUR

Listening tips
1 Read the instructions and questions carefully.
2 Do not worry if you miss the answer first time.
3 Use the second listening to check your answers.
4 Transfer your answers carefully to the Answer Sheet.

Questions 23–30

- 🎧 2.04 Listen to a Head of Department talking to an employee about her performance.
- For each question 23–30, mark the correct letter A, B or C.
- You will hear the conversation twice.

23 Sharon started working for the company
   A some time last year.
   B one year ago.
   C over a year ago.

24 Sharon found out about the vacancy from
   A a friend.
   B a newspaper.
   C an internal memo.

25 Sharon does not enjoy
   A answering the telephone.
   B typing invoices.
   C preparing price lists.

26 The biggest problem with her PC is that
   A it doesn't run the stock-control system.
   B it doesn't have enough memory.
   C it doesn't run the sales-tracking system.

27 Sharon would like the company to buy
   A better software.
   B a new PC.
   C more IT support.

28 When dealing with complaints, she would like to
   A take more responsibility.
   B pass the customer on to her boss.
   C give the customers money back.

29 Sharon's boss thinks that some customers
   A often receive faulty orders.
   B often make mistakes.
   C are not always honest.

30 Sharon's main aim for next year is to
   A get to know the customers a lot better.
   B make fewer mistakes.
   C learn more about the products.

Unit 13a   Production

Bread production

Listening 1 1.36

1 Brian Benfield, Production Manager in the UK branch of Gosardi, an international food group, explains how baguettes are produced. Before you listen, put the following stages of the process into the correct order.

- ☐ cool the baguettes
- ☐ box the baguettes
- ☐ mix the dough
- ☐ wrap the baguettes
- ☐ form the baguettes
- ☐ bake the baguettes
- ☐ weigh the ingredients (flour, yeast and water)

Now listen and check your answers.

2 Look at the floorplan below. Listen again and write the correct numbers next to the following:

- ☐ circuit
- ☐ first prover
- ☐ baguette former
- ☐ mixers
- ☐ divider
- ☐ second prover
- ☐ oven
- ☐ cooler

Floorplan of the bakery

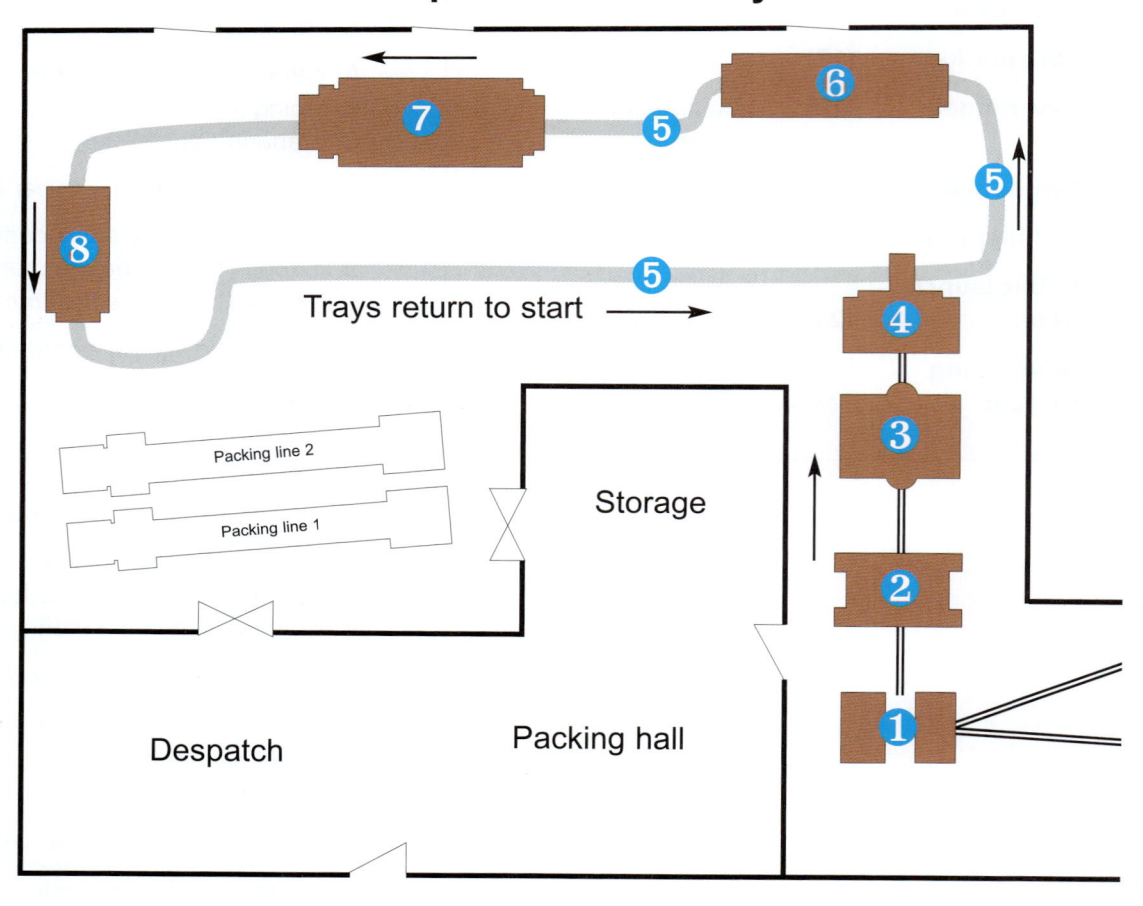

Speaking

3 What happens at each of the machines on the production line?

4 Complete the information below.

> Don't forget
>
> **The Passive**
> The passive is formed with the verb _____
> (in the correct tense) and the _____ of the verb.
> *The ingredients* **are weighed**.
> *The company* **was set up** *in 1982*.

Vocabulary

5 Which verbs can be used with each noun? Tick (✓) the correct boxes.

	weigh	mix	bake	cool	wrap	box	despatch
ingredients	✓						
dough							
baguettes							
boxes							

Now think of another noun to go with each verb.

weigh .... wrap ....
mix .... box ....
bake .... despatch ....
cool ....

Speaking

6 Work in pairs. Think of three processes. How many of the verbs below can you use to describe each process?

| check | cool | cut | despatch | heat |
| mix | press | weigh | wrap | collect |

Sending a parcel

First the object **is wrapped**. Then the parcel **is weighed**. It is taken to the post office or **collected** by a courier. Then the parcel **is dispatched**.

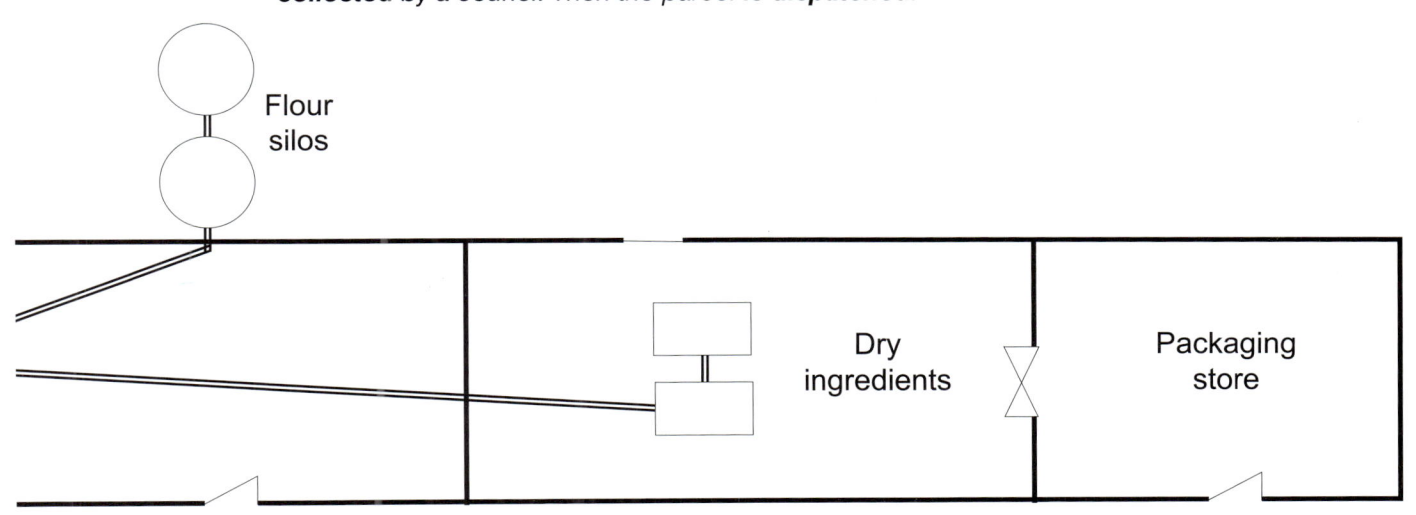

Flour silos

Dry ingredients

Packaging store

Production problems

Listening 2 1.37

1. Brian Benfield talks about production problems at the bakery. Before you listen, decide which of the following would cause problems most often. Then listen and compare your answers.
   - human problems
   - electronic problems
   - mechanical problems

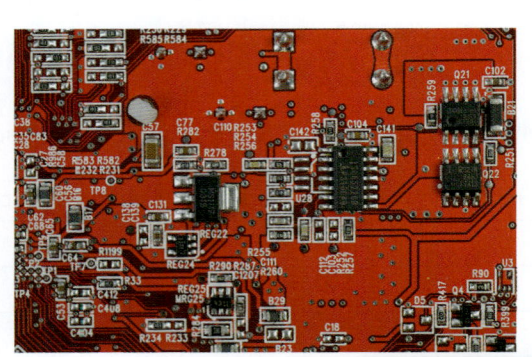

2. Listen again and complete the sentences.

   1. The computer stops the whole process _____
   2. If the computer gets the mix wrong, _____
   3. If a mixerman forgets the yeast and additives, _____
   4. When an old tray loses its shape, _____
   5. We can lose up to an hour and a half of production _____

> **Don't forget**
>
> **When or if?**
> - **When** is used when we expect something to happen.
>   *The trays pass through a sensor **when** they enter the oven.*
> - **If** is used when we are unsure if something will happen.
>   *We can lose an hour and a half **if** we have a really bad day.*

Grammar

3. Match the following sentence halves and complete the sentences with *when* or *if*.

   The trays pass a sensor when they enter or exit any machine.

1 The trays pass a sensor	they get jammed in them.
2 The baguettes do not rise	they enter or exit any machine.
3 The line produces 6,000 baguettes an hour	the oven temperature is too high.
4 The baguettes are taken off the trays	the dough does not prove first.
5 Old trays can damage machines	everything runs properly.
6 The baguettes burn	they have left the cooler.

Speaking

4. Work in pairs. What goes wrong at your partner's place of work? What does he/she do when things go wrong?

Self-study 13a

1 Rewrite the following sentences using the passive.

1 We weigh the ingredients.
   The ingredients are weighed.

2 The system feeds the ingredients into the mixers.
   _____

3 A machine drops the baguettes onto a tray.
   _____

4 Ovens bake the baguettes for ten minutes.
   _____

5 A blower blows cool air over the baguettes.
   _____

6 Packing machines pack the baguettes in boxes.
   _____

2 Look at the flow chart below. Write a short text describing the start-up process for the baguette production line. Add any words which are necessary (articles, sequencers, etc.).

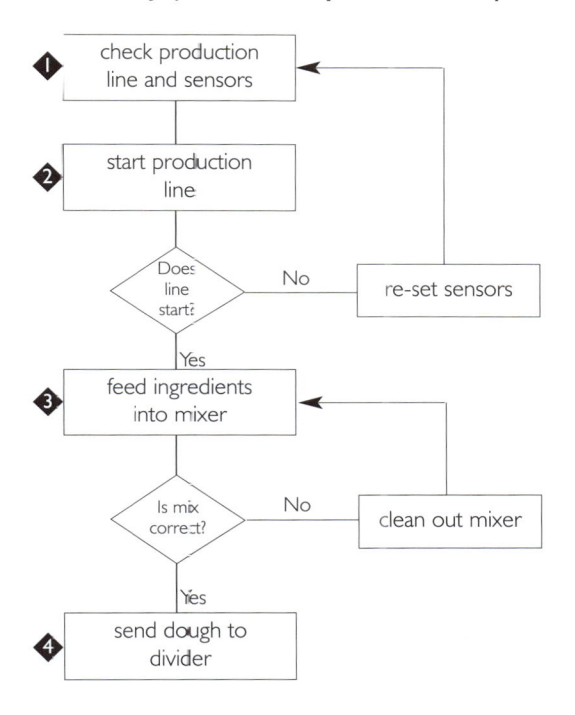

1. check production line and sensors
2. start production line
   - Does line start? No → re-set sensors
3. Yes → feed ingredients into mixer
   - Is mix correct? No → clean out mixer
4. Yes → send dough to divider

3 Complete the diagram with vocabulary from the audioscript for Listening 1 on pages 146–147.

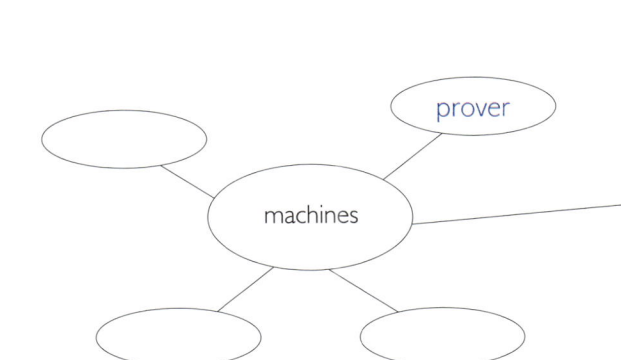

machines: prover, ...

ingredients: flour, ...

processes: weigh, ...

4 Exam practice

- You are the Production Manager at a factory.
- You notice that some packing machines are not set correctly for some new packaging.
- Write an email to all packing machine operators:
  * explaining the problem
  * saying which machines are having problems
  * asking them to check the machine settings.
- Write 30–40 words.

To: All packing machine operators
From: Production Manager

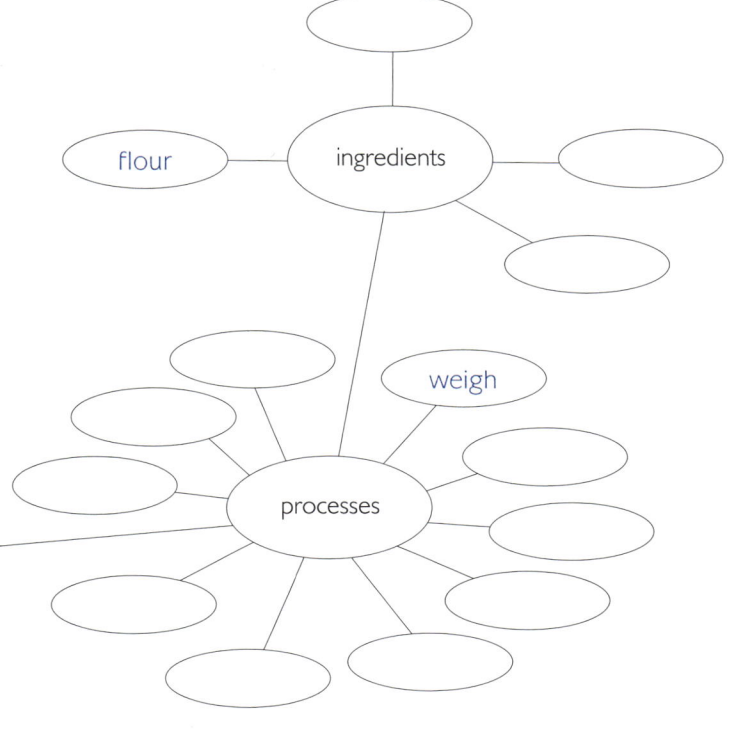

_____
_____
_____
_____
_____
_____
_____
_____
_____

Unit 13a 95

Unit 13b Quality control

Monitoring quality

Speaking 1 What does the job of a quality control (QC) manager at a snacks factory involve? Use the verbs below.

> check   monitor   inspect   sample   reject

Listening 1 2 Mazli Amhar is Head of Quality Control at Alibaba, a Malaysian snack producer. (1.38) She talks about monitoring quality. Listen and complete the table below.

Quality Control at Alibaba
Inspection points

1 Suppliers	2 Goods in	3 _____	4 Finished goods
• QC processes	• quantities	• cooking oil	• _____
• _____	• _____	• flavouring	• packet seal
	• _____	• _____	• _____
		• crispness	

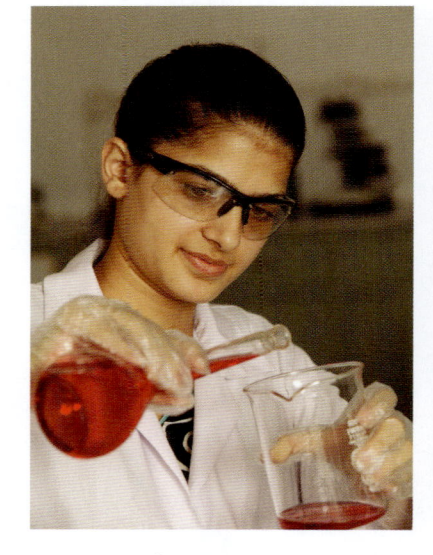

3 Listen again and answer the questions.

1 Why is hygiene very important for the supplier?
2 Why is it important to check transport packaging?
3 What happens if the snacks are too oily?
4 How do they check the taste of the snacks?

Speaking 4 Work in pairs. What QC processes are there at your partner's place of work?

Improving quality

Listening 2 1.39 **1** Mazli is in a meeting with Amrit Singh, the Production Director, and Lu Wei, the Operations Manager. Read the memo below. Then listen to their discussion and answer the questions.

1 What is the problem?
2 What causes it?
3 Which proposals do Lu Wei and Mazli each support?
4 What action does Amrit decide to take?

Alibaba Quality Snacks
Internal Memorandum

To: Mazli Amhar
cc: Lu Wei
From: Amrit Singh
Date: 8 March 2011

Re: QC Meeting   9 March 2011

Our reject levels have risen by over five per cent in three weeks. Chemical analysis shows that fat levels are above the acceptable maximum.

Here are some ideas for dealing with the problem. Please be prepared to discuss them at the meeting.

1 Increase the sampling rate
2 Change the cooker temperature sensors
3 Change the cooking oil more often

---

2 Listen again and choose the best option to complete the sentences.

1 The samples do not pick up the high fat levels because
   A the cooker does not work properly.
   B the oil temperature changes too quickly.
   C the factory is running at full capacity.

2 Mazli does not want to increase the sampling rate because she
   A thinks the rate is already good enough.
   B has not got enough staff in her department.
   C does not think it will make a difference.

3 Lu Wei does not want to change the sensors because
   A the sensors are very expensive.
   B it would mean losing production.
   C he has already changed them.

4 The temperature sensors do not work properly
   A when the cooker oil gets dirty.
   B if samples are not taken regularly.
   C because the cookers are old.

5 Lu Wei does not want to change the oil more often because
   A it will be expensive and cut production.
   B he thinks changing sensors is a better idea.
   C he does not think it will make a difference.

Grammar

3 Look at the audioscript on pages 147–148. Underline examples of the present simple. What are the different uses of the present simple in the conversation?

> **Don't forget**
>
> **Conditional 1 (real)**
> - We can use the following conditional forms to talk about the possible results of an action:
>
>   If + present simple, will
>   going to + infinitive
>   might
>
> - We can use **will / going to** when we are sure of the result.
> - We can use **might** when we are not sure of the result.

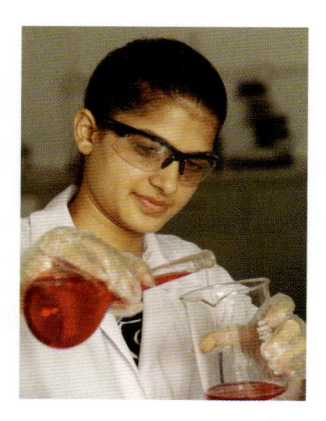

4 You are discussing changes to the place where you work. Here are some of your colleagues' suggestions. Your thoughts are in brackets. Write responses using conditional sentences.

1 'I think we should buy new machinery.' (Very expensive!)

   If we buy new machinery, it'll be expensive.

2 'We need to spend more on training.' (Possibly improve quality)

   _____

3 'We have to work more overtime.' (Problems with the workforce!)

   _____

4 'Why don't we increase the workforce?' (Spend too much time training new people)

   _____

5 'Let's increase our QC activities.' (Possibly reduce reject levels)

   _____

6 'We can only offer workers a 2% pay rise.' (Never accept it!)

   _____

Speaking

5 You are the directors of a small soft drinks producer. You are going to hear descriptions of different problems at your company and possible solutions. Discuss the problems and decide what action to take. Use some of the words below.

| Let's … | Why don't we …? | We should … |

Self-study 13b

1 Match the words. Then use them to complete the sentences below.

1	quality	life
2	inspection	control
3	shelf	analysis
4	finished	in
5	goods	goods
6	chemical	points

1 All _____ are stored in a warehouse ready for despatch.
2 There are five main _____ in our quality control programme.
3 The _____ department is next to the production hall.
4 The _____ of our ingredients is about two weeks. After that we throw them away.
5 We check all _____ when they arrive at our warehouse.
6 The _____ is carried out in a laboratory in the QC department.

2 Match the words with their opposites. Then complete the text with the correct form of the words. Do not use any word more than once.

1	demand	fall
2	goods in	increase
3	rise	accept
4	reject	supply
5	reduce	finished goods

The problems started about six months ago. We were already at full capacity when (1) _____ suddenly went up by 30%. We only had one warehouse so both (2) _____ and (3) _____ were in the same place. There was no way we could (4) _____ our storage space so we worked very closely with our (5) _____, who delivered the ingredients just when we needed them and not before. On the production side, both workers and machinery had to work overtime and our quality levels began to (6) _____. We soon noticed a (7) _____ in our (8) _____ levels and we had to throw away more and more finished goods. But we couldn't really do anything about it without (9) _____ capacity so we just had to (10) _____ the situation.

3 Complete the following sentences with the correct form of the verb in brackets.

1 We ____'ll need____ (need) to increase capacity if we ____get____ (get) any more orders.
2 Even if we _____ (change) the sensors, it _____ (not/make) any difference.
3 If it _____ (not/make) any difference, we _____ (talk) about it again next week.
4 If demand _____ (increase), we _____ (have to) increase overtime.
5 What _____ (happen) if we _____ (keep) the oil in the cooker longer?
6 We _____ (have to) spend more on training if we _____ (want) to improve quality.
7 If the goods _____ (not/arrive) soon, we _____ (look) for a new supplier.
8 The QC department _____ (not/be) happy if we _____ (increase) the sampling rate.

4 Exam practice

- Look at the notice below. It shows the different divisions of a manufacturing company.
- For questions 1–5, decide where each person should go.
- For each question, mark the correct letter A–H.
- Do not use any letter more than once.

A	Production line
B	Warehouse
C	Despatch
D	Research & development
E	Quality control
F	Packing line
G	Canteen
H	Washrooms

1 Sam needs to get changed and freshen up after her shift.
2 Vince wants to research how the goods are currently manufactured.
3 Kate needs to take sample products for inspection.
4 John needs to check the quality of the storage facilities.
5 Ian wants to see what happens to the goods after they have been packed.

Unit 14a Direct service providers

The call centre

Speaking 1 Call centres are a growing business sector across the world. Why do you think companies invest so much money in them?

Listening 1 2 Gabe Steele, the National Sales Manager at American Life, talks about call centres. Listen and complete the journalist's notes.

Notes: American Life

Products
- Insurance lines: auto insurance (**1**) _____ , home and travel insurance
- Vehicle breakdown service
- Financial services: mortgages, personal (**2**) _____ savings and (**3**) _____

Company statistics
Number of call centres: (**4**) _____
Total number of staff: (**5**) _____

Advantages of call centre service
Lower insurance (**6**) _____ for the client and lower (**7**) _____ for the company. When customers call, they get an immediate (**8**) _____ .

Future
Offshoring is not the answer because labour (**9**) _____ are likely to rise in places like India. Call centres will probably find it difficult to find and keep (**10**) _____ . Gabe Steele believes that (**11**) _____ call centres are the future – they make it possible for companies to hire new staff from across the (**12**) _____ .

3 Listen again and choose the correct option to complete the sentence.

1 Using calls centres keeps costs lower because the company does not have to
  A employ lots of workers.
  B rent shops or pay commission.
  C pay for advertising.

2 In the future, American Life
  A will probably relocate its call centres where labour is cheaper.
  B might relocate its call centres in India.
  C won't 'offshore' its call centres.

3 American Life is starting to hire new staff
  A who can work from home.
  B who can do a wider range of different jobs.
  C who live within a fifty-mile radius round each call centre.

4 When companies use virtual call centres,
  A they don't need to hire so many staff.
  B they have more potential staff to choose from.
  C they don't need to train staff.

American Life

40,000

American Life's motor telesales operators handle around 40,000 incoming calls a day.

Vocabulary

4 Match the words with the meanings.

1 broker — money you pay for insurance
2 premium — person who buys and sells things, e.g. insurance, for other people
3 claim — money paid to a salesperson for every sale he/she makes
4 policy — loan to buy a house
5 mortgage — request for money to be paid by an insurer
6 commission — insurance contract

Don't forget

Future possibility and probability

- We can express possibility in different ways.
  *In the future, companies **might** relocate their call centres back to the USA.*
  *Virtual call centres **will possibly** replace most of our existing call centres.*

- We can also talk about probability in different ways.
  *Companies **will probably** have difficulty finding staff.*
  *Labour costs **are likely to** rise fast in places like India.*

Speaking

5 Work in pairs. Are the following situations likely in your country? Are they already happening?

1 Customer-service companies will outsource and offshore almost all their business.
2 Automated customer services systems with 'virtual' agents will completely replace people.
3 Call centres will use video-phones for face-to-face contact.

Working in a call centre

Listening 2

1.41

1 Work in pairs. Gabe Steele talks about working conditions in a call centre. Before you listen, decide whether the following statements are true or false. Then listen and check your answers.

1 The computer system monitors the workers every minute of their shift.
2 Call centre agents can earn productivity bonuses for selling a lot of policies.
3 Agents normally work a lot more hours than office workers.
4 Agents work the same hours every month.
5 The call centre is open from 9 am until 5 pm on weekdays.
6 Call centres employ a lot of young people and women.
7 The company tries to make working in the call centre more interesting.

Reading

2 Which of the following people would be interested in working in a call centre? Why?

Zoe Connolly, 22

I've just finished university and I'm looking for a job. I've got a degree in business studies but I'm not really sure what I want to do. I'd like to take some time off and travel around the world but I don't have any money.

Vernon Eliot, 32

I'm unemployed at the moment. I've worked in sales a lot and I'd like to continue in that area. I really enjoy working with people and visiting customers. Sales is always interesting because you know you can always sell more, so you never relax.

Marisol Cara, 26

I worked as a secretary after leaving school but I stopped work last year to start a family. My daughter is now nearly six months old and I would like to go back to work. My husband works in an office from nine till five.

Speaking

3 Work in pairs. More and more organisations sell their services and products directly to customers online. What are the advantages and disadvantages of the internet business model a) for customers and b) for a business? What kinds of business is it NOT appropriate for?

Self-study 14a

1 Look back through the unit (including the audioscripts). How many words connected with *insurance* can you find? Now write words which go before the word *insurance* and words which go after.

.... auto .... broker ....

....

.... **insurance** ....

....

2 Which is the odd one out?

1 contract	policy	agreement	memorandum
2 cost	claim	premium	price
3 premium	location	price	commission
4 instant	immediate	exciting	fast
5 life	loan	auto	house
6 volume	total	quality	number
7 loan	mortgage	provider	pension

3 Complete the sentences with the words below.

supervisor	loan	premium
policy	monitor	broker
claim	commission	enquiry

1 I changed my car insurance because the _____ was lower.
2 I bought the car with a _____ from the bank.
3 We know a _____ who advises us on insurance.
4 As an insurance salesman he earns _____ on everything he sells.
5 A new customer phoned me to make an _____.
6 The system lets us _____ what the operatives are doing at any time.
7 My car has just been stolen so I need to make a _____.
8 Her house insurance _____ ran out last month.
9 A _____ makes decisions if operatives have to deal with large or unusual risks.

4 Exam practice

- Read the newspaper article below about call centres.
- Choose the correct word from A, B or C below.
- For each question, mark the correct letter A, B or C.

Call centre creates 2000 jobs in the Phillippines

HJC Bank is setting up a call centre in Boracay in the central Philippines (1) ..... of the growth of its internet and telephone banking service. This is a welcome decision for the area, (2) ..... companies considered less attractive (3) ..... regions such as India, Malaysia or Singapore in (4) ..... list of the best locations for call centres. Opening early next year, the centre (5) ..... expected to employ 2,000 people over the next three years.

HJC Bank, the internet and telephone banking service, (6) ..... introduced in 2010 and has (7) ..... than 600,000 customers. The service is helped by the well-developed telecoms infrastructure of the Philippines and the high standard of English. HJC Bank is (8) ..... 25,000 new customers every month and the bank expects one million customers (9) ..... the next two years. One director said: 'Opening another call centre shows (10) ..... popular our internet and telephone banking service is (11) ..... our customers. HJC Bank will continue to invest to satisfy their needs.'

1	A because	B despite	C due
2	A where	B what	C which
3	A that	B than	C as
4	A there	B their	C its
5	A are	B be	C is
6	A was	B were	C have
7	A more	B many	C much
8	A attractive	B attracted	C attracting
9	A at	B over	C on
10	A why	B very	C how
11	A with	B between	C through

Unit 14a 103

Unit 14b The banking sector

The banking revolution

Reading 1 Read the article and match the headings with the paragraphs.

| The question of customer service | Paperless billing – always a good thing? |
| Twenty years on from the banking revolution | The Three C's |

The new face of banking in the 21st Century

1. _____

The banking revolution of the last two decades has caused huge changes in the way that banks conduct their businesses and interact with their customers; but what are the results of these changes in real terms? Are bank customers getting a better service, and are the banks themselves more efficient?

2. _____

Martha Hogan, head of customer relations at YourBank, believes the answer is 'yes'. 'Customers are delighted they don't have to stand in long queues at the bank anymore. Now they can check their bank balance without leaving the house. But, most importantly, internet banking puts the customer in complete control. We see it as a good thing that our customers depend on us less. They can use the computer to control their money and to manage it directly.' Hogan talks about 'The Three C's – control, comfort and convenience.' As online banking becomes more developed, customers can choose to do their banking on the move. Nowadays you can use your mobile phone to pay your electricity bill on the train on the way home from work.'

3. _____

So, is the banking revolution all good news? Not all bank customers think so. Banks invested heavily in developing new technology to create their internet banking systems and this led to cost-cutting in other areas. Many banks cut thousands of jobs and closed smaller branches to save money. Setting up call centres to service hundreds of branches from just a few locations made it possible to reduce staff numbers even more. However, there are customers that say they still prefer direct contact with their local branch, even if this is only possible during business hours. Whilst the banks are making record profits, many customers believe they are getting a poorer service.

4. _____

It's not just customer service that is a problem. Some customers who changed to paying all their bills online are now changing back. They feel they actually have less control with online billing than paper bills. 'Electronic bills don't always contain all the information I need,' says Bill Snowdon, who cancelled his 'paperless billing' service last month. 'Whenever I want to find out information and see my account, it's always very complicated and takes a long time. If online banking does save money for the banks, they should pass this benefit on to the customers by improving their services.'

Page 27

Writing

2 Take notes from the text under the following headings.

Main changes made by banks	Advantages for customers	Disadvantages for customers
• Closed lots of local branches		

3 Choose the correct option to complete the sentences or answer the questions.

1 Martha Hogan thinks internet banking gives customers more control because
   A paperless billing saves them money.
   B they don't rely on the banks so much to manage their money.
   C they don't have to stand in queues at the bank any more.

2 At the beginning of the banking revolution, banks had to cut staff costs
   A so they could pay for better IT.
   B so they could open more call centres.
   C so they could increase customer service in the smaller branches.

3 Why don't some bank customers like call centres?
   A Because they don't have enough staff.
   B Because they can't see the people they are talking to.
   C Because they can never speak directly to their own branch.

4 How are the banks performing?
   A They are making more money than ever before.
   B The cost of IT investment has reduced profits.
   C They have lost customers and lost money.

Grammar

4 Find words ending in *-ing* in the article. Write them in the groups below.

-ing as a noun	*-ing* after prepositions	*-ing* in the present continuous
banking		

Don't forget

Preposition + *-ing*
- Prepositions are usually followed by *-ing* or a noun.
  Banks invested heavily **in** develop**ing** new technology.
  Customers are delighted they don't have to stand **in queues** at the bank anymore.

The banking sector Unit 14b 105

Vocabulary 5 Complete the table with the correct verb or noun.

Verb	Noun	Verb	Noun
merge	merger	compete	....
....	increase	invest	....
reduce	....	....	closure
....	cut	....	development

Speaking 6 Work in pairs. What changes are taking place in your partner's sector?

Home banking

Listening 1 1 Denise Le Blanc enquires about internet banking. She has noted down some questions. Listen and take notes to answer her questions.
(1.42)

- Check transactions on accounts
- Check your balance
- Order a statement
- Transfer money
- Pay bills

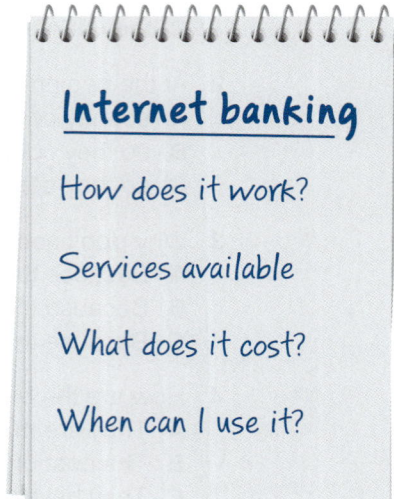

Internet banking

How does it work?

Services available

What does it cost?

When can I use it?

Listening 2 2 Denise applies for the internet banking service. Listen and complete the form.
(1.43)

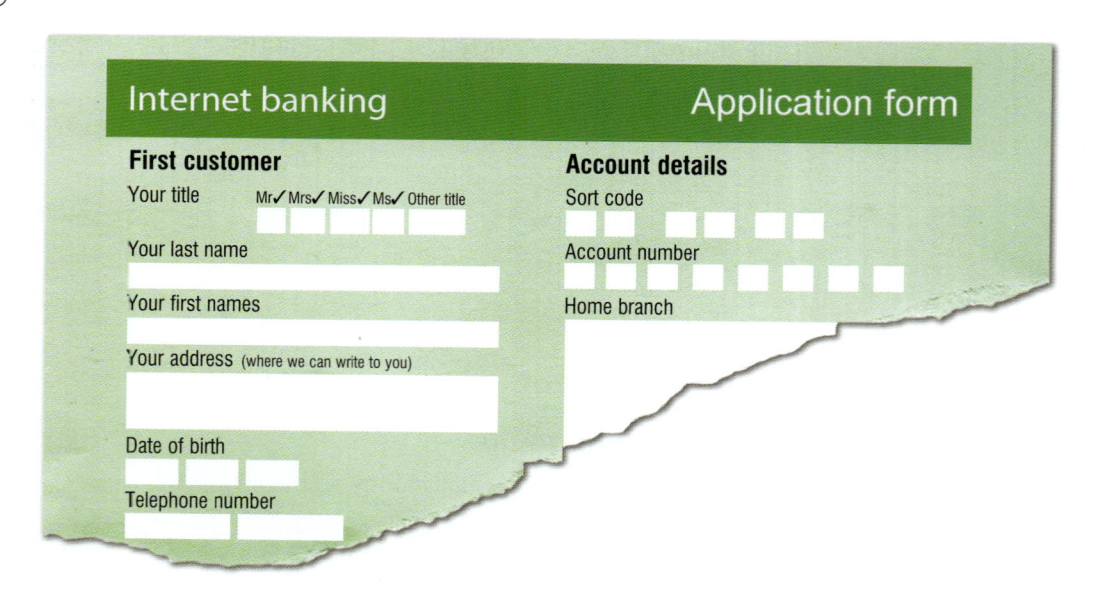

Internet banking — Application form

First customer
Your title Mr ✓ Mrs ✓ Miss ✓ Ms ✓ Other title
Your last name
Your first names
Your address (where we can write to you)
Date of birth
Telephone number

Account details
Sort code
Account number
Home branch

Speaking 3 Work in pairs. What internet banking services does your partner's bank offer? Does your partner use any of them? What other services would he/she like?

Self-study 14b

1 Complete the crossword.

Across

2 When you receive your bills online, this is known as _____ billing.
4 The amount of money you have in the bank.
6 The place in a bank where your money is.
9 The banks are still making a lot of it.
10 A type of bank account for everyday expenses.
11 When two organisations become one, they ___.

Down

1 The places that banks use to outsource their customer services.
2 You need one of these to access your account online.
3 The people who work for an organisation.
4 The bank's local office that you can visit.
5 Internet banking offers customers control, comfort and _____.
7 The verb for when you move money from one place to another.
8 A print-out with information about your account.

2 Match the verbs and nouns.

1 check — bills
2 transfer — a balance
3 pay — a form
4 order — a PIN number
5 sign — a statement
6 follow — money
7 key in — instructions

3 Match the words below to make phrases.

1 compete — in — a service
2 deal — with — a form
3 invest — down — another company
4 pay — in — some details
5 fill — for — problems
6 note — with — new technology

4 Exam practice

- Read the email and the note below.
- Complete the email to Giancarlo Pirelli.
- Write a word, phrase or number in spaces 1–5.

To: bruni.edit@pirellidesign.com
From: jaycee.tranco@topcomputers.com
Subject: internet security

Dear Edit,

Here's the information you needed about the Pro-Protect internet security software. Giancarlo bought a two-year licence for up to six Macs, and the licence period begins from when he installs it on the first one. This licence period applies to any other Macs you install it on.

I have some good news for you. Pro-Protect have a special offer at the moment – they are giving away free additional anti-virus protection to all customers. You can download this online when you install the internet security software from the disk. The attached note tells you about the system requirements.

Anyway, you should have all the information you need, but please let me know if you or Giancarlo require more assistance.

Best wishes,
Jaycee

Jaycee Tranco
IT consultant

- Pro-Protect internet security – system requirements
- Mac system with Intel®processor
- 512 MB RAM
- 270 MB of hard drive space (depending on the size of your anti-virus database)
- Internet connection (to activate the product and for updates)

To: Giancarlo Pirelli
From: Edit Bruni

Jaycee, the IT (1) _____ from Top Computers, contacted us with the information you wanted about the Pro-Protect internet security. The licence is for (2) _____ years and for up to (3) _____ computers. You need to check that all the Macs have (4) _____ MB of memory space. We can also have free additional anti-virus protection – you can (5) _____ it when you install the software.

Unit 14b 107

Unit 15 Exam focus: Speaking

The Speaking Test

The Cambridge BEC Preliminary Speaking Test always takes place with two or three candidates and two examiners.

Part	Format	Input	Task
1	Examiner talks to both candidates	Examiner asks questions	Speaking about yourself Expressing preferences
2	Candidate talks to candidate	Written prompt	Giving a one-minute presentation
3	Candidates discuss a topic together	Written prompt or visual prompt	Completing a collaborative task

Length: A total of 12 minutes.

How to succeed

During the Speaking Test one examiner will ask questions and give instructions. The second examiner in the Speaking Test does not speak to the candidates but is also there to assess your English. Here are some simple tips to remember in the test.

Interactive communication

- Listen carefully to all instructions and respond appropriately. Perfect grammar is useless if you do not answer the question you are asked.
- Ask the examiner to repeat any instructions you are not sure about.
- Give full answers, not just one or two words.
- Keep to and complete the task. Do not talk about other things.
- Good communication means helping the other candidate by asking questions, checking understanding and giving very clear information.
- Work **together** with the other candidate to complete the task in Part Two. Remember to speak to the other candidate and not the examiner.

Organisation of ideas

Show that you can organise your ideas. They can be organised in many ways, such as:
- sequence (*first of all, then, after that, etc.*)
- importance (*I think the most important thing is ...*)
- contrast (*but, although, etc.*).

Grammar and vocabulary

- Do not try to use complicated words and structures. It is better to use simple words well than difficult ones badly.

Pronunciation

- Speak clearly and at a natural speed.
- Relax and think before you speak. It is better to pause before a sentence than in the middle of it.

Personal information

1 After introducing himself/herself, the examiner will check that the information on the entry form is correct. He/she will then ask both candidates a few general questions. Write three questions for each of the topics below.

| family | transport | free time | places to live |

Now work in pairs. Ask and answer questions about the topics.

Speaking

2 Work in pairs. Your teacher will give you some cards with possible Cambridge BEC Preliminary conversation topics on them. Take a card and ask your partner about the topic on it. Then take another card and find a different partner.

Listening (2.05)

3 Listen to Caroline and Cénéric doing Part One of a Speaking Test. Read the exam tips again and listen to the test. What do they do wrong?

(2.06)

4 Now listen to the same candidates doing Part One of the test again. Is it better this time? In what way?

Presentation

Speaking

1 The examiner will ask each candidate to talk about a given topic. Look at the following topic. Think of two things to say about each point.

> What is important when ...?
>
> **Choosing which airline to fly with**
>
> - Price
> - Safety record
> - Customer service

2 Now look at the tips for Part Two of the Speaking Test below.
- Give an opinion about all the main points in the question.
- Use words such as *and*, *but*, *as well*, *because*, *so*.
- Think of a question to ask the other candidate.

Work in pairs. Discuss how you could improve your answer.

Listening (2.07)

3 Listen to Cénéric doing Part Two of the Speaking Test. What does he do wrong?

(2.08)

4 Now listen to Caroline doing Part Two of the Speaking Test. What is the difference? Think of a question to ask her.

Speaking

5 Work in pairs. Look at the Activity sheet on page 138. Take it in turns to pick a topic and give a short talk. Remember to ask each other questions.

Collaborative task

Speaking

1 In Part Three of the Speaking Test the examiner will ask you and the other candidate to discuss a situation and try to reach a decision.

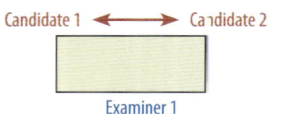

Candidate 1 ⟷ Candidate 2

Examiner 1

Examiner 2

Look at the tips for Part Three of the Speaking Test below.
- Listen to the examiner very carefully.
- Ask the examiner to explain if you do not fully understand.
- Ask your partner what they think and react to their ideas.
- If you do not agree, say why and give a reason.

2 Work in pairs. Your teacher will read you a scenario. Look at the prompt below. Discuss the situation together to complete the task.

The Seated Buddha Thai Restaurant

24 WEST STREET

AUTHENTIC T

The White Hart

Real Ale and Good Pub Food
Sunday Lunch - no booking required
14 High Street, Alton

Charity Soccer Match

Kick-off 7.00pm
Long Road Football Ground
Featuring
Premier Division Players
and
Familiar TV Personalities

Spangles Nightclub

Fridays & Saturdays
10.00pm - 2.00am

Entry €10
Free drink with this flyer

The New Shakespeare Company

Romeo And Juliet
William Shakespeare
A romantic tragedy
Saturday Matinee 2.30 pm
Evenings 8.00pm

Listening

3 Now listen to Caroline and Cénéric complete Part Three of the Speaking Test. What do they do wrong? (2.09)

4 Now listen to the same candidates do Part Three again. What are the differences between the way they do the two tests? (2.10)

Speaking

5 Work in pairs. Look at the Activity sheet on page 139. Use the information to practise Part Three of the Cambridge BEC Preliminary Speaking Test.

Exam practice

Exam practice: Reading

Questions 1–5

- Read the email and the information about office laser printers.
- Complete the form below.
- Write each word, phrase or number in CAPITAL LETTERS.

To: rachel.wells@close-and-sons.co.uk
From: tim.nichols@close-and-sons.co.uk
Subject: New colour laser printer
Date: 10.12.10

Rachel,

We'll have to order the new printer today or it won't be delivered before Christmas. Could you look at these three printers and choose one? We need a printer that is fast but not the most expensive. Could you place the order for me this morning and leave me a copy of the order form?

Thanks

	560Pro	Tek200	Pro-jet
Width	50cm	40cm	62cm
Depth	53cm	50cm	49cm
Height	40cm	33cm	37cm
Pages per min.	3	6	4–5
Memory	12MB	24MB	20MB
Price	€2995	€3495	€3900

ORDER FORM

Company name: (1) ....
Contact person: (2) ....
Date of order: (3) ....
Product: (4) ....
Price: (5) ....

Exam practice: Writing

Part One

- You have decided to work at home tomorrow.
- Write a note for your colleague:
  * saying you won't be in the office tomorrow
  * explaining why you are going to work from home
  * giving your home telephone number.
- Write 30–40 words.

Part Two

- You are visiting a trade fair in Barcelona with your boss. You have seen this hotel in a brochure.

Hotel Gaudí
Rambla de Catalunya 38, Barcelona

The Hotel Gaudí is situated in the heart of Barcelona city centre with its exciting nightlife. The hotel has 120 rooms including forty-two business rooms specifically designed for the business traveller and fully-equipped with communication facilities.

The hotel enjoys direct bus and train connections to the airport (35 mins) and exhibition centre (25 mins). Other facilities include express check-in and check-out, twenty-four hour room service, two bars, restaurant, fitness room and full business centre.

- Write an email to your boss:
  * mentioning the hotel in the brochure
  * describing some of the facilities listed
  * saying why you think you both should stay there
  * asking him which dates you should book.
- Write 60–80 words

Unit 16a Delivery services

Parcel carriers

Speaking 1 Work in pairs. Complete the information about ParcelExpress CH with the figures below.

2 59,200   3 billion   35,0000   10   4 million

1 Its turnover is more than _____ euro a year.

2 ParcelExpress CH delivers _____ parcels and documents every day.

3 The company owns _____ vehicles (cars, vans, trailers, etc.).

4 The ParcelExpress CH customer service centres are listed in the top _____ best call centres in Europe.

5 Home shoppers know the exact time within _____ hours when their ParcelExpress CH parcel will arrive.

6 The company employs about _____ people worldwide.

Reading 2 Now read the first part of the Parcel Express CH brochure and check your answers.

ParcelExpress CH – Parcels to the people

We are one of the world's fastest-growing and most dynamic package distribution companies with an annual revenue of €3 billion. As leading operators in the express parcels sector, we offer a range of specialist solutions and services and have an outstanding record in customer service. We employ 59,200 people in 150 countries and operate more than 35,000 vehicles from over 80 locations. Our customers understand our commitment to quality service and trust us to deliver over four million of their parcels across the world every day.

ParcelExpress CH is recognised as one of the most innovative parcel carrier companies in operation today. We have won many awards for our services particularly in the e-commerce sector. We are particularly well-known for our 'Expect' service, which gives home shoppers a two-hour window of time in which their parcel will arrive. So customers don't have to stay at home all day waiting for the courier to come. The ParcelExpress CH call centres are listed in the top ten best call centres in Europe and offer the highest quality customer service in the industry.

Services

Express Priority Plus
This is ParcelExpress CH's fastest services for your most urgent documents and packages. It guarantees delivery by 8.30 am the next day to hundreds of cities across Europe and Central Asia. The service also includes automatic confirmation of delivery by email as soon as your shipment is delivered.

Express Priority
This is the ideal service for your urgent deliveries. It guarantees delivery by 10.30 am the next business day to over 200 countries. Full electronic tracking means confirmation of delivery is available within minutes in many cases.

Express Expedited
Express Expedited offers quality, reliability and scheduled delivery for your less urgent shipments. The service guarantees door-to-door deliveries within forty-eight hours. Full electronic tracking means confirmation of delivery is available within minutes in many cases.

Express Standard
The ParcelExpress CH Standard offers the benefits of ParcelExpress CH quality,

Reading

3 Match the phrases below with one of the features of the services.

1 Only our Express Priority Plus guarantees ...
2 Three services provide ...
3 With the Express Expedited service, you can arrange ...
4 Both Express Priority Plus and Express Priority guarantee ...

> A same day delivery
> B next day delivery
> C delivery to only EU countries
> D next day delivery by 8.30 am
> E confirmation of delivery
> F worldwide next day delivery by 10.30 am
> G delivery on a particular day

Vocabulary

4 Read through the brochure again and find examples of the following.

- words and phrases that are repeated several times
- words and phrases written to impress the reader

Don't forget

Prepositions of time

- **By/until.** By refers to a point in time. **Until** refers to a period of time.
  *I can do it **by** 10 o'clock. (I can finish it sometime before 10 o'clock.)*
  *We'll wait **until** 10 o'clock (We'll wait for the period between now and 10 o'clock.)*

- **Within** refers to a period of time. It can always be replaced by **in**.
  *We can deliver the package **within** two days.*

- **In/on time.** You arrange to meet a colleague at 1 o'clock.
  *Don't worry, she'll arrive **in** time. (She'll arrive before 1 o'clock.)*
  *Don't worry, she'll arrive **on** time. (She'll arrive at exactly 1 o'clock.)*

5 Match the following sentence halves.

1 Don't worry, an Express Expedited parcel will arrive in	3.30.
2 An Express Priority parcel will get there within	two days.
3 To arrive tomorrow, the package needs to leave by	on time.
4 I'll stay here until	in time.
5 It arrived at 8.30, which was exactly	twenty-four hours.
6 We sent it by ParcelExpress CH Premium so it should arrive	ParcelExpress CH collects the parcel.

Speaking

6 Work in pairs. Which three of the following features do you think are the most important for a parcel delivery service?

next day delivery	reliability	global network
confirmation of delivery	low prices	high quality of service

Delivery services Unit 16a 113

Sending a parcel

Reading

1 Your company wants to send three packages to different countries. How much will each item cost?

- Weight: 3000g
  To: Helsinki
  To arrive by tomorrow morning

- Weight: 1200g
  To: Warsaw
  To arrive within 48 hours

- Weight: 2400g
  To: United States Seattle
  To arrive Thursday

PARCELEXPRESS CH

How to use the guide
All shipping charges are based on three criteria: the service selected, the weight of the shipment and the zone number for the destination. To find the correct rate for your shipment, follow these three steps:

1 Choose your service
ParcelExpress CH offers a choice of Express Priority Expedited or Standard. Refer to the zone chart to see which services are available.

2 Choose the zone
Find the destination country and find its zone number.

3 Find the rate
Turn to the rate chart and match the shipment rate with the correct zone number.

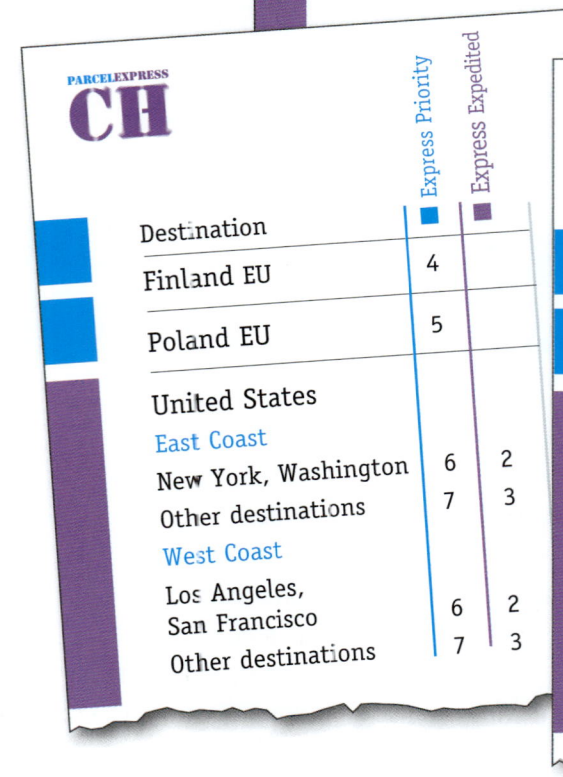

Destination	Express Priority	Express Expedited
Finland EU	4	
Poland EU	5	
United States		
East Coast		
New York, Washington	6	2
Other destinations	7	3
West Coast		
Los Angeles, San Francisco	6	2
Other destinations	7	3

■ Worldwide Express Priority Packages

Weight	zone 4 €	zone 5 €	zone 6 €	zone 7 €	zone 8 €
0.5 kg	37.70	43.50	48.50	44.00	47.50
1.0 kg	41.90	46.80	41.00	47.00	52.00
1.5 kg	44.50	49.40	43.00	50.00	56.50
2.0 kg	47.10	42.00	45.00	53.00	59.10
2.5 kg	49.70	54.60	57.00	56.00	61.70
3.0 kg	52.30	57.20	48.80	58.30	64.30

■ Worldwide Expedited Packages

Weight	zone 1 €	zone 2 €	zone 3 €	zone 4 €	zone 5 €
1.0 kg	45.80	37.40	44.25	47.80	47.80
2.0 kg	50.80	41.20	48.75	53.40	53.40
3.0 kg	55.80	44.60	53.25	58.90	58.90
4.0 kg	60.00	48.00	57.75	64.30	64.30
5.0 kg	64.20	51.40	62.25	69.70	69.70
6.0 kg	67.20	53.00	65.05	73.70	74.10

Speaking

2 Work in pairs. What kind of parcel delivery service does your partner's company use? Why?

3 What other ways are there to send documents and parcels abroad? What are the advantages and disadvantages of each method?

4 Work in pairs. Your teacher will give you two sets of cards showing items and destinations. Take one from each set and decide the best way to send the item to that destination.

Self-study 16a

1 Complete the sentences with the prepositions.

in	on	by	until	within

1 We sent it by Express Priority Plus so it should arrive __by__ 8.30 tomorrow morning.
2 We chose ParcelExpress CH Expedited in order to guarantee delivery _____ twenty-four hours.
3 She's very punctual. She always arrives exactly _____ time.
4 If you email it, it'll get there _____ minutes.
5 We can't send it _____ we've weighed it.
6 If you want delivery _____ a particular day, you should request a scheduled delivery.
7 It needs to arrive _____ tomorrow so we'll have to send it Express Priority.
8 Please wait _____ I inform you that I have received the package.

2 Complete the sentences with the words below.

destinations	urgent
charge	weight
documents	packages
vehicles	rate

1 ParcelExpress CH will deliver both your _____ and parcels.
2 If you have the zone and the weight, you can work out the delivery _____.
3 Most ParcelExpress CH delivery _____ are vans.
4 You can send really _____ parcels to arrive before 8.30 am the following day.
5 There is a standard postal _____ for EU countries.
6 They deliver to _____ in almost every country.
7 It is more expensive to send heavy _____ by post than by parcel delivery services.
8 The cost of the service depends on the _____ of the package and the speed of the service.

3 Exam practice
- Look at questions 1–5.
- In each question, which phrase or sentence is correct?
- For each question, mark the correct letter A, B or C.

1
> For additional charges, please refer to page 10.

You should turn to page ten
A to see about possible discounts.
B to find out about extra costs.
C for information about the product.

2
> Guaranteed delivery within forty-eight hours.

The parcel will arrive
A in less than two days from now.
B in exactly two days' time.
C in at least two days' time.

3
> Export documentation may be required for non-EU destinations.

Packages sent outside the EU
A must be documents only.
B will need special documents.
C might need special documents.

4
> Payment to be made by cash on delivery.

The invoice has to be paid
A after the shipment arrives.
B before the shipment arrives.
C when the shipment arrives.

5
> Transport papers must include an approximate value of the shipment.

The transport documents have to show
A how much the shipment is worth.
B the delivery charges for the shipment.
C a list of what is in the shipment.

Unit 16b Trading

An import agent

Listening 1.44

1 Krallpack GmbH is a small company based near Düsseldorf. Listen to Joachim Krall, the Managing Director, and complete the factfile.

Krallpack FACT FILE

Company Krallpack GmbH

Activities Agent for Korean packing machine manufacturers.

Services
- Provides European sales network.
- (1) _____ documents, specifications and (2) _____ lists.
- Deals with customer enquiries and (3) _____.
- Arranges (4) _____.

Founded In (5) _____.

Customers Major companies include GlaxoSmithKline, Bayer Schering, Rhône-Poulenc and (6) _____.

2 Listen again and choose the best phrase to complete the sentence.

1 Joachim Krall left his job in 1992 because
 A he did not like the company.
 B he saw a good business opportunity.
 C the company had financial problems.

2 Krallpack expanded because
 A its suppliers built very good machines.
 B the whole market grew very quickly.
 C its prices were very low.

3 Krallpack became known for the
 A fair prices of its products.
 B quality of its products and service.
 C skill of its sales people.

116

4 Krallpack's suppliers will have to develop
   A their machines and customer support services.
   B reliable and low priced machines.
   C technically advanced and reliable machines.

Product Collator

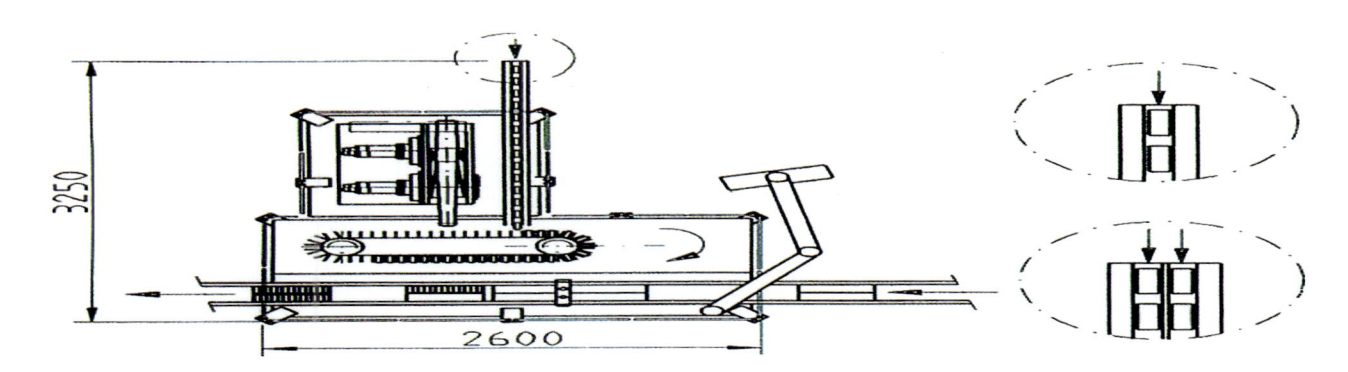

Speaking

3 Work in pairs. Your teacher will give you some cards describing how a customer orders parts through Krallpack. Read the cards and put the process into the correct order.

Decide which of the **emails,** faxes or letters is
- an enquiry
- a quotation
- confirmation
- an invoice

Grammar

4 Look at the audioscript on page 149. Underline examples of the following tenses. How does Mr Krall use them?

1 Present simple — *company activities (e.g. we translate their documents)*
   opinions (e.g. I think)

2 Past simple

3 Present perfect

4 Present continuous

Speaking

5 Work in pairs. Ask your partner questions and write a factfile for his/her company.

Trading Unit 16b 117

Ordering parts

Reading

1 **A customer has received a quotation from Krallpack. Read the attachment and Todd's note and choose the best phrase to complete the sentences.**

krallpack

Date:	18.04.12
To:	Al Shamai Dairy
FAO:	Jaleel Al Fahim

In der Loh 47
407149 Düsseldorf
Tel +49 (0)211 - 10 07 98 67
Fax + 49 (0)211 - 10 07 98 65
email: sales@krallpack.com

Dear Mr. Al Fahim
Re: Parts Quotation for SM300/Machine type 3000.002.93
Thank you for your enquiry. We are pleased to quote as follows:

Qty	Description	Parts No	Unit Price
100	Tension spring	RZ-0531 9907.15	
10	Starting disc	3000.010.19	
4	Grooved bearing	6007-2RS1 9908	
1	Level switch	WF02	

Could you write back to Krallpack and order their spares? Could you also ask how much the extra costs will be and how long they'll take to get here. Thanks.
Todd

The above prices are quoted in euros and are ex works in Korea. These prices do not include packing, transport, insurance and VAT. Our standard terms and conditions apply. The parts would be ready for despatch from Busan approximately four weeks after receipt of the order.
Kind regards

Gisela Mason

Gisela Mason
Krallpack

1 The customer would like to
  A buy some spare parts for a machine.
  B buy a new packing machine.
  C enquire about a new machine.

2 The letter is in reply to a
  A confirmation of an order.
  B request for information.
  C letter of complaint.

3 The customer has to pay
  A no extra costs.
  B only import tax.
  C all extra costs.

4 The order could
  A leave the factory in about four weeks.
  B be delivered in about four weeks.
  C leave the factory immediately.

Speaking

2 Work in pairs. Find five things your partner's company orders. Does it order them by telephone, fax, email or letter? Which type of communication is best? Why?

Writing

3 Work in pairs. Read the note again and write a reply to Krallpack. Write 50–60 words. Plan your letter carefully with your partner before you write it.

Self-study 16b

1 Look at the audioscript on page 149. Find the nouns that go with the verbs below.

1. deal with — *customers* / .... / ....
2. translate — .... / .... / ....
3. provide — .... / .... / ....

2 Match the sentence halves about the history of Krallpack.

1. Mr Krall began by ... G
2. The company's smaller suppliers wanted ...
3. So Mr Krall set up ...
4. His suppliers were very good at ...
5. Moreover, his company developed a name for ...
6. Krallpack is now looking for new staff ...
7. In the future, suppliers will have to develop the machines technically without ...
8. And Krallpack will have to continue ...

A. the quality of its products and service.
B. developing technically advanced machines.
C. someone to sell only their machines.
D. to provide the best possible service.
E. to help the company grow.
F. losing any of their reliability.
G. working in sales for an international company.
H. his own company.

3 Re-arrange the words to make phrases from a written quotation.

1. you / enquiry / thank / your / for

   _____

2. pleased / to / follows / we / quote / are / as

   _____

3. apply / our / conditions / terms / standard / and

   _____

4. in / is / price / quoted / euros / the

   _____

5. does / price / include / the / not / VAT

   _____

6. hearing / forward / from / look / we / to / you

   _____

4 Exam practice

- Look at the checklist below. It shows the documents A–H which are needed to export machinery.
- For questions 1–5, decide which documents A–H the people are talking about.
- For each question, mark the correct letter A–H.
- Do not use any letter more than once.

> A Shipping papers
> B Drawings
> C Invoice
> D Specifications
> E Handbook
> F Parts list
> G Registration form
> H Guarantee

1. Two per cent discount if payment is within ten days.
2. The customer fills it in and returns it in order to go on our customer mailing list.
3. If they aren't correct, the machine won't get through customs.
4. It's translated so the engineers know how to operate the machine properly.
5. We normally mark on it the spares that we think the customer should always keep in stock.

Unit 17a Recruiting staff

Recruitment methods

Speaking 1 Work in pairs. How many different ways can a company recruit applicants to fill a job vacancy?

Reading 2 Read the magazine article about recruiting staff and complete the diagram on the opposite page.

PROFILE

The right person for the right job

Finding the right job applicant to fill a vacancy is never easy. **Julie Bain** *looks at the pros and cons of different recruitment methods.*

Recruiting the right candidate to fill a vacancy can be a difficult and costly task. Appointing the wrong person could be an expensive mistake which could cause personnel problems for the whole department. And, as every HR Manager knows, it is much more difficult to get rid of someone than it is to employ them.

The HR Manager's first decision is whether to recruit internal applicants or advertise the vacancy outside the company. Internal applicants are easy to recruit by memo, email or newsletter. Furthermore, they are easy to assess and know the company well. However, they rarely bring fresh ideas to a position. Moreover, a rejected internal candidate might become unhappy and leave the company.

Recruiting outside the company means either advertising the vacancy directly or using an employment agency. If the company decides to advertise the vacancy directly, it has to decide where to place the advertisement. Traditionally this has meant newspapers and professional journals but now the internet is also very popular. The decision normally depends on the vacancy. Companies advertise blue-collar or clerical jobs in local newspapers and senior management positions in national papers or professional journals, while the internet is one of the best ways of advertising IT vacancies or recruiting abroad. However, with the internet there is a risk of receiving unsuitable applications from all over the world.

An employment agency can be either a private business or a local government employment centre. A company often uses a local government employment agency to recruit blue-collar workers but normally prefers a commercial agency for its white-collar staff. However, a commercial agency could be very expensive and the applicants are less likely to stay with the company for a long time.

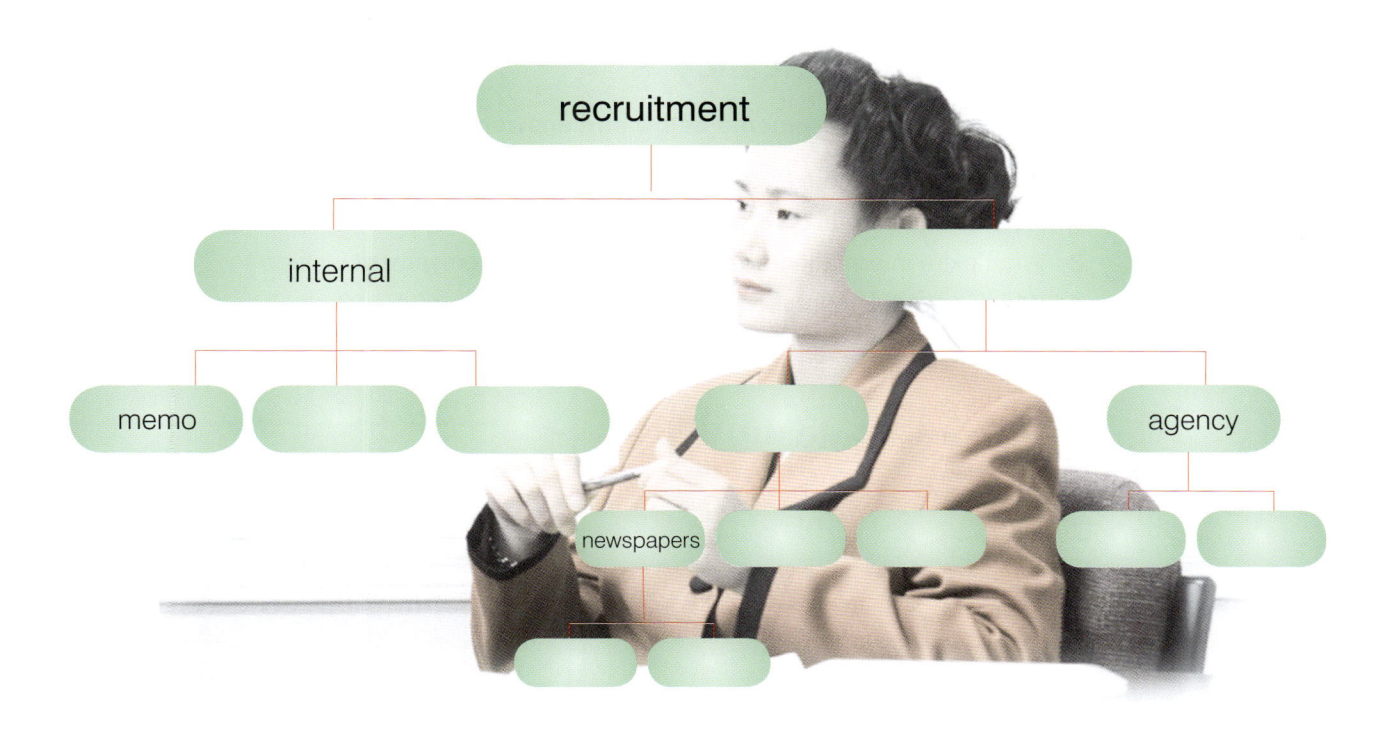

```
              recruitment
         /         |        \
    internal              agency
    /   |   \             /  |  \
  memo       newspapers
```

3 What are the advantages and disadvantages of each recruitment method?

4 Look at the following extracts from the article and answer the questions.

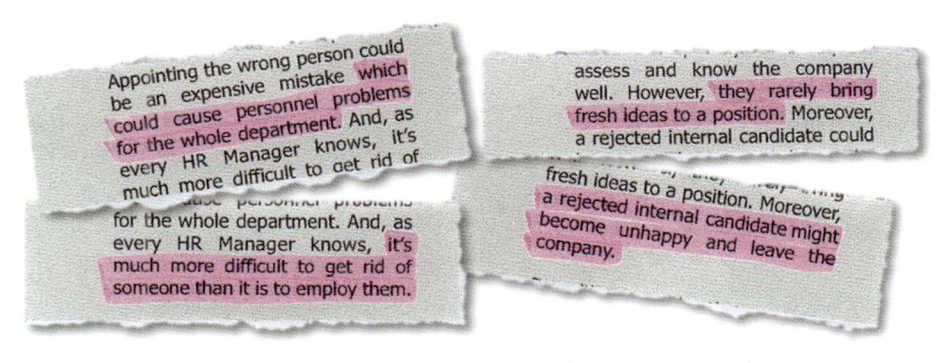

> Appointing the wrong person could be an expensive mistake *which could cause personnel problems for the whole department*. And, as every HR Manager knows, *it's much more difficult to get rid of someone than it is to employ them.*

> assess and know the company well. However, *they rarely bring fresh ideas to a position.* Moreover, a rejected internal candidate could

> fresh ideas to a position. Moreover, *a rejected internal candidate might become unhappy and leave the company.*

1 How could the wrong candidate cause problems for the whole department?
2 Why is it difficult to get rid of someone?
3 Why don't internal applicants have fresh ideas?
4 Why might an unsuccessful candidate leave the company?

Don't forget

Hypothetical situations
- We can use **would** to talk about the expected results of a hypothetical situation.
  *A large company **would** advertise in a national newspaper.*
- We can use **could/might** to talk about the possible results of a hypothetical situation.
  *Appointing the wrong person **could/might** be an expensive mistake.*

Speaking

5 Work in pairs. How would you advertise the following vacancies?

| finance director | graphic designer | marketing manager |
| bilingual secretary | truck driver | computer programmer |

Recruiting staff Unit 17a

Advertising a vacancy

Reading

1 Read the two advertisements below and answer the questions.

1 Where would the advertisements appear?
2 How is the information organised in the two advertisements?
3 What extra information does the newspaper advertisement include?
4 Which advertisement tries to "sell" the position more? How?

Goldsmiths HOLIDAYS

To: All offices
From: Rick Hayward
Date: 6 March 2012
Re: Vacancy for Senior Marketing Assistant

Senior Marketing Assistant – London

Goldsmiths Holidays has a vacancy at its main London offices for an assistant to the Marketing Director.

The successful candidate will be a graduate with at least three years' marketing experience and preferably a second European language. Key responsibilities will include helping to plan and manage our range of package holidays and building relationships with partners.

If you wish to apply for the vacancy, please speak with your office manager and contact Rick Hayward at Heath Villas by 13 March.

Goldsmiths HOLIDAYS

requires a

Senior Marketing Assistant

Goldsmiths, one of Europe's largest package holiday companies, requires a **Senior Marketing Assistant** at our main London offices. Working closely with the Marketing Director, you will help plan and manage our range of quality products and maintain relationships with our partners worldwide.

A confident and skilled communicator, you will be a graduate with a minimum of three years' marketing experience within the travel industry. A second European language would also be an advantage.

The rewards in terms of salary, benefits and career development will fully reflect your contribution to the success of Goldsmiths Holidays Ltd.

If you think you have the ability and the confidence, please email your CV to: Goldsmiths Holidays, 24 Heath Villas, The Vale of Heath, London NW3 1AW. email: refsma@goldsmiths.com

---

Listening 🔊 1.45

2 Two HR managers discuss the vacancy at Goldsmiths. Listen to the conversation. Which advertisement do they decide to place first? Why?

3 Listen again. What are the disadvantages of each type of advertisement?

Grammar

4 Look at the audioscript on page 149. Underline all the verbs in the past simple. How many of them refer to the past? What do the others refer to? Now complete the information below.

> **Don't forget**
>
> **Conditional 2 (hypothetical)**
> - We can use the following conditional forms to talk about the results of an action which we do not expect to happen.
>
>   *would*
> If + _____ tense, _____ + infinitive
>   _____

Speaking

5 Work in pairs. How would your partner recruit people for his/her own job?

Self-study 17a

1 **Choose the best word to complete the sentences.**

   1 We had over thirty *applicants/assistants* for the vacancy we advertised in the local paper.
   2 I had to fill in *a CV/an application form* and return it to the HR Department.
   3 We *appointed/filled* someone to the position over two weeks ago.
   4 We advertised the *employment/vacancy* on the internet.
   5 We need to *apply/recruit* ten more people before the summer.
   6 I am going to interview the *candidates/appointments* tomorrow.

2 **Look back through the unit and audioscript on page 149. Find three words to go with each of the following.**

   1 .... / .... / .... → a vacancy

   2 .... / .... / .... → applicants

   3 recruit ← .... / .... / ....

   4 advertise ← .... / .... / ....

3 **Complete the sentences below. Use your own words.**

   1 If I decided to change my job,
      I'd look for a different type of work.

   2 If you wanted to recruit more people to work in your department,
      _____

   3 If I lost my job,
      _____

   4 If I worked abroad,
      _____

   5 Would you accept it if
      _____

4 **Exam practice**

   - Look at the graphs below. They show the passenger volumes for eight different airlines.
   - Which airline does each sentence 1–5 describe?
   - For each sentence, mark the correct letter A–H.
   - Do not use any letter more than once.

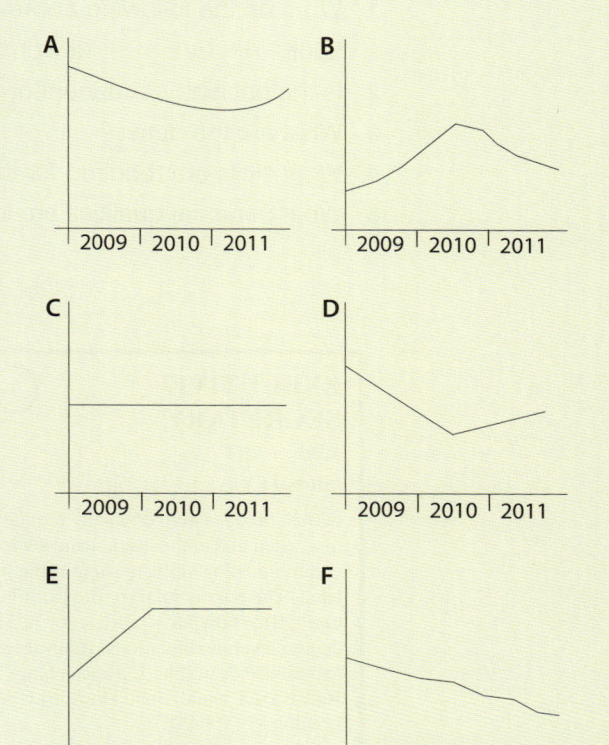

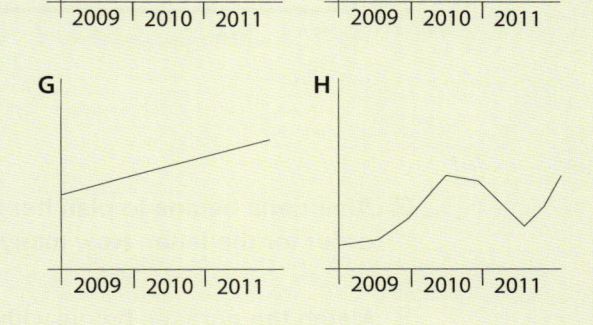

   1 After a sharp fall in 2010, business recovered slightly the following year.
   2 Passenger volumes showed strong growth in 2009 but levelled off in 2010.
   3 The number of passengers decreased steadily throughout the three-year period.
   4 Passenger volumes peaked in 2010 and then fell steadily afterwards.
   5 The number of passengers remained steady between 2009 and 2010.

Unit 17a   123

Unit 17b Applying for a job

Application letters

Reading

1 Almudena Ribera is a secretary in Madrid. She is looking for work in Britain and replies to the advertisement below. Read the advertisement and answer the questions.

1 What do the following abbreviations mean?
   £30K   O/T   60wpm   langs
2 Is the position permanent or temporary?
3 What are the duties?
4 What skills are required for the job?
5 What personal qualities are looked for?

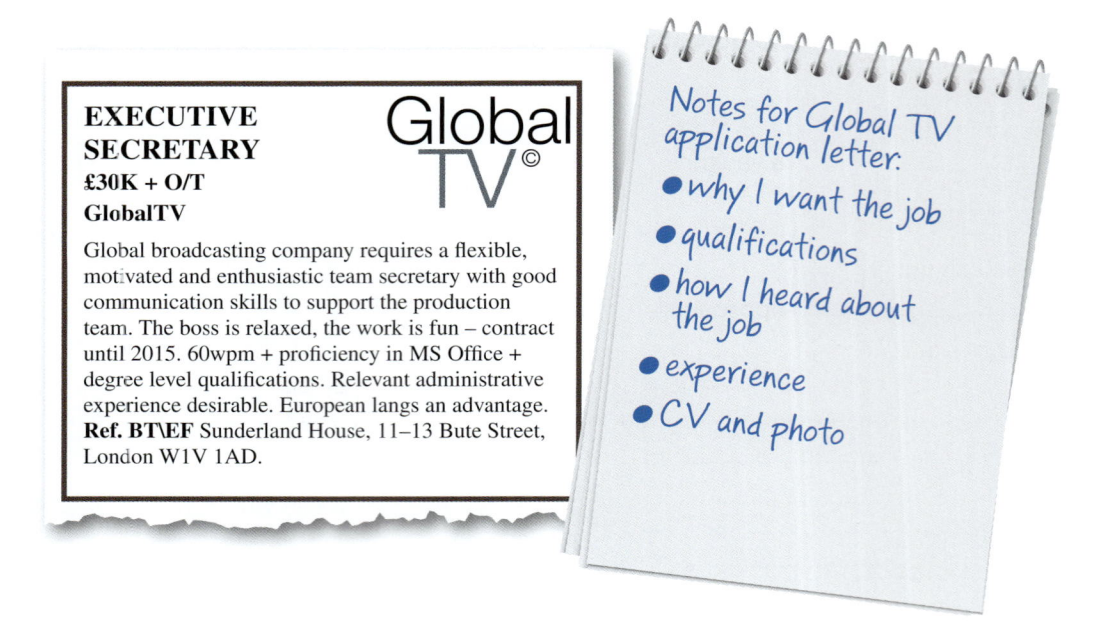

EXECUTIVE SECRETARY
£30K + O/T
GlobalTV

Global broadcasting company requires a flexible, motivated and enthusiastic team secretary with good communication skills to support the production team. The boss is relaxed, the work is fun – contract until 2015. 60wpm + proficiency in MS Office + degree level qualifications. Relevant administrative experience desirable. European langs an advantage.
Ref. BT\EF Sunderland House, 11–13 Bute Street, London W1V 1AD.

Notes for Global TV application letter:
- why I want the job
- qualifications
- how I heard about the job
- experience
- CV and photo

2 Almudena begins to plan her application letter. Put her notes above into the correct order for the letter. How many paragraphs should there be?

3 Match the phrases below with Almudena's notes.

1 I am writing with reference to your advertisement in the ...
2 I graduated from Madrid University with a degree in ...
3 Since 2010 I have been working as ...
4 I am very interested in the position because ...
5 Please find enclosed ...

Writing

4 Work in pairs. Write Almudena's letter of application to GlobalTV. Decide what information you should include. Use the phrases above and the information in the curriculum vitae (CV) on the opposite page.

Attending an interview

Listening 1.46

1 Almudena attends an interview at GlobalTV. Before you listen, read the HR Manager's notes about Almudena's CV. Change his notes on the CV into polite questions. Then listen and compare your questions with his.

CURRICULUM VITAE
ALMUDENA RIBERA

Name: Almudena Ribera
Address: c/ Lozano n°24 1°B 28019 Madrid
Telephone: 00 34 91 6342918
Marital status: Single
Nationality: Spanish

*Duncan
Thanks for agreeing to do the interview for me on Tuesday. Here's the candidate's CV – I've marked a few things you should ask her about. And don't forget to take notes!
Thanks*

Key skills

- Ability to work to deadlines.
- Experience of dealing with clients in **different countries**. – *Which countries?*
- Good written and spoken knowledge of **English and Italian**. – *What about French?*
- **Good keyboard skills** and knowledge of current software packages.

Work experience   *WPM?*

2010–present
Ediciones Gómez S.A., Madrid
Currently working as a bilingual secretary for Ediciones Gómez, a Madrid-based publisher. Duties include dealing with international partners both on the phone and in writing, sending invoices, organising meetings and travel for the editors and general office duties.

2007–2010 – *Why did she leave?*
Informática S.A., Madrid   *Which software?*
Support Secretary for the Training Director. **Used various software packages.** Assisted the Director in the organisation of training courses for software designers and **presentations** to IT managers. Responsibilities also included dealing with correspondence and general office duties.
What kind of presentations?
Experience with PowerPoint?

Summer work 2005–2007
Instituto Calderón de la Barca, Madrid
Teaching Spanish as a foreign language. Duties included planning and teaching Spanish lessons to adults. I also organised cultural trips to museums and exhibitions.

Qualifications

2001–2005
Complutense University, Madrid
Graduated with an honours degree in Modern European Languages, specialising in English and Italian. The degree also included French language studies, English commercial correspondence and IT skills.

---

2 Now listen again and write down Almudena's answers to the questions.

Grammar

3 Look at the direct and indirect forms of the question below. What are the grammatical differences?

- Which programs do you use?
- Could you tell me which programs you use?
- Can you leave your present job immediately?
- Could you tell me if you can leave your present job immediately?

Speaking

4 Work in pairs. Imagine your partner is applying for a job at GlobalTV. Complete the application form with your partner's details.

GlobalTV

Please write clearly in BLOCK CAPITALS.

- Position applied for:
- Title:
- Full name:
- Nationality:
- Marital status:
- Date of birth:
- Address:
- Phone number:
- Email:
- Current employment:
- Higher education:
- Professional qualifications:
- Computer skills:
- Language skills:
- Interests:
- Signature:
- Date:

---

5 Work in pairs. Look at the interview questions below. How would you answer them?

What don't you like about your current position?
Where does your employer think you are today?
What are your professional objectives?
What are your weaknesses?

Now look at the text *Attending interviews* on the opposite page. It contains a recruitment consultant's advice on how to answer these questions. Do you agree?

Self-study 17b

1 Rewrite the following as indirect questions.

1 Where is the interview room?
   Could you tell me where the interview room is?

2 Where do you work at the moment?

3 Does the position include a pension?

4 How did you hear about the vacancy?

5 Is there any training?

6 What is your present salary?

2 Complete the diagram with vocabulary from the unit.

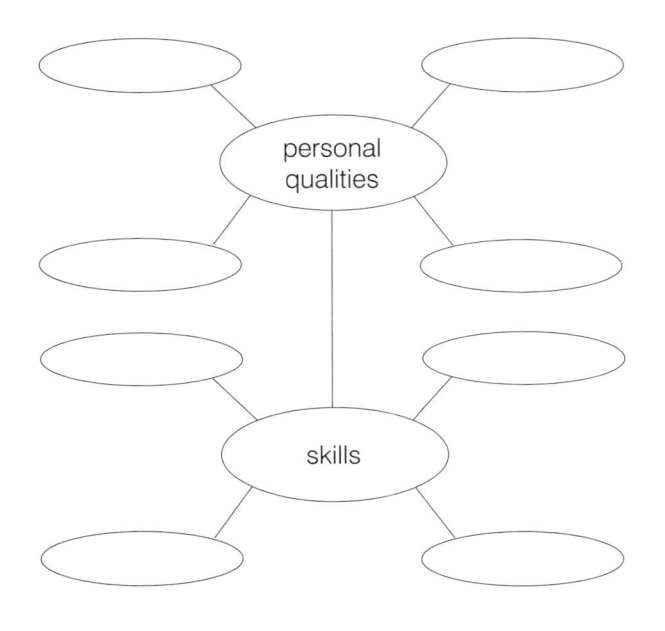

(diagram: central bubbles labelled "personal qualities" and "skills", each with four empty bubbles connected)

3 Re-arrange the following words to make phrases from a letter of application.

1 Please / copy / my / CV / a / find / enclosed / of

2 I / because / position / am / in / the / interested / very

3 Since / as / been / have / 2006 / I / working

4 I / reference / am / advertisement / writing / with / to / your

4 Exam practice

- Read the text below which advises candidates how to answer difficult interview questions.
- Are the sentences below 'Right' or 'Wrong'?
- If there is not enough information to answer 'Right' or 'Wrong', choose 'Doesn't say'.
- For each question, mark the correct letter A, B or C.

Attending interviews

Good interviewers prepare their questions carefully in advance according to the candidate's application and CV. So candidates need to prepare just as carefully. Here are some useful tips on answering interview questions.

1 What don't you like about your current position?
No job is perfect; there's always something we don't like. Be honest but don't give a list of complaints. The important thing is to talk positively about how you deal with problems at work.

2 Where does your employer think you are today?
Be honest. If you lie to your current employer, you'll lie to your next employer. Don't phone in sick on the day of the interview. Take a day's holiday but don't say why.

3 What are your professional objectives?
Think about these before the interview. Your objectives should be relevant to the job you have applied for and achievable. If the new job can't offer you everything you want, the interviewer will think that you probably won't stay with the company very long.

4 What are your weaknesses?
Be honest: no-one is perfect. Think about this before the interview and choose your answer carefully. Talk about how you deal with a weakness; this is far more important than the weakness itself.

1 Interviewers ask every candidate the same questions.
   A Right   B Wrong   C Doesn't say

2 You shouldn't mention problems with your current job.
   A Right   B Wrong   C Doesn't say

3 You should arrange to have a day off for the interview.
   A Right   B Wrong   C Doesn't say

4 You should give your personal objectives.
   A Right   B Wrong   C Doesn't say

5 Your objectives should suit the position you apply for.
   A Right   B Wrong   C Doesn't say

6 You should practise your answers at home.
   A Right   B Wrong   C Doesn't say

7 You shouldn't discuss things you aren't good at.
   A Right   B Wrong   C Doesn't say

Unit 18

Exam practice

Reading and Writing Test

Reading

Questions 1–5

- Look at questions 1–5.
- In each question, which phrase or sentence is correct?
- For each question, mark the correct letter A, B or C.

1
> **The Supplies Department will provide overalls.**

The company provides
A an overcoat.
B a uniform.
C a suit.

2
> Mrs Rothe called – she's unavailable for the meeting tomorrow.

Mrs Rothe will
A be late for the meeting tomorrow.
B take part in the meeting tomorrow.
C not be at the meeting tomorrow.

3
> 8.7.11
> Mike called yesterday to say he's flying to Turkey tomorrow.

Mike is flying to Turkey on
A 7 July.
B 8 July.
C 9 July.

4
> European sales have recovered this year.

Compared to last year, European sales have
A improved.
B remained steady.
C decreased.

5
> Thank you for your enquiry of 18 February.

The company received a letter asking for
A a delivery date.
B information.
C an order.

Exam practice

Questions 6–10

- Look at the graphs A–H below. They show how eight different companies used websites for recruitment over a four-year period.
- Which company does each sentence 6–10 describe?
- For each question, mark the correct letter.
- Do not use any letter more than once.

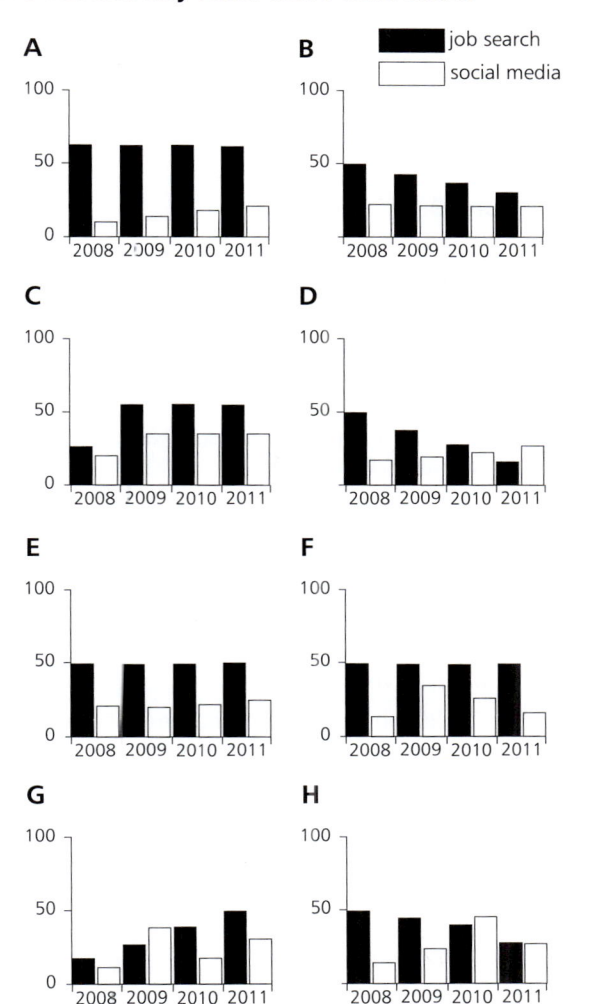

6 While recruitment through job search websites fell, the number of employees recruited via social media rose steadily throughout the period.

7 Recruitment through job search websites remained constant, whereas after an increase in 2009, recruiting via social media fell steadily.

8 The number of staff recruited through both methods levelled off after a sharp rise.

9 Recruitment through job search websites peaked in 2010, while recruiting via social media fell steadily from 2009 to 2011.

10 While the rate of recruitment via social media fluctuated over the four-year period, there was a steady rise in recruitment through job search websites over the same period.

Questions 11–22

- Read the newspaper article below about a new alliance in the packaging industry.
- Choose the correct word from A, B or C below.

Packaging alliance

This week sees more changes in the packaging world. DD Holdings, the UK group, has (11) ..... an alliance with three other European packaging companies. The company hopes the alliance will help (12) ..... members to win more orders from multinational pharmaceutical groups.

There is a (13) ..... trend in the pharmaceutical industry for large multinationals to use pan-European suppliers. (14) ..... has presented problems particularly for small and medium-sized companies (15) ..... produce in just one country.

DD Holdings, based in Yorkshire, is teaming up (16) ..... partners in France, Germany and Spain to form an alliance called Pharmapak. (17) ..... the partners will continue to work (18) ..... separate companies, they will share (19) ..... of their sales and marketing resources. The deal (20) ..... customers with the opportunity to negotiate Europe-wide contracts.

DD is the (21) ..... of the four companies, with fifteen production facilities throughout Europe and (22) ..... annual turnover of about £120m.

11	A announced	B advised	C alerted
12	A our	B its	C their
13	A grown	B growth	C growing
14	A These	B This	C That
15	A which	B what	C who
16	A with	B to	C in
17	A However	B Despite	C Although
18	A as	B than	C that
19	A some	B any	C lot
20	A provided	B provides	C provide
21	A largest	B larger	C large
22	A some	B a	C an

Unit 18 129

Exam practice

Questions 23–27

- Read the email and the information about theatre performances.
- Complete the form below.
- Write each word, phrase or number in CAPITAL LETTERS.

> **To:** jane.little@Abstrakt.com
> **From:** enrique.garcia@Abstrakt.com
> **Subject:** Theatre tickets
>
> **Epcom visit on Friday**
>
> Could you book some theatre tickets for tomorrow for the five Epcom visitors and me? We'll be in a meeting all day until about 4.30 and then we'll have an early dinner together at the hotel. Could you phone the ticket agency and find a play or something that starts after half past seven? Use the company VISA card to pay for the tickets.
>
> Enrique

> **What's on: Theatre**
>
> *Hamlet* at the Barbican.
> Performances start at 19.15.
> Tickets £17.50–£75
>
> *West Side Story* at the Play house.
> Show starts at 19.00.
> Tickets £15.50–£80
>
> *Buddy Holly* at the Palace Theatre.
> Performances at 15.30 and 20.00.
> Tickets £16.50–£65

BOOKING

Name of show:	(**23**) ....
Venue:	(**24**) ....
Method of payment:	(**25**) ....
Time:	(**26**) ....
No. of tickets:	(**27**) ....

Writing

Question 28

- It is the beginning of December and you have been asked to find out how many days' holiday staff in your department intend to take over Christmas.
- Write an email to all staff in the department:
    * saying on which days the company is closed
    * asking them to confirm their holidays
    * giving a deadline for filling in holiday forms.
- Write 30–40 words.

Question 29

- You had arranged to meet Christine Hendrikson but had to cancel the meeting at short notice. You receive the email below from her.

> **To:** f.andrews@brit-tech.com
> **From:** christine.hendrikson@arton.se
> **Subject:** Our meeting
>
> Dear Fiona
>
> I received a message this morning saying that our meeting on Friday 12 April had been cancelled. Unfortunately, the message didn't give any more details or any alternative dates.
>
> Could you just confirm that the meeting has indeed been cancelled and possibly suggest another date?
>
> Best regards
> Christine

- Write an email to Christine:
    * apologising for cancelling the meeting
    * giving a reason for the cancellation
    * offering a new date and time
    * asking her to confirm the new date and time.
- Write 60–80 words.

Exam practice

Listening

Questions 30–37

- For questions 30–37, you will hear eight short recordings.
- For each question, mark one letter A, B or C.
- You will hear each recording twice.

30 What does Alison order?
   A Fish
   B Steak
   C Chicken

31 Which is the flight to Sydney?

LH4521	LH4152	LH4125
A	B	C

32 Which hotel does Graham's colleague recommend?
   A The Orion
   B The Grand Hotel
   C The Plaza

33 Which machine are the people talking about?
   A A fax machine
   B A printer
   C A photocopier

34 What happens to the phone call?
   A The receptionist puts the caller through.
   B The receptionist takes a message.
   C The caller offers to ring back later.

35 How much does the retailer pay for each game?
   A $7 a unit
   B $8 a unit
   C $9 a unit

36 How long will the order take to arrive?
   A three days
   B four days
   C five days

37 What is wrong with the printer?
   A It has run out of paper.
   B The paper has jammed.
   C It needs a new ink cartridge.

Questions 38–45

- Listen to the Manager talking to staff about the way they answer the telephone.
- For questions 38–45, mark the correct letter A, B or C for the correct answer.
- You will hear the conversation twice.

38 The information was
   A recorded by the company.
   B given by the company's customers.
   C collected by a consultancy.

39 The company's staff answer the phone
   A very quickly.
   B reasonably quickly.
   C far too slowly.

40 The groups average friendliness score was
   A six out of ten.
   B seven point five out of ten.
   C eight out of ten.

41 When dealing with enquiries, staff usually
   A know who to pass the caller on to.
   B can't answer the caller's questions.
   C have to take a message.

42 When putting a call through, staff should always
   A ask for the caller's name.
   B play the hold music.
   C ask the caller to wait.

43 Employees should answer the phone after
   A two rings.
   B three rings.
   C four rings.

44 The company is most worried about how
   A quickly staff answer the phone.
   B efficiently staff deal with enquiries.
   C friendly staff sound on the phone.

45 The handout has a list of
   A pieces of good hold music.
   B useful telephone phrases.
   C extension numbers.

Student A Unit 4a

1. You have an appointment with Andrew Jones of Collingwood Pharmaceuticals on 14 May at half past two. Telephone him to:
   - confirm the date
   - change the time to three o'clock
   - give the name of the colleague who is attending the meeting with you.

2. You are a receptionist at Isis, a company based in Los Angeles. Someone calls to speak to Rosemary Burton. She is not in the office today. Offer to take a message.

Message for ....
From ....
Message ....

Student A Unit 5a

Describe the graph below to your partner.

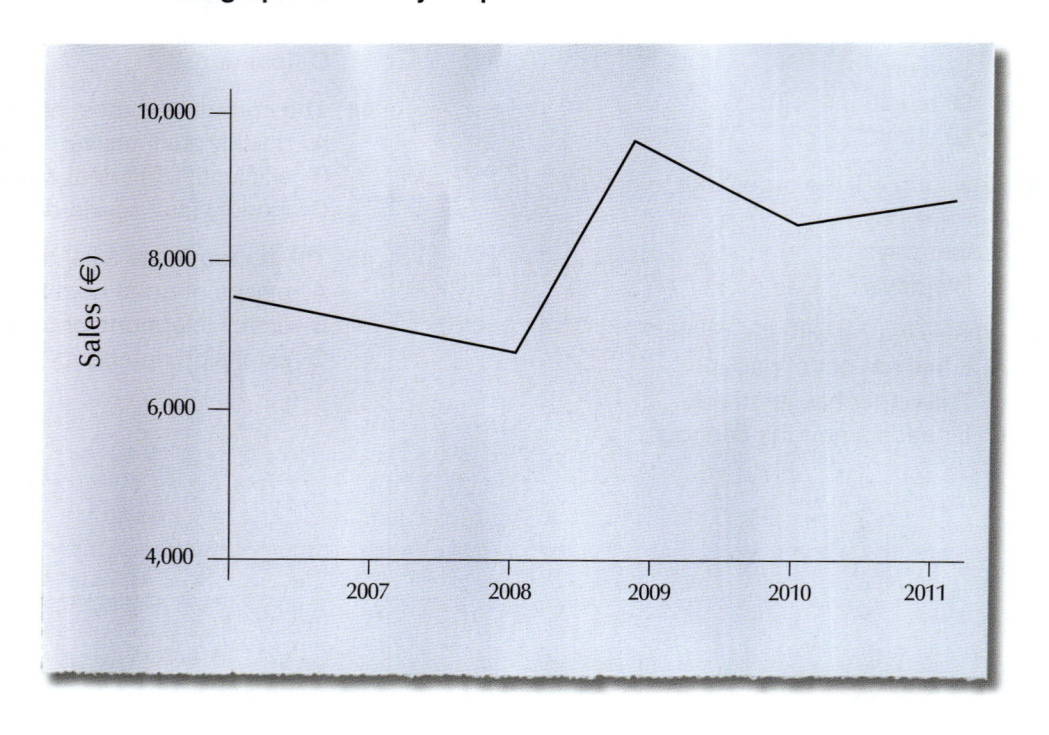

Student A Unit 5a

Draw the graph your partner describes.

[Graph: y-axis labeled "Sales (€)" with values 4,000, 6,000, 8,000, 10,000; x-axis with years 2007, 2008, 2009, 2010, 2011]

Student A Unit 11a

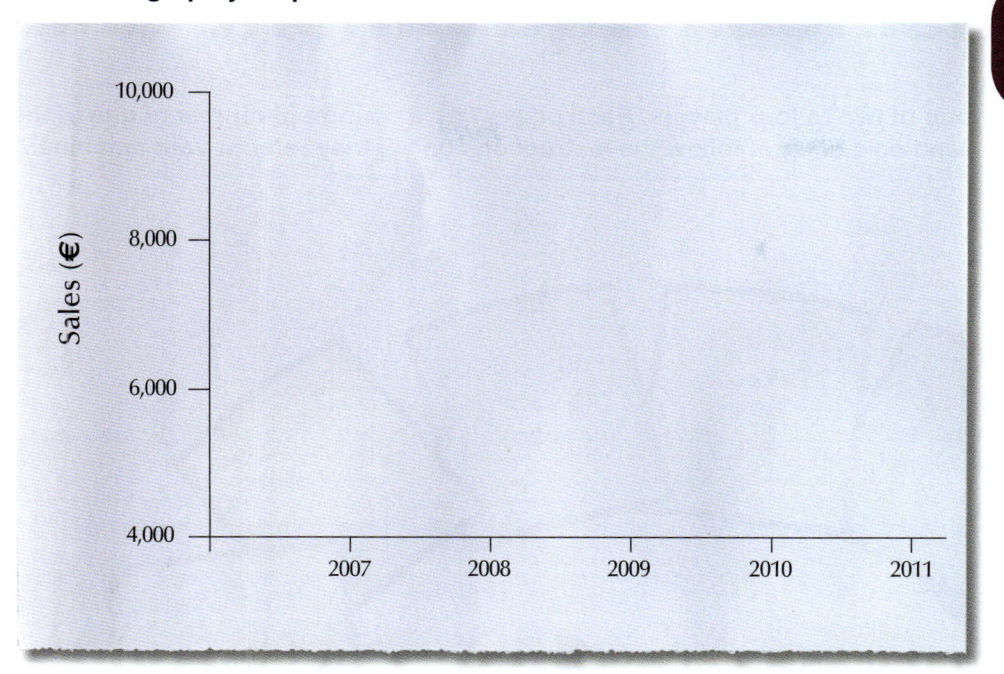

Ask your partner for the information to complete the conference programme below.

Amtech Marketing Conference 2012 Programme

Hotel
The Central Hotel
120-126 Chater Road,
Central Hong Kong

Tel +852 3422 2678   Fax +852 3422 2660
Email: info@thecentralhotel.com

Friday 21 September
_____   Drinks reception (hotel bar)
19.30   Dinner at _____

Saturday 22 September
9.00   Opening session (Dragon Lounge)
11.00   Coffee
11.30   Plenary session
13.00   Buffet lunch
14.00   Workshops (Dragon Lounge and Emperor Room)
_____   Coffee
16.30   Plenary session
18.00   End of session
_____   Dinner at a local restaurant

Sunday 23 September
9.30   _____ (Dragon Lounge and Emperor Room)
11.00   Coffee
11.30   Plenary session
13.00   End of conference
13.15   _____
14.45   Departure from hotel

Activity sheets 133

The Business Equipment Game

Play the game in a group of two to four players. Each player has a counter to represent one of these machines. When you land on a square, follow the instructions only if they refer to your machine.

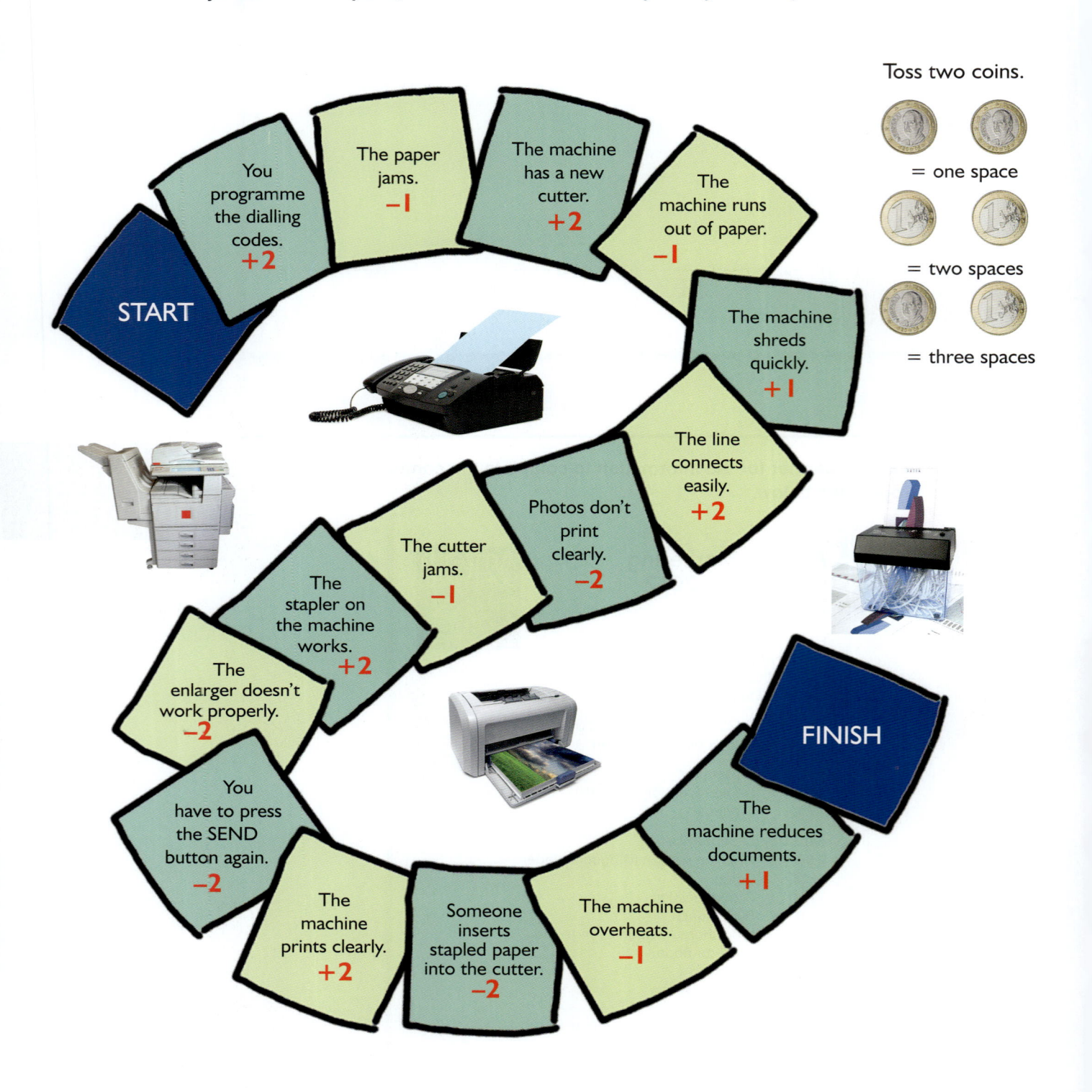

Toss two coins.

= one space

= two spaces

= three spaces

START

You programme the dialling codes. +2

The paper jams. −1

The machine has a new cutter. +2

The machine runs out of paper. −1

The machine shreds quickly. +1

The line connects easily. +2

Photos don't print clearly. −2

The cutter jams. −1

The stapler on the machine works. +2

The enlarger doesn't work properly. −2

You have to press the SEND button again. −2

The machine prints clearly. +2

Someone inserts stapled paper into the cutter. −2

The machine overheats. −1

The machine reduces documents. +1

FINISH

The Commuter Game

You have to get to work for a very important meeting at 9.00. When you land on a red or green traffic light, another player will pick up a card and tell you what to do or ask you a question. If you decide to break the law, toss a coin to see whether the police catch you. Heads: the police catch you and you return to the start. Tails: they don't and you continue as normal. If you land on amber, do nothing. The first person to arrive at work is the winner.

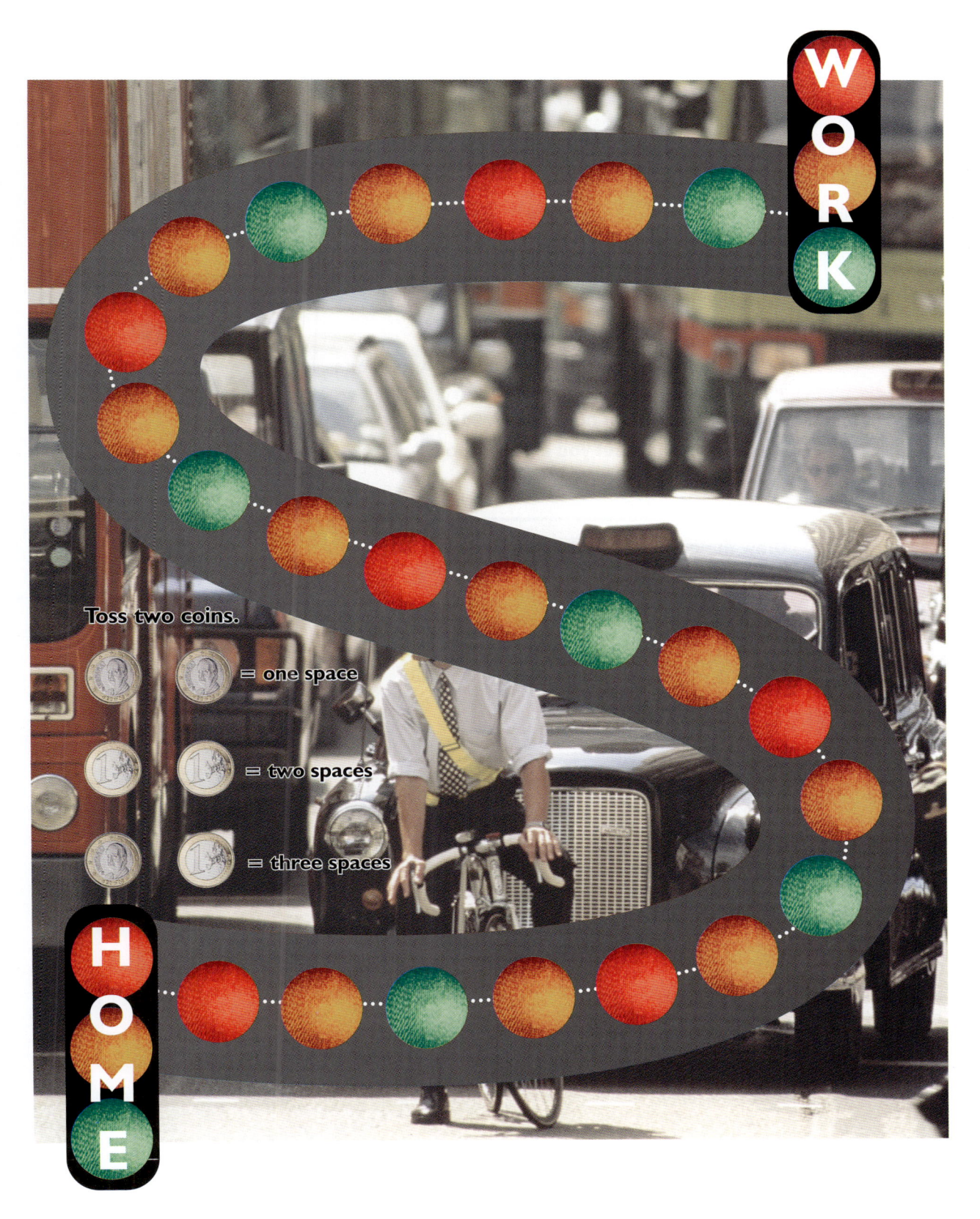

Toss two coins.

= one space

= two spaces

= three spaces

Student B Unit 4a

1 You are a receptionist at Collingwood Pharmaceuticals. Someone calls to speak to Andrew Jones. He is in a meeting. Take a message.

Message for ....
From ....
Message ....
....
....

2 You are flying to Los Angeles to visit Rosemary Burton at a company called Isis. Telephone her to:

- say that your flight on Thursday 22 April lands at 10.00 not 14.30
- confirm the flight number: BA 348
- ask who will meet you at the airport.

Student B Unit 5a

Draw the graph that your partner describes.

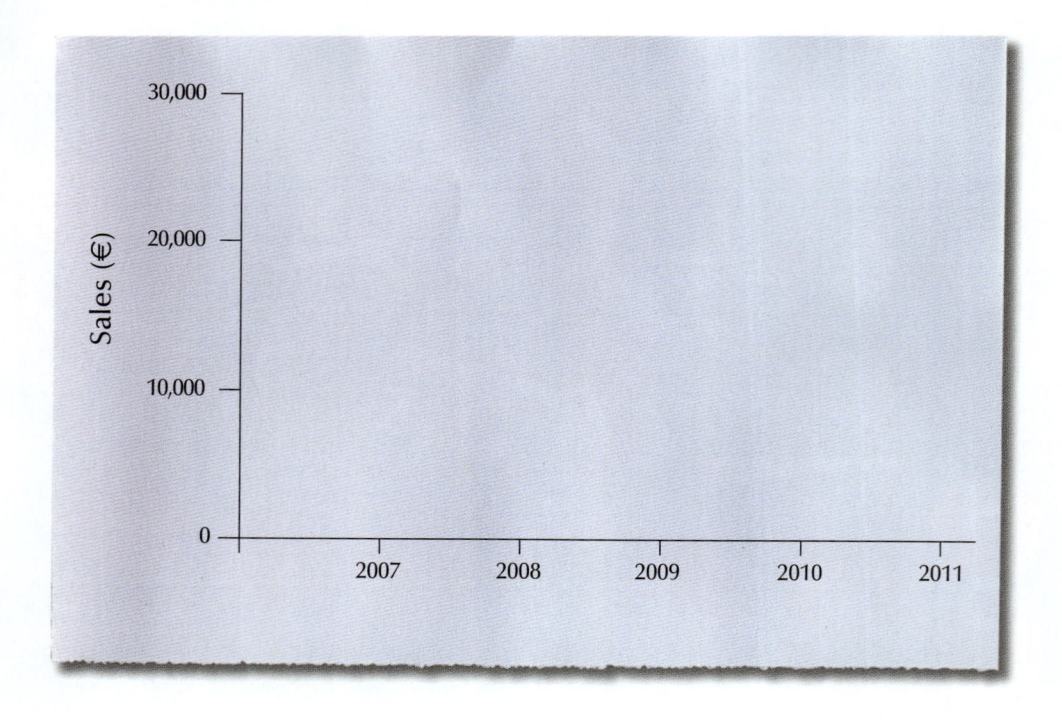

[Graph with y-axis labelled Sales (€) from 0 to 30,000 and x-axis showing years 2007, 2008, 2009, 2010, 2011]

Describe the graph below to your partner.

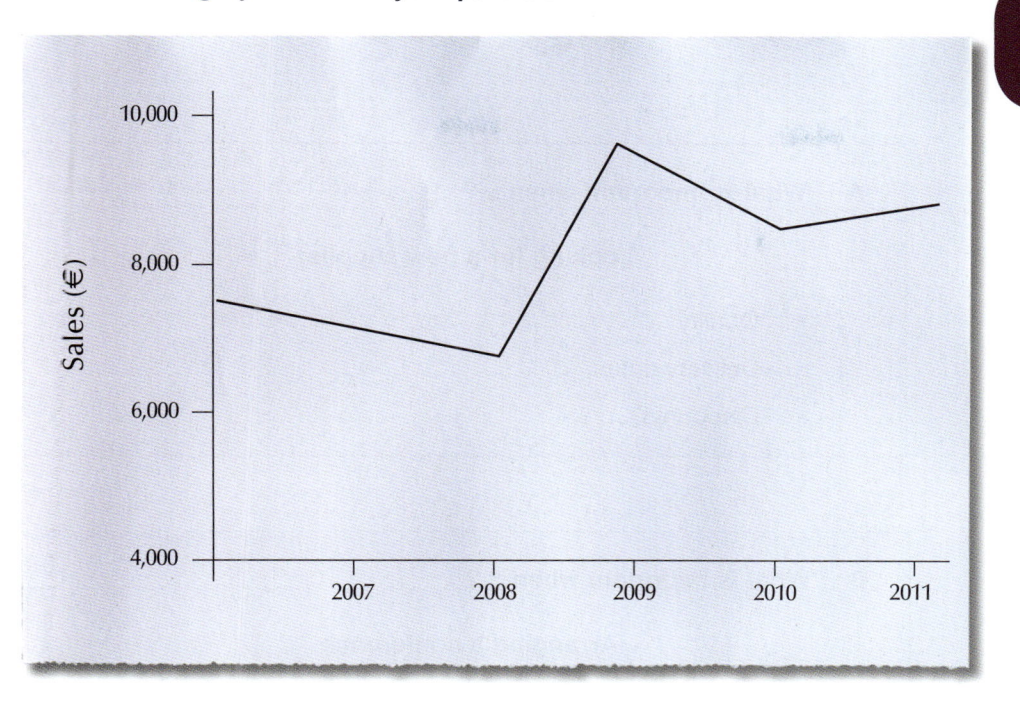

[Graph: Sales (€) from 2007 to 2011. 2007: ~7,500; 2008: ~6,800; 2009: ~9,500; 2010: ~8,500; 2011: ~8,800]

Student B
Unit 5a

Ask your partner for the information to complete the conference programme below.

Amtech Marketing Conference 2012 Programme

Hotel
*The Central Hotel
120-126 Chater Road,
Central Hong Kong*

Tel +852 3422 2678   Fax +852 3422 2660
Email: info@thecentralhotel.com

Friday 21 September
18.30   Drinks reception (hotel bar)
19.30   Dinner at hotel

Saturday 22 September
9.00   _____ (Dragon Lounge)
11.00   Coffee
11.30   Plenary session
13.00   _____
_____   Workshops (Dragon Lounge and _____ room)
16.00   Coffee
16.30   Plenary session
18.00   End of session
19.30   Dinner at a local restaurant

Sunday 23 September
9.30   Workshops (Dragon Lounge and _____ room)
_____   Coffee
11.30   Plenary session
_____   End of conference
13.15   Lunch
14.45   Departure from hotel

Student B
Unit 11a

Activity sheets   137

Unit 15 — Speaking Test Part Two

A What is important when ...?

Looking for a new supplier

- Quality
- Delivery times
- Discounts

B What is important when ...?

Arranging a conference

- Location
- Hotel facilities
- Number of delegates

C What is important when ...?

Recruiting staff

- Qualifications
- Experience
- Age

D What is important when ...?

Applying for a job

- Curriculum Vitae
- Interview
- Appearance

Speaking Test Part Three

Unit 15

1 English lessons

- Lesson times?
- Who pays?
- Location?
- Number of students?

2 New office

- Computer
- Desk chair
- Armchair
- Printer
- Fax machine
- Video-conferencing equipment
- Water cooler / drinks machine
- Plant

3 Choosing a hotel

- Price
- Location near city centre / airport / exhibition centre
- Business facilities
- Leisure facilities
- Food

Map of London

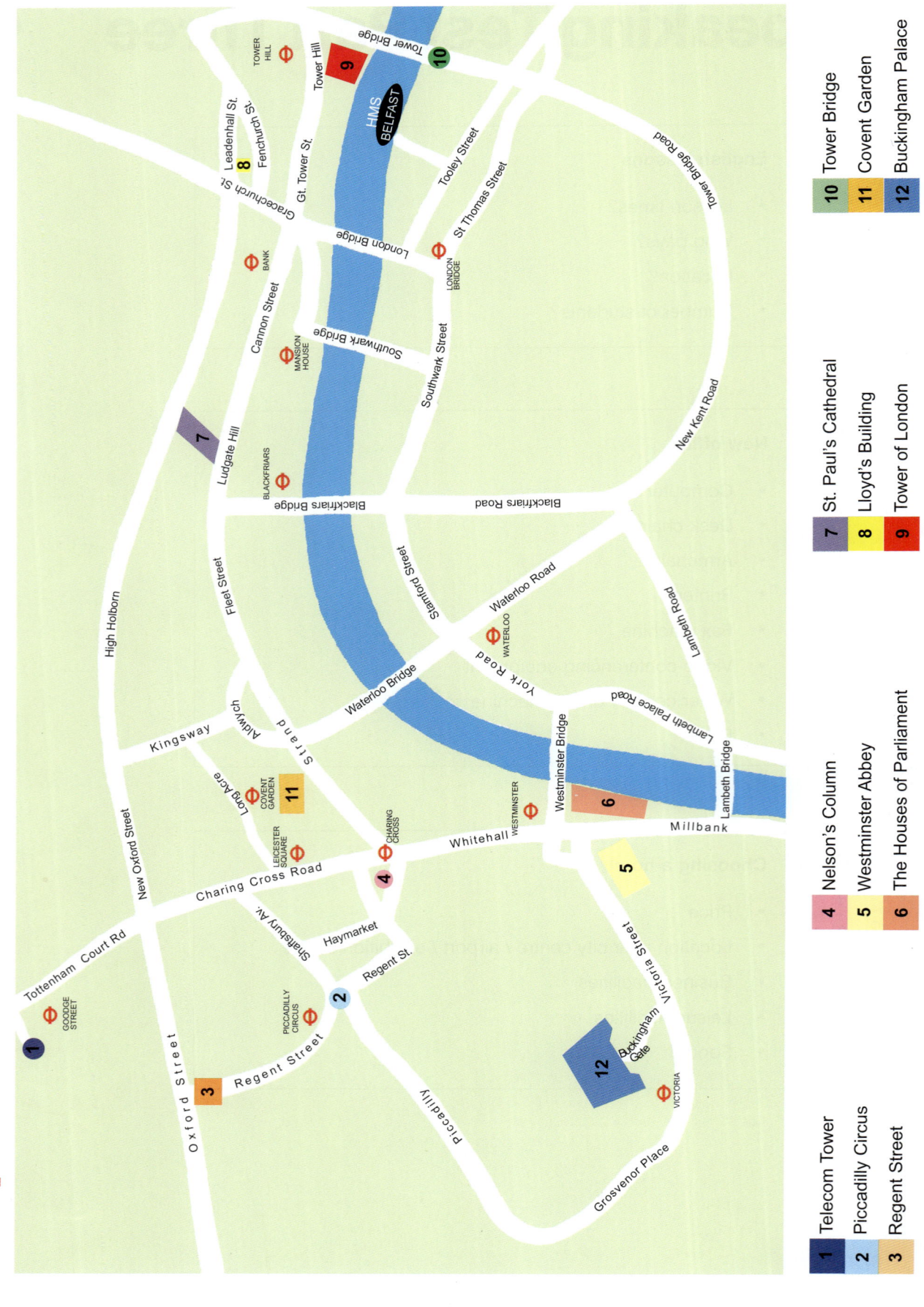

1 Telecom Tower	**2** Piccadilly Circus	**3** Regent Street
4 Nelson's Column	**5** Westminster Abbey	**6** The Houses of Parliament
7 St. Paul's Cathedral	**8** Lloyd's Building	**9** Tower of London
10 Tower Bridge	**11** Covent Garden	**12** Buckingham Palace

Audioscripts

Unit 1a: Job descriptions

Listening 1 (1 01–1.06)

Si = Silvio El = Elif Ha = Hans
Ad = Adrianna Ku = Kurt Su = Sunita

Conversation 1
Si So, Do you live in Geneva then – or are you just here for the meeting?
El No, I'm from Istanbul, but my company has an office here.
Si What kind of company is it?
El I work for an IT company. I'm a consultant.

Conversation 2
Ha Where do you work?
Ad I work for a large pharmaceutical company.
Ha And what do you do?
Ad I'm the head of the Marketing Department.

Conversation 3
Ku So what kind of products do you sell?
Si Anything that helps people make money.
Ku How do you mean?
Si Financial services. I sell investment products.

Conversation 4
El Tell me, does your consultancy work with big companies?
Su No, we do the accounts for small and medium-sized companies.
El Ah, I see. Are all of your clients in London?
Su Most of them. But we also work for some international charities in Geneva.

Conversation 5
Si So, you work in the food industry?
Ha Yes, I'm a factory manager.
Si Oh, really? What do you make?
Ha We produce frozen food.

Conversation 6
Su And what do you do?
Ku I manage a human resources department.
Su What kind of company do you work for?
Ku We make packaging for fresh food.

Listening 2 (1.07–1.08)

1
Hello, I'm Adrianna Marek I work as a marketing manager for a large pharmaceuticals company. My department produces vaccines against hepatitis and so on. We normally sell our vaccines directly to doctors so one of my jobs is to discuss our new products with doctors. Marketing managers don't always do this, but I do as I'm a qualified doctor. I'm also responsible for our publicity material so I have to deal with designers and printers. I'm responsible for the whole of central Europe, so I have to deal with the health authorities in the different central European countries. That means my job involves a lot of travelling. And finally, when we produce a new vaccine, it's my job to organise a conference for the medical press so they can ask us questions about it.

2
Hello, I'm Kurt Bjornson. I work for a company called Vacupack. I'm responsible for employing most of the people in the company. I write the job advertisements and then I have to choose which applicants I want to interview. Usually, I interview the applicants with the head of the department where the vacancy is. I then have to contact the applicants after the interview, both the successful and unsuccessful ones. Another duty is dealing with employees' problems. Of course many of them are work-related, but people do sometimes come to discuss personal problems with me. My job also involves informing employees if the management isn't satisfied with their work, which isn't a pleasant part of the job.

Unit 4a: Telephoning

Listening 1 (1.09–1.14)

Cl = Clare Ca = Caller

Call 1
Cl Good morning, Baker and Kerr. Can I help you?
Ca Could you put me through to Elaine Pearson, please?
Cl Who's calling, please?
Ca Lewis Taylor of SRT.
Cl One moment please, Mr Taylor ... Hello, Mr Taylor. I'm afraid the line's busy. Can I take a message?
Ca No, it's all right, thank you. I'll call back in about ten minutes.
Cl OK. Thank you for calling.

Call 2
Cl Good morning, Baker and Kerr. Can I help you?
Ca Yes, please. Could I have extension 184, please?
Cl Who's calling, please?
Ca Jack Symes.
Cl Thank you. I'll put you through.
Ca Thank you.

Call 3
Cl Good morning, Baker and Kerr. Can I help you?
Ca Can I speak to William Grogan, please?
Cl I'm afraid he's in a meeting. Can I take a message?
Ca Do you know when he'll be free?
Cl He should be available after lunch.
Ca Right, I'll call back then. Thanks.

Call 4
Cl Good morning, Baker and Kerr. Can I help you?
Ca Jasmine Singh, please.
Cl I'm afraid she's interviewing all day. Can I take a message?
Ca Yes, my name's Mary Banks, from Walkers. She called me earlier. I'm returning her call.
Cl Mary Banks, from Walkers. Right. I'll tell her you called back.
Ca OK. Thanks.

Call 5
Cl Good morning, Baker and Kerr. Can I help you?
Ca Hi Clare. It's Fiona. Is Keith available?
Cl I'm afraid the line's busy, Fiona.
Ca It's OK. I'll hold.
Cl Fiona?
Ca Yes.
Cl The line's free now. I'll put you through.
Ca Thanks.

Call 6
Cl Good morning, Baker and Kerr. Can I help you?
Ca Hi. It's Fiona again. We were cut off.
Cl Oh, sorry about that. I'll try to reconnect you. Hold the line.
Ca Thanks.

Listening 2 (1.15)

Cl = Clare D = David

Cl Good afternoon. Baker and Kerr. Can I help you?
D Good afternoon. Can you put me through to Sharon Thomson, please?
Cl I'm afraid she's out of the office at the moment. Can I take a message?

D Yes, my name's David Whelan from the Health and Safety Council.
Cl I'm sorry. Could you spell your surname, please?
D W-H-E-L-A-N.
Cl And it's the Health and Safety Council. Right. And what's the message, please?
D I'm calling about the First Aid course Ms Thomson's arranging with us. I'd like to confirm the week beginning the thirteenth May but I'm not ...
Cl Sorry, did you say the thirteenth or thirtieth?
D The thirteenth, one, three.
Cl OK ... yes?
D Yes. The date's fine, but we can only take twenty-five participants, not twenty-nine.
Cl So that's the First Aid course for the week commencing thirteenth of May and you can only take twenty-five people.
D That's right, yes.
Cl Right. I'll give her the message.
D Thanks.
Cl You're welcome. Bye.

Unit 4b: Internal communication

Listening 1 1.16

H = Henry Wallace   S = Sarah Longman

H Hello, Henry Wallace speaking.
S Hello, Henry, it's Sarah Longman from Accounts.
H Oh hello Sarah. What can I do for you?
S I'm calling all of the heads of department about expenses. I just wanted to remind you that if someone claims any expenses, they must enclose receipts with the claim.
H OK. I'll send a memo to remind my salespeople.
S Thanks, Henry. Bye.

Listening 2 1.17

M = Monica   E = Evan

M Hello. Monica Sanchez.
E Hello Monica, it's Evan.
M Oh hi Evan. How are you?
E I'm fine thanks. Look, I got your note yesterday about the meeting. I'm sorry I didn't get back to you.
M That's OK. But I'm flying out to Paris next week and we need to meet before I leave. Is Thursday all right for you?
E Not really, no. How about Tuesday?
M Fine, I've got to be in the office on Tuesday morning anyway. How about lunchtime?
E Well, that's fine by me, but we should find out if Steve's available then, as well.
M That's true. I'll send him an email and see if lunchtime's OK for him.
E If it's OK with Steve, let me know and we can fix a time.
M I'll email him now. Thanks Evan. Bye.
E Bye.

Unit 5b: Performance

Listening 1 1.18

Good afternoon. My name is Shelley Cohen and I'm here to talk about Railwork West's performance. As you all know, Railwork West has only been a private company since the privatisation of the national railway network in 1997. Between 1997 and 2007, Railwork West was owned and run by the Conaxus Group. However, the period of change from publicly-owned transport system to private company was not an easy one. Conaxus had considerable problems – asset management was difficult, passenger revenues fell and customer satisfaction dropped dramatically. In 2007 Transcon bought Railwork West and since that time, we have made a lot of changes. Today I'd like to talk to you about these changes and show you how they've affected the company's performance since 2006. To do this, I'd like to draw your attention to figures three and four on page eight of your information brochures.

I'd like to begin with a look at the bar chart, which shows annual growth in passenger revenue from 2006 to 2010. As you can see, growth slowed from 2.4% in 2006/2007 down to just 1% in 2007/2008. However, reduced costs and more efficient sales practices resulted in growth reaching 9.9% in 2008/2009. This was followed by 7% in 2009/2010. The bar chart clearly shows that the changes have made a big difference financially and have improved customer satisfaction, as we'll see.

I'm sure you've all heard the recent stories in the media about bad service on the privatised rail network, so I'd like you to look at figure four, which shows Railwork West's reliability and punctuality figures. As you can see from this graph, the company has an excellent reliability record. Reliability improved steadily from 99.1% in 2006 to 99.3% in 2008, where it has remained. Punctuality also rose steadily, going from 90% in 2006 to 91% in 2008. You'll notice the drop to 88% in 2009, which I'll explain later. Although we haven't received the final figures yet, I can tell you that punctuality improved in 2010 and has continued to improve this year as a result of further investment.

Listening 2 1.19

S = Shelley Cohen   I = Investor

S So, that's the end of my presentation. Does anyone have any questions?
I Yes. Earlier you mentioned the drop in punctuality in 2009. What was the problem?
S Sorry, I said I'd explain that, didn't I? Well, it was mainly because of problems with the railway track. As you know, we have to lease both the track and our trains from other companies. The track belongs to a company called Network Rail. Although we receive penalty payments from them for any delays due to the track, it doesn't help our reliability figures. We don't like the situation, none of the train-operating companies like the situation, and we hope that it may change in the future, but for the moment, there is nothing we can do about it. Next question, please.
I2 Could you tell us a bit about the company's future investment plans?
S Of course. At the moment Railwork West is investing £9m in upgrading its stations. This includes facilities, information systems and security. We're also investing in new trains, which will lead to improved reliability levels. The gentleman at the back, please ...
I3 Earlier you said that Railwork West wants to make sure the service it offers doesn't become too expensive for passengers – so you don't plan to increase ticket prices this year. Can you tell us how you hope to improve profits in the future?
S That's a good question. As I said, we have to lease both the track and our trains, so our biggest costs are fixed. The only way the company can improve profits is by increasing passenger volumes. That's why we're spending so much on improving customer satisfaction. Next question, please.

Unit 7a: Product description

Listening 1 1.20

Morning everybody. Now, as you know, this morning we're going to talk about our latest products in our range of games. Before we talk about the selling points of each game, I'd just like to describe them briefly. I'll begin with this general knowledge game called Mindtwist, which comes in two versions: a standard size and a travel size.

As you can see, the differences are size, weight and, of course, cost. The standard version has a normal size board, two packs of

cards, six wooden playing pieces, a timer and two dice. The travel size, Mindtwist Travel, is obviously smaller: it has a thin, light-weight, magnetic board which measures just 23cm square. The cards are smaller and the four playing pieces are magnetic counters which are made of coloured plastic. The total weight is only 300 grammes. The standard version will retail at €24.99 and the travel size at €14.99.

And now I'd like to show you another new game called Collect. This is a game ...

Listening 2 (1.21)

R = Robert   S = Sophie

R   So Sophie, how are our products selling?
S   Board games are the big seller at the moment. They're selling better than ever before?
R   Good, so you might be interested in having a bigger range of our board games then.
S   Yes, if there's anything different.
R   We've got Mindtwist. It's our newest board game. The game itself comes in two versions: standard and travel. The games are basically the same but the travel version's lighter and smaller. There are also fewer playing pieces.
S   I stock several general knowledge games already, but I don't have a travel size. I might be interested in that.
R   Right. This is it. You can see it's nice and compact.
S   Mmm, it looks interesting. Are the instructions easy to follow? Some of your games have very complicated instructions.
R   Yes, other customers have told us that as well. So we've made the instructions easier. But I have another travel size game, called Collect. It's even easier to play. Let me show you. It's a card game based on the television programme Collectables. You know, antiques.
S   Oh yes.
R   And it isn't as big as the board game either.
S   Hmm, well, it sounds different, but I'm not sure it'll sell as well as the board games. Not everybody's interested in antiques. Anyway, what's the recommended retail price for the Mindtwist travel version?
R   €14.99.
S   That sounds reasonable. And what would you be willing to sell it to us for?
R   €12.99.
S   Would there be a discount on large orders?
R   Not on Mindtwist on its own, no. But if you were to buy both versions of Mindtwist, I could give you 5% on both games.
S   OK, I'll take them both, but I'll order just a few to start with.
R   Good. I'll get an order form.

Unit 7b: Product development

Listening (1.22)

J = Journalist   M = Marketing Manager

J   So, you're launching a new product for arthritis – Arthran. Who is Arthran for exactly?
M   Anybody who suffers from the condition.
J   And how soon is this product going to be on the market?
M   Well, we're launching it in five weeks' time, on the twenty-fifth of May, but obviously we're starting the publicity campaign before then.
J   Right, and is it going to be available from the chemists' as well as doctors?
M   No, it's a powerful drug and will only be available in hospitals or on prescription from doctors – not over the counter.
J   I see. And what are the side effects?
M   The main one is tiredness. Doctors need to advise their patients not to drive while they're taking this drug. Of course, we're going to give doctors and patients all the necessary information about the drug and how to use it.
J   And how are you going to do that?
M   Well, at the beginning of May we're visiting doctors in hospitals and surgeries. But we're sending them detailed information packs at the end of April so they can read all about the drug and prepare for our visits.
J   And what information is there for patients?
M   Well, about a week before the launch, we're going to give general information posters to doctors for them to display in their waiting rooms.
J   What's the purpose of those?
M   To make patients aware of the new drug so they'll ask their doctors about it. And we're also producing information leaflets at the moment for patients who'll take the drug. They'll be available just after the launch on 25 May.

Unit 8a: Business equipment

Listening (1.23)

Z = Zoltan   A = Anna

Z   Purchasing.
A   Hi Zoltan. It's Anna from Accounts here.
Z   Hi.
A   Zoltan, you know that shredder we've just bought?
Z   Yes?
A   Well, everyone keeps asking how to use it and I can't find the operating instructions.
Z   Ah! Now I think they may still be here. Hold on a second ... Yes, I've got them here, Anna. What do you want to know?
A   Well, what to do if it doesn't work. You know, things like that.
Z   Well. It says here that the machine jams if you insert too much paper into it. If that happens, press the red button, remove the excess paper and start again with less paper.
A   Right. Are there any other possible problems?
Z   The motor overheats sometimes. If that happens, it switches off automatically. Just leave it for fifteen to thirty minutes before you switch it on again.
A   OK, I've got all that. Is there anything else I should know?
Z   Yes, there are a few things to be careful about – like never put your fingers in the shredder.
A   That's a bit obvious, isn't it?
Z   And be careful with long hair and loose articles of clothing like ties. And that's it.
A   Thanks, Zoltan. I'll put a notice with the instructions on the wall next to the shredder.
Z   Good idea.

Unit 10a: Business hotels

Listening 1 (1.24)

I = Interviewer   K = Kara

I   So, what special needs do business travellers have?
K   One of the most important things is a quick check-in and check-out. After a long trip it's annoying to have to wait at the hotel reception for five minutes. Room service is also very important. Guests often stay in their rooms working and don't have the time to go out to a restaurant, so they want their meals to be served in their rooms.
I   And what facilities are there in the rooms?
K   Well, nowadays broadband is very important, especially for business people who need to stay connected with what's happening in the office. That's why all our rooms have free Wi-Fi access.

Audioscripts 143

I   That's great!
K   The lighting is also very important. We've just spent a lot of money upgrading the lighting in our rooms. As I said, guests often spend their evenings preparing work, so they need good lighting at their desks.
I   And what about facilities in the hotel in general?
K   The bars are important. Corporate guests tend to spend more time in the hotel bars than tourists. It's very important to provide a business centre, too.
I   What services does the business centre provide?
K   Photocopying, scanning and document delivery services and we also rent out laptops. We also have a professional conference planner available attached to the business centre who can coordinate conferences for clients and organise catering for them on request. Our corporate clients find this service very helpful.
I   Right, and what about distance to the airport and city centre? Is that important?
K   Yes. We're in the east of London so we're near City Airport. A lot of our guests have meetings in this area, so they don't want to be near Heathrow airport or right in the city centre. But it is easy to get to the centre of London from here. It only takes about fifteen minutes with our courtesy bus. And there's a river taxi, as well.
I   Are your corporate guests interested in using your fitness centre or swimming pool?
K   Not really. They're more popular with tourists. Our corporate guests are more interested in getting in and out of the hotel as quickly as possible and working while they're here.

Listening 2 1.25

R = Reception   M = Montse

R   Good morning. Can I help you?
M   Yes. Could you tell me the best way of getting into the centre of London, please?
R   Well, there is a courtesy bus, which leaves every twenty minutes during the rush hour, or the river taxi service to London Bridge.
M   And when is the rush hour?
R   It's between seven and nine in the morning and five and seven in the evening.
M   And after nine in the morning?
R   After nine, the courtesy bus service runs every forty minutes.
M   Ah ha. And how long does it take?
R   The bus takes about fifteen minutes, depending on the traffic.
M   And which way does it go?
R   Here, I'll show you on the map. From the hotel it goes along the river bank and then on to Brunel Road. It crosses the river at Tower Bridge and then stops just after Tower Bridge at Tower Hill Underground Station.
M   And what about the river taxi, does that change after rush hour?
R   Yes, it's a half hourly service during rush hour and after that it runs to a timetable. It takes about fifteen minutes. It's a really nice trip. You go across to Canary Wharf Pier first, then you go along the river, under Tower Bridge and you stop at a pier just before London Bridge. It costs £3.30 each way.
M   OK. Thanks very much.
R   You're welcome. Bye.

Unit 10b: Commuting

Listening 1.26 – 1.31

Speaker 1
I think it's a stupid idea. The motorways are already too full and now they're going to stop cars using one of the lanes. It's crazy. The traffic'll be twice as bad and there'll be a lot more accidents as well. People will spend hours and hours stuck in traffic jams and be late for work all the time.

Speaker 2
OK, I know cars are bad for the environment and all that, but big increases in petrol prices aren't going to make any difference. What about industry? Higher petrol prices are only going to increase companies' costs and put jobs at risk.

Speaker 3
It's about time! When I go shopping there are thousands of people all on a narrow little pavement trying to walk along. It's impossible to relax. Car drivers should use park and ride schemes and leave their cars out of the city centre. Shopping should be fun and not stressful.

Speaker 4
It's difficult to say, really. Paying every time you use a road might be a good idea. I suppose some people might leave their cars at home a bit more often, which would be good. But there isn't any public transport where I live, so it would be more expensive for me personally.

Speaker 5
How am I going to get to work if I can't leave my car there? It takes twice as long to get to work on the bus and it costs twice as much, as well. So, of course I'm not going to use public transport.

Speaker 6
I think it's a good idea. I hate it when you don't have the right money on the buses. They don't accept notes so you need a pocket full of change all the time. I like the idea of a plastic card – especially if it makes them cheaper to use as well.

Unit 11a: Arranging a conference

Listening 1 1.32

J = Jessica Yeung   D = Daniel Black

J   Good morning, Events Asia. Can I help you?
D   Good morning. My name's Daniel Black from Amtech. Could you give me a quotation for the organisation of a marketing conference, please?
J   Yes, of course. I'll need to take some details first. So, it's Daniel Black from Amtech. Can you spell the company name, please?
D   Yes, it's A-M-T-E-C-H.
J   And what's the address?
D   152 Jalan Pemimpin – that's J-A-L-A-N, Jalan, and P-E-M-I-M-P-I-N Pemimpin 02-08, and the postcode is 6553 6839 Singapore. The phone number is 65 for Singapore, 6211 4789.
J   65 6211 4789. And it's a marketing conference. How many delegates will there be?
D   Between thirty-five and forty.
J   Do you have a preferred location?
D   Yes. Well, we're thinking of Hong Kong, if it's affordable.
J   That's always the big question, isn't it? Could you tell me what your budget is, please?
D   70,000 American dollars maximum.
J   OK. And when do you want to hold the conference?
D   In September or October.
J   How long would you like it to last?
D   A weekend. We'd like the delegates to arrive for dinner on the Friday evening and leave after lunch on the Sunday.
J   Will you want to have the delegates in one room for the whole conference or will you need seminar rooms?
D   Well, we plan to break into two discussion groups during the day, so we'll need one seminar room in addition to the main conference room.
J   Right, Mr Black. That's all I need to ask you for the moment. I'll look at your requirements and make a written proposal before the end of the week.
D   Fine. Thanks very much.

Listening 2 (1.33)

D = Daniel Black   J = Jessica Yeung

D Good morning. Daniel Black.
J Hello. This is Jessica Yeung from Asia Events.
D Hello. How are you?
J Fine thanks. I'm phoning about the marketing conference. I'd like to check some details before I send you the letter of confirmation.
D Sure, go ahead.
J So, the conference will be held on September the twenty-fifth to the twenty-seventh for thirty-seven delegates and all of the delegates will require accommodation for two nights. You will have the use of one conference room plus a smaller seminar room. Is that correct?
D Yes, that sounds right.
J Now there's just one thing I'm not sure about. Did you say that you want the delegates to pay their own bar and phone bills before they depart?
D No, just their phone bills.
J So all drinks should go on the master account?
D That's right, yes.
J Fine. That's all I need to know, thanks.
D And are you going to be in the hotel at the time of the conference?
J No, it won't be me as I'll be at another conference then. One of my colleagues will be waiting for you at the hotel when you arrive. I'll be able to give you the name of your contact person in a few days.
D Great, thanks.
J So, I'll confirm the whole thing in writing. You should receive the letter before the end of the week.

Unit 11b: At a conference

Listening 1 (1.34)

Good morning everybody. Welcome to the 7th Annual International Sales Conference. It's great to see so many of you – old faces and new ones! Now we're going to have two very busy days as usual, but I am sure you'll enjoy them. As soon as I finish, which won't be long, I promise you, we'll begin with our first session, which is our Sales Managers giving their National Sales Reports for their own countries.

We'll stay together for that session as I feel it's useful for everybody to see the overall picture. Then, after we've had lunch, we're going to divide into groups to discuss our targets for next year and how to reach them. At four o'clock we'll come back together again when Amy Carter, our guest speaker, gives her presentation. As you all know, the consultants Allman & Partners have been looking at the way we answer the telephone throughout the group and Amy is going to give a short report on their findings. Her presentation will probably finish just before 5.30.

Dinner this evening is at eight o'clock. We'd like everyone to meet in the bar for drinks from about seven o'clock. That way we can enjoy a drink together until the coach leaves for the restaurant at 7.45.

Tomorrow morning we're starting at nine o'clock with a look at ways of marketing the new product. This'll also be a workshop session. Then there'll be a coffee break before we come back together again and share our ideas with a feedback session. And that will bring us to the end of the conference and a farewell lunch. So, that's enough from me. I'd just like to wish you all an enjoyable and successful two days and hand you over to Jodie Cox, who's going to start with a look at Canadian sales.

Listening 2 (1.35)

C = Colleague   J = Jodie

C So, how did the conference go, Jodie?
J Oh it was good. All the sessions were interesting and all the speakers were really good. The organisation was a lot better this year as well. I think having a smaller number of people there made a big difference. You know, you could actually get things done in the workshops and make decisions a lot more quickly. There were about thirty delegates altogether, which was just perfect.
C And how was the hotel?
J Fine. The conference rooms were a good size and the hotel rooms were clean and very comfortable. I really liked the hotel a lot. I think we should go there again next year.
C And how was dinner on Saturday?
J Ah, that was probably the only thing that people really complained about. The food wasn't very good and the service was slow. If we go back to the same hotel again, we'll have to find another restaurant.

Unit 12: Exam focus

Part One: Questions 1–8 (2.01)

For Questions 1–8, you will hear eight short recordings. For each question, mark A, B or C for the most suitable picture or phrase. You will hear each conversation twice.

1 **What is Maria's job title?**
   A So, you work in Sales, don't you, Maria?
   B Sort of, I'm actually in the Marketing Department.
   A Oh I see. And what do you do there?
   B I'm the Manager.

2 **Where are they taking the visitors?**
   A Where should we take the visitors this evening?
   B Good question. What kind of food will they like?
   A I know a place that serves great Asian food.
   B Not everyone likes spicy food, though. I know a place that does great pasta. Why don't we go there?
   A OK.

3 **What was the final decision about the meeting?**
   A Did you see the memo about tomorrow's meeting?
   B Yes, I saw it was postponed until next week.
   A Well, forget the memo. It's back on again at the same time.

4 **Which part of the job offer was George unhappy about?**
   A Are you going to take the job, George?
   B I don't know. The salary was OK.
   A What about the hours?
   B They were long but I don't mind that. I'm just a bit worried about the amount of paid leave, that's all.

5 **Which graph is the Head of Department talking about?**
   A So, as you can see, sales rose at the start of the year and then levelled off in the summer. But I'm happy to say there was a big increase in orders for toys at Christmas.

6 **When are the visitors arriving?**
   A Oh you stupid machine!
   B Hey. What's all the excitement for?
   A Because it's already half past ten. I've got visitors arriving in half an hour. I need to photocopy some reports and this stupid machine isn't working!

7 **Which photocopier do they decide to buy?**
   A So which of these photocopiers should we buy?
   B This one looks nice, the X40.
   A Hmm. Bit expensive. The RX200 looks fast. It does twenty-five copies a minute.
   B So does the BT100. And it's cheaper and smaller.
   A But it hasn't got many functions, has it?
   B That's true. OK, we'll get the bigger one.

8   Which part of the factory does Alan want to change?
    A   How can we increase production, Alan? Should we buy some more machines for the production line?
    B   That's not necessary. The real problem is that we can't store any more raw materials. We need to increase storage space.
    A   Hm. And the packing area, is that OK?
    B   For the moment. As I said, storage is the problem.

Part Two: Questions 9–15 (2.02)

You will hear two people discussing an invoice. Listen to the conversation and write the missing information in the spaces. You will hear the conversation twice.

A   Hello, Accounts. How can I help you?
B   I'd like to check an invoice please.
A   Certainly. Can you give me the invoice number please?
B   Of course, it's HP420Y.
A   HP420Y?
B   That's right.
A   OK, that invoice is dated the fifteenth of February, what seems to be the problem?
B   I just wanted to check the details, my copy isn't very clear.
A   Right, go ahead.
B   Well, can you confirm that we ordered nine boxes of paper for the photocopier?
A   No, you ordered ten boxes of paper at fourteen euro ninety-nine each.
B   OK. That's a hundred and forty-nine euro ninety, isn't it?
A   Yes, but that price is exclusive of VAT, which is 17.5%.
B   Oh, how much is the actual total then?
A   That's one hundred and seventy-six euro and thirteen cents to pay.
B   Thirty cents?
A   Thirteen.
B   Oh, right and that needs to reach you by the seventeenth?
A   Please.
B   OK. Can I have your name in case I have any more problems?
A   Of course, it's Natalia Kosor.
B   Kosor, how do you spell that?
A   K-O-S-O-R.
B   And have you got a direct line?
A   Yes, the number is 0176 688 820.
B   688 120?
A   688 820.
B   Great thanks, thanks for your help.
A   You're welcome. Bye.

Part Three: Questions 16–22 (2.03)

You will hear a woman talking to some journalists about a new product range. Listen to the talk and write one or two words or a date in the spaces. You will hear the talk twice.

Good morning ladies and gentlemen. My name is Jade Ritchie and today I'd like to introduce you to our new product range, but first let me welcome you to NatureSoft Skincare. I hope you all had a pleasant journey here to our Head Office. Although we have a sales office in London and Milan, NatureSoft Skincare has made its home here, in York, for the past fifty years. During this time we have built up a loyal customer base of older, more mature women who appreciate our products for their high quality and no-nonsense packaging. However, we felt it was time to broaden our appeal and move into new markets and so we have developed our 'Feel Good' cosmetic range. As I said earlier, Feel Good is aimed at a different type of consumer but of course we are not going to abandon our traditional, more mature market and will continue producing all our original ranges. The Feel Good consumer is a young, modern, professional lady who expects the quality enjoyed by previous generations but wants a fresh-looking product. This brings me to what we believe to be Feel Good's unique appeal – the price. What we have achieved is a serious quality product which won't break the bank.

If you look in your welcome pack you will see we have included some samples for you to try, but when will the general public be able to test our claims for themselves? Well, as I'm sure your must be aware, we have already started to run advertisements in some women's magazines. Our celebrity party, with special guests Vicky and Veronique from the TV series Little Sister, is September 14th, with products going on sale to the public the following day. We will also be running a number of nationwide promotions all based on the Feel Good promise 'Look Great'. All that remains is for me to thank you for coming here today.

Part Four: Questions 23–30 (2.04)

Listen to the conversation between a head of department and an employee. For Questions 23-30 mark the correct phrase to complete the sentence. Mark one letter, A, B or C for the phrase you choose. You will hear the conversation twice. You have 45 seconds to read through the questions.

A   Come in Sharon and take a seat.
B   Thanks.
A   So, where do we start? Should we begin with a look at last year and then go on from there?
B   Fine.
A   So, how do you feel you've done in your first full year with the company?
B   Overall, I think I've done quite well. I feel quite confident now about what I do.
A   And are you happy with your duties?
B   Well, the job is exactly as it was advertised so there have been no surprises. I like dealing with customers and I don't mind answering the phone and preparing invoices. Sometimes it's a bit boring typing long price lists, but then everyone has to do it.
A   That's true. Does anything make your job difficult?
B   Well, as you know, we all have problems with the new stock control system. It's still not working properly, but I know people are trying to fix it. But, unfortunately, since the sales-tracking software was upgraded, I've had difficulties with this, too. It runs really slowly. IT Support says it's because my PC is so old and I really need a new machine with more memory.
A   OK, we'll see what we can do about that. But apart from getting a new PC, is there anything else you would like to change?
B   Erm, let me see. I'd like the authority to issue credit notes without having to ask you first. You're often away on business and sometimes customers ring up with a complaint. And if we can't contact you, then we can't deal with the complaint properly. It's a bit embarrassing at times.
A   Yes, but some of our customers always find something wrong and try and get a credit note with every order. You can't believe everything they say, you know. What about your objectives for the future?
B   Well, I need to get to know the customers a bit better and maybe try to make fewer mistakes. But I think the most important thing is to increase my product knowledge, so I don't get embarrassed when customers make enquiries.
A   Don't worry, you'll learn. What I'd like to ask you about now is ...

That is the end of the Test.

Unit 13a: Production

Listening 1 (1.36)

B = Brian   V = Visitor

B   So, this is a diagram of the bakery. Now it all begins with the main ingredients – those are flour and water. They're weighed and fed

automatically into mixers. Yeast and additives are then added by hand and everything is mixed together for twelve minutes to make the dough.
V What are the additives for?
B They're just to increase the shelf-life of the baguettes. The dough is then divided into pieces. And after the weight is checked, the dough enters the first prover for ten minutes.
V The first what?
B Prover.
V What's a prover?
B I can tell you haven't baked bread before.
V No, that's very true!
B Well, you can't bake the dough straight away. You have to let it stand for a while so the yeast can react before you form it. This is called proving. Well now, the yeast makes the dough rise, and gives the bread shape and volume.
V Oh, right. I see.
B So, the dough is then formed into a baguette and dropped onto trays, which then continuously go round a circuit. The trays take the baguettes into another prover for 60 minutes. The temperature in the prover is perfect for the yeast to make the bread rise even more.
V 60 minutes, that long?
B Well, the prover stage is very important. If the bread doesn't prove properly, you can't bake it. Now the trays then continue around the circuit to the oven, where the bread is baked for ten minutes. And after leaving the oven, the trays enter the cooler. That's where cool air is blown over them for forty minutes. The baguettes are then taken off the trays and dropped into plastic baskets for packaging. And the trays continue around the circuit and go back to the start again.
V And what happens to the baguettes?
B They're taken to the packing hall, where they're wrapped, boxed and despatched.
V And how long does the whole process take?
B From flour to boxed products takes about two and a half hours.

Listening 2 🔘 1.37

V = Visitor   B = Brian

V So, Brian, what problems do you have with the production line?
B Well, we have a lot of problems with sensors. These are electronic sensors that tell the computer when a tray enters or leaves a prover or oven. The computer monitors the circuit and controls the speed of the trays. The computer stops the whole process when a sensor stops working properly – a complete shutdown.
V Really?
B Well, you have to remember that the line produces 6,000 baguettes an hour. The timing has to be perfect or the system stops. The sensors have to be set up exactly right. If they aren't, the computer won't start the system.
V What other problems do you have?
B Well, sometimes we have problems with the mixers. If the computer gets the mix wrong, we have to clean out the whole mixer.
V Do you have any problems with your workers?
B Not often, no. The system produces a new mix every twelve minutes, so it is possible that a mixerman can forget to put in the yeast and additives. If he forgets the extra ingredients, we lose the whole mix.
V Any other kinds of problems?
B Occasionally we have mechanical problems. Like when an old tray loses its shape, it can jam in a prover or oven. That can be a big problem because it can damage a machine and jam the whole system.
V So how much time do you lose a day on average?

B That's difficult to say, really. On a good day maybe six minutes. We can lose up to an hour and a half of production if we have a really bad day. And that means nearly 10,000 baguettes.

Unit 13b: Quality control

Listening 1 🔘 1.38

V = Visitor   M = Mazli

V Could you tell me a bit about quality control at the factory?
M Well, there are four main quality control inspection points. We begin by visiting our suppliers to make sure we are happy with their quality control. Next, we inspect all goods in on arrival at our factory and the third inspection point is during production. And the final stage is chemical analysis of our finished goods.
V And what do you look for at each of the four inspection points?
M Well, each stage is different. With our suppliers, for instance, we inspect their QC processes and, even more importantly, their factory hygiene. If we're not happy with their hygiene, we'll cancel the supply contract. At the goods in stage we make sure that order quantities are correct and the quality is OK. We also check the transport packaging. If the packaging is damaged, the warehouse shelf-life can be reduced.
V And what quality checks do you run during production?
M We take samples to check there isn't too much cooking oil on the snack and that each snack has the minimum amount of flavouring. We also check the size of the snacks and their crispness. If the snacks are too oily, they go soft.
V So that leaves the finished goods. What do you check for at the final QC stage?
M We check individual bags to make sure that the packet weight is above the acceptable minimum and that the packet is sealed properly. We also check the taste.
V And how do you do that?
M Well, we eat them. How else? We also do chemical analysis to check things like fat levels and other information that we have to put on the packets.

Listening 2 🔘 1.39

A = Amrit   LW = Lu Wei   M = Mazli

A OK, so we all know there's a problem with reject levels, but before we look at ways of dealing with it, what I'd like to know is why don't we find the rejects sooner. How can they get all the way to the finished goods chemical analysis before we find them? Lu Wei?
LW Well, Amrit. The problem is the oil temperature in the cookers. It keeps falling or rising suddenly. And that's why the samples don't always pick up high fat levels. The problem is worse when demand is high and we're running at full capacity, well, like we are at the moment.
A So what can we do about it?
LW Well I think the first idea on your memo is the best one. We should increase the sampling rate. You see, if we take samples more often, we'll pick up the rejects sooner.
M That's true, but if we do that, we'll need extra human resources in the QC department. I prefer the second idea. I'd rather just change the temperature sensors in the cookers.
LW We've already tried that, but it didn't make any difference. The problem is the oil in the cookers. When it gets dirty the temperature sensors don't work properly.
M So why don't we change the oil more often?
LW Well it would help, but we have to stop production to change the oil. We're going to lose production capacity if we stop the line more often. And the extra oil will increase our costs, of course.
A Hmm. That's a point.

M Yes, but if it reduces the reject levels, a bit of lost production won't be a problem.
LW It might not be a problem if we can reduce reject levels to zero, but I don't think that's possible.
A OK let's try it anyway. Lu Wei, I'd like you to change the oil more often and monitor the sensors. Mazli, I'd like you to increase the sampling rate by just ten per cent. That means you won't need extra staff. Let's do that for the next two weeks and see what happens. OK?
M Right.

Unit 14a: Direct service providers

Listening 1 1.40

J = Journalist   G = Gabe

J American Life was the first direct provider of insurance in the United States when it started twenty-six years ago. Can you tell us a bit about the products you offer?
G Well, most people when they think about American Life, they think about car insurance. Over the last ten years we've become one of the biggest direct auto insurers in the USA – and we've recently started to offer a vehicle breakdown service. However, as our name suggests we were originally best known for our life insurance policies and our home and travel insurance products. We also offer financial services such as mortgages, personal loans, savings and pensions.
J And how many call centres does the company now operate?
G We have 200 regional centres across the United States which employ between 300 and 600 people each. So, in total we have over 100,000 staff in our centres. Almost one in fifty working Americans has some kind of insurance policy with us.
J So what are the advantages of using call centres to buy and sell insurance directly?
G Well, the biggest advantage of direct service is the same for both the company and our customers – we all save money. Direct auto insurance means there is no middleman; consequently the price of the insurance is lower for the client. And the costs are lower for the company because call centres are cheap to run. We don't have to pay high rents for good main street locations or pay commission to brokers and agents. This means we can offer our customers lower premiums.
J OK. And how does a call centre affect the quality of service a customer gets?
G When a customer calls, they get an instant response. The computer database shows all the customer's details, which saves a lot of time. When people say they don't like call centres, they forget how much slower things were in the past. For example, we can now process insurance claims up to three times more quickly. Our call centres allow us to offer our customers much quicker service as well as lower prices.
J So far, American Life hasn't followed the trend of 'offshoring' its call centres to locations outside the United States where labour is cheaper and costs are even lower. Is this something that might happen in the future?
G No. And at American Life we don't believe that offshoring is the future for the call centre industry. You see many companies who have off-shored their call centres are not happy with the result. The different language and culture create a lot of problems and isn't always as cheap as they hoped. Labour costs are likely to rise fast in places like India and as the economy develops, companies will probably have difficulty finding and keeping staff. In the future, companies might relocate their call centres back in the States. We've kept our call centres right here and we believe this was the right decision.
J So how do you see the future for call centres?

G I believe virtual call centres are the future. We're starting to use more home-based agents who do the same jobs as our call centre staff but who work from home. That way we can hire new staff from across the whole country instead of in a fifty-mile radius round a call centre. We have a lot more possible candidates to choose from for each new job, so we can find people with just the right skills and experience. We can deliver our staff training online, too. In the future, virtual call centres will possibly replace most of our existing call centres because they offer us a way to keep growing our customer service teams without lots of capital investment.

Listening 2 1.41

J = Journalist   G = Gabe

J Gabe, we sometimes read negative stories about working conditions in call centres. Is it true, for example, that you know exactly where workers are for every minute of their shift?
G Yes, the computer system does monitor whether agents are at their desks, but we make sure that they get an hour for lunch and plenty of other breaks.
J Does the monitoring affect their pay?
G Yes, but in a positive way. Agents receive bonuses based on the number of calls they take, the products they sell and the mistakes they make. This way we reward good work. Every team also has a supervisor whose role it is to support the agents and to help them with difficult or unusual customer enquiries. Agents don't have to make any difficult decisions themselves.
J So what kind of hours do the agents work?
G They work flexible shifts of thirty-five hours a week. Plus overtime if they want it.
J What do you mean by flexible shifts?
G Well, the computer system works out a shift plan based on the calls it expects and plans exactly the right number of agents for each time of day. So shift times are flexible.
J So, do the agents also work evenings?
G We're open from eight till eight Monday to Friday and from nine till five on Saturdays. A lot of our agents are young mothers or students, so they're happy to work evening shifts.
J And what about job satisfaction?
G Some people believe that working in a call centre isn't the most exciting job in the world – so it's very important to remember that your agents are human. So we organise them into teams. The team that sells the most policies, for example, wins a prize. We also organise fun competitions during big sporting events like the World Cup or the Olympics.

Unit 14b: The banking sector

Listening 1 1.42

Cl = Clerk   Cu = Customer

Cl Hello. Can I help you?
Cu Yes, I'd like some information on your internet banking service.
Cl Certainly. Do you have an account with us?
Cu Yes, I do. This is my home branch.
Cl Well, with our internet banking service you can do all your day-to-day banking online at any time of day or night.
Cu How does it work?
Cl All you do is log in, key in your PIN number, choose the service you want and then just follow the instructions. It's as easy as that.
Cu And what can I actually do online?
Cl You can check your balance, pay bills, order a statement or transfer money. All your normal day-to-day banking.
Cu Does it cost anything?
Cl No. The service is part of your normal bank account.
Cu Oh right. And can I log in at any time of the day

Cl Yes, you can. The service is available 24 hours-a-day, seven days a week.
Cu Could I fill in a form now?
Cl Certainly. One moment, I'll just get an application form ...

Listening 2 (1.43)

Cl = Clerk   Cu = Customer

Cl Right, could I have your full name, please?
Cu Yes, it's Miss Denise Le Blanc.
Cl And your address, Miss Le Blanc?
Cu 4, Manor Road, Winchester.
Cl And the postcode?
Cu SO23 9DY.
Cl Could I have your date of birth, please?
Cu Yes, it's thirty-first October 1968.
Cl Thank you. And your daytime phone number?
Cu 01962 866 155.
Cl And all I need now are your account details. So, the sort code is 77 25 09 and could I have the number of your current account please?
Cu 60877422.
Cl 60877422.
Cu That's right.
Cl If you could sign the form here, Miss Le Blanc, and then that's it. I'll register you and then we'll send you your information pack and membership number.

> Unit 15 contains extracts from a Speaking Test.
> No tapescript is provided.

Unit 16b: Trading

Listening (1.44)

J = Journalist   K = Mr Krall

J Could you tell me about Krallpack and its activities?
K We're an agent for Korean manufacturers of packing machinery. We provide them with a European sales network and translate their documents, specifications and parts lists into English and other European languages, as required. We also deal with the British customers and all their enquiries and correspondence. And we arrange customers' visits to Korea.
J Mm, that's very interesting. How did this company begin?
K Before I started Krallpack, I worked in sales for eight years for an international company here in Germany. We had to use some small suppliers of packing machinery to complete our product range. But working with both large and small suppliers caused problems. The smaller companies wanted someone to sell only their products, so in 1992 I left and set up my own company, Krallpack GmbH.
J That was a big step. And how has this company developed since then?
K Well, I began selling to the drinks industry. Our suppliers began developing excellent new machines that were technically more advanced than our competitors'. These machines helped us to expand into the food and pharmaceutical industries. And our sales people were very good at understanding and selling these new machines so Krallpack got a name for delivering excellent products and providing a service that was fair to both customers and suppliers. Since then turnover has grown to nearly £10m a year and our customers now include companies such as GlaxoSmithKline, Bayer Schering, Rhône Poulenc and Merck. We moved into these new offices last year and at the moment we're looking for new staff to help the company grow further.
J Very good. And the future? How do you see the future?

K I think technical development is the key to the industry. Companies have to produce and pack more and more specialised goods to satisfy their customers. So, in future, our suppliers will have to develop their machines technically but without losing any reliability. Our job, of course, is going to be to sell these new machines and continue to provide the best possible support for both our customers and our suppliers.

Unit 17a: Recruiting staff

Listening (1.45)

R = Rick   P = Patricia

R So Patricia, have you given any more thought to taking on an assistant in marketing?
P Yes and I'm still not sure about it. If we decided to take someone on, where would we advertise the vacancy?
R Well, I guess we'd advertise the position internally as we always do.
P But if we advertised the job internally, we'd have the same old problems – not enough applicants and lots of internal political problems. Couldn't we advertise the job outside the company for once?
R Well, I suppose we could. But if we did, a lot of people wouldn't be very happy about it.
P So? Would that be a problem?
R Well, yes. I mean, the company always talks about how we like to promote our own people and how you can develop a career with us. So it would look a bit funny if we didn't advertise it internally first.
P But even if we promoted one of our own people, the other internal applicants wouldn't be happy anyway. So what's the difference? Why couldn't we just advertise it in the national papers and online?
R But it's company policy. You know that. We always advertise internally first.
P Yes, I know. But why can't we try something different for a change? If we took someone on from outside the company, we'd bring some new ideas into the department. It's what we need, Rick.
R Look, why don't we just advertise it internally as we always do, right? That'll keep everyone happy and then, after a couple of weeks, we can put an advert online as well. What do you say?
P Oh all right. But I'm not going to do the interviews. You can. I had to do the interviews last time and the people who didn't get the job didn't speak to me for weeks afterwards.

Unit 17b: Applying for a job

Listening (1.46)

I = Interviewer   A = Almudena Ribera

I So, Ms Ribera, I'd like to ask you a few questions about your professional experience and qualifications, if I may?
A Sure.
I Now your CV says that you've experience of dealing with clients from different countries. Could you tell me which countries you've dealt with?
A My department publishes translations of foreign books. Most of them are English language books so I deal with America a lot and Britain. And sometimes Italy, too.
I So, America, Britain and Italy. So your English is obviously very good and you speak Italian too. Could you tell me how good your French is?
A It's OK. I did French as part of my degree but it isn't as good as my English or Italian.

I So, that's reasonable French. Now, on your CV you say you have good keyboard skills. Could you tell me how many words a minute you can type?
A About sixty. I'm a bit out of practice at the moment since I don't do a lot of typing in my present job, but I could soon get up to speed again.
I OK, fine. Now, you are obviously an experienced Word user, but what about Excel and PowerPoint?
A At the moment I use Excel a lot because I need it for all the cost sheets and the expenses forms, and also to help the editors with the figures for the publishing proposals. In my last job I also used PowerPoint for our presentations.
I You used PowerPoint? Did you design the presentations yourself?
A The Training Director planned them but I had to do the actual computer work and make sure it worked properly during the presentations.
I So that was at Informática. But it says here in your CV that you left in 2007. Could you tell me why you left?
A I think the main reason was languages. I liked my job at Informática but all our clients were Spanish so I never got to use my languages. Then one day I saw the advertisement for the job at Ediciones Gómez and I'd always been interested in publishing, so I applied.
I So why do you want to change jobs now?
A Well, I still feel that I don't get enough practice with my languages ...

Unit 18: Exam practice

Questions 30–37 (2.11)

For Questions 30–37, you will hear eight short recordings. For each question, mark A, B or C for the most suitable picture or phrase.

30 What does Alison order?
A So, Alison. Do you know what you want?
B I'm not sure. The chicken sounds nice, but so does the fish. What about you?
A Well, I think I'm going to have the fish.
B OK. I'll have that, too.

31 Which is the flight to Sydney?
Would all passengers for flight LH4521 to Brisbane please go to gate number forty. Flight LH4152 to Sydney is now also boarding at gate number forty-two.

32 Which hotel does Graham's colleague recommend?
A Have you booked a hotel room yet, Graham?
B No, I'm just looking at the brochure now.
A Well, don't go to this one here.
B Why? What's wrong with the Grand?
A It's too expensive. So's this one, the Orion. I'd go to the Plaza if I were you.

33 Which machine are the people talking about?
A Karen. Could you help me for a moment?
B Sure. What's the problem?
A I'm not sure how to use this machine.
B It's very simple. Just insert the paper, key in the number and press the send button.

34 What happens to the phone call?
A Hello, North Seas Shipping. Can I help you?
B Hello. Could I speak to Amanda Collins, please?
A One moment please, I'll just try her office. Hello, I'm afraid she's in a meeting. Can I take a message?
B It's OK. I'll try again this afternoon.

35 How much does the retailer pay for each game?
A The games look interesting, but how much do they cost per unit?
B The unit price is eight dollars.
A And are there any discounts on large orders?
B We could give you a dollar off per unit on orders over 500 units.
A Hm. Then I'll just take 200 units to begin with.

36 How long will the order take to arrive?
A When are those samples arriving?
B Well, they sent them on Friday and it normally takes four working days.
A But Monday was a bank holiday.
B Oh yes. So they should be here on Friday then.

37 What is wrong with the printer?
A Oh! The stupid machine isn't working again!
B What's wrong with it?
A Oh I don't know. I think it needs some more paper or it's run out of ink or something.
B Oh no, look here. There's some paper stuck in it.

Questions 38–45 (2.12)

Listen to the manager talking to staff about the way they answer the telephone. For Questions 38–45, mark the correct phrase to complete the sentence. Mark one letter, A, B or C for the phrase you choose. You will hear the conversation twice. You have forty-five seconds to read through the questions.

So, if everyone is here, I'll make a start. Now, as you might know, a few months ago we asked some consultants to take a look at the way we answer the telephone across the group. They telephoned our offices and made enquiries as customers normally would. They recorded information such as how quickly the call was answered, how friendly people were and how efficiently they dealt with the enquiry.

So, I'll begin with what they found out. Right, now, first of all, they found out that on average we answer the phone after four rings, which isn't bad, but we can still improve on it. Secondly, friendliness. Now, although some offices scored as high as eight out of ten for friendliness, the consultants only gave the company as a whole six out of ten. Once more, this wasn't as good as it should be. The consultants said that seven point five is the minimum we should be aiming for throughout the group. And finally, efficiency. Now here, we did quite well. It seems that the people who normally answer the phone can either deal with enquiries themselves or put the caller through to the right person. However, there were one or two negative points which we still have to work on, such as always remembering to ask the caller's name before putting them through. So, as you can see, we need to do a lot of work.

Going back to the first point, about the phone ringing four times, everyone will now be responsible for answering the phone after the third ring. This way there is no excuse for keeping a caller waiting. The point about friendliness, however, is the most important. People want to hear a cheerful voice when they call the company and feel good when they do business with us. So we're going to choose some new hold music and the consultants have given us some good phrases to use on the phone. They're on the handout I gave you at the beginning. Does everyone have a copy? Right, good.

So, moving on to efficiency ...

That is the end of the Test.

Answer key

Unit 1a: Job descriptions

Ex 1:
2 provide a service
3 interview an applicant
4 deal with a problem
5 attend a meeting
6 keep a record
7 organise a conference

Ex 2:
1 give a presentation
2 provide support
3 interview a candidate
4 deal with people
5 attend a training session
6 keep a diary
7 organise a holiday

Ex 3:

product	produce
sale	sell
organization	organise
interview	**interview**
applicant	apply
advertising	advertise

Ex 4:
1 interview
2 organise
3 advertise
4 applicants
5 products
6 discussion
7 sales

Ex 5:
1 A 2 C 3 B 4 A 5 A 6 A
7 B 8 A 9 C 10 C 11 A 12 B

Unit 1b: Working conditions

Ex 1: *Suggested answers:*
- paper, stationery, supplies, time, money
- holidays, overtime, salary, problems
- holidays, overtime, orders, stock
- computers, telephone calls, customers

Ex 2:
1 with 2 about 3 at 4 of 5 of
6 in 7 at / in 8 with 9 in 10 with

Ex 3: *Suggested answers:*
I rarely work 35 hours a week.
I usually work over time.
I get 21 days leave a year.
I wear a suit but employees in the factory wear overalls.
There is a health and safety representative in every department.

Ex 4:
1 Mohammed Baddou
2 32
3 29/11/01
4 Leave
5 Production

Unit 2a: Company history

Ex 1:
1 tried 2 visited 3 found
4 were 5 decided 6 sold
7 expanded 8 began 9 had
10 bought 11 had 12 set up
13 went 14 opened 15 continued

Ex 2:
in: December, 1992, summer, the 1980s
at: 10.30, Christmas, the weekend (UK)
on: Friday, 23 July, Tuesday morning, the weekend (USA)

Ex 3: 1 stop 2 produce 3 make

Ex 4: 1 E 2 C 3 A 4 F 5 D

Ex 5: *Suggested answer:* (35 words)
Copies of the new company brochure have just arrived from the printers. Could you collect your copies as soon as possible, please? You'll find them in John's office in the marketing department.
Thanks

Unit 2b: Company activities

Ex 1:
1 is / are building 2 are developing
3 are growing 4 are modernising
5 is investing 6 are earning

Ex 2:
1 are working 2 spends
3 are thinking 4 isn't earning
5 are building 6 isn't developing
7 is growing 8 believe, is growing
9 wants, is offering 10 are increasing

Ex 3:
2 Nokia is a Finnish communications company.
3 Reuters is a British press agency.
4 Timberland is an American clothes manufacturer.
5 ABN Amro is a Dutch bank.
6 Tata is an Indian car manufacturer.
7 Godiva is a Belgian chocolate manufacturer.
8 Swatch is a Swiss watch manufacturer.
9 Softbank is a Japanese software distributor.
10 Danone is a French food group.

Ex 4:
1 C 2 B 3 B 4 A 5 B 6 A
7 C 8 C 9 A 10 C 11 A 12 B

Unit 4a: Telephoning

Ex 1:

[11] Thank you Mr Abraham. I'll give Mr Green the message.
[4] I'm afraid the line's busy. Can I take a message?
[13] You're welcome. Bye.
[1] Good morning, Priory Hotel.

[7] And what's the message, please?
[5] Could you spell your surname, please?
[9] Did you say 7.15 or 7.50?
[4] Yes, please. Could you tell him Alan Abraham called?
[12] Thank you very much.
[8] Could you tell him I've booked a table at Marcel's restaurant for 7.15 this evening and I'll meet him there?
[6] A-B-R-A-H-A-M.
[2] Hello, could you put me through to Mr Green in room 105, please?
[10] 7.15. Quarter past seven.

Ex 2: Suggested answers:
1 Can I take a message?
2 Could you spell your surname, please?
3 Sorry, did you say
4 I'm calling about
5 Could you tell her
6 I'll give her the message.

Ex 3: 1 C 2 B 3 A 4 A 5 C

Unit 4b: Internal communication

Ex 1: Suggested answer: (35 words)
We're having a meeting on Tuesday 21 Jan to discuss the new training schedule. Could you prepare your proposals by 18 Jan please, and can you give everyone a copy before the meeting.
Thanks.

Ex 2: Suggested answer: (32 words)
There will be a meeting on 21 January at 10.45 in the boardroom to discuss the new brochure. Could all staff please attend. The meeting is scheduled to last approximately one hour.

Ex 3: Suggested answer: (37 words)
Elizabeth Sharp, the new Human Resources Manager, will be visiting us on Tuesday 11 April. The aim of her visit is to learn more about the company so please make sure that you introduce yourselves to her.

Unit 5a: Facts and figures

Ex 1: A fall   B rise   C level off
D remain steady   E recover   F peak

Ex 2:
1 Last year there was a drop **in** net sales **of** 9%.
2 Market share increased **by** 3%, up to 8%.
3 Net sales peaked **at** £22m in 2007.
4 European sales went **from** £4.2m to £3.0m.
5 Sales levelled off **at** £5m in 2008.
6 Costs rose **by** £3.3m. This was a rise **of** 10%.
7 Office software sales fell **by** 10% in 2007.
8 A strong pound meant a fall **in** exports in 2008.

Ex 3: 2 product launch   3 net income
4 top-selling brand   5 annual report

Ex 4: Suggested answer:
The most successful product was adventure games. Sales increased steadily from 30% to 45% in the period from 2005 to 2008. There was strong growth in action games for the first three years of the same period. They peaked at 25% in 2007 but dropped sharply in 2008. Sales of sports games fell from 25% to 15% in 2006 then levelled off in 2007 and rose to 20% in 2008. Sales of other computer games remained steady at 10% in 2005 and 2006, fell slightly in 2007 and then recovered in 2008.

Ex 5: 1 F 2 H 3 G 4 C 5 A

Unit 5b: Performance

Ex 1: 2 I'd like to begin with a look at
3 As you can see
4 The graph clearly shows
5 I'd like you to look at
6 I'd like to draw your attention to

Ex 2: 1 has been   2 has already achieved
3 have worked   4 has performed
5 had   6 were
7 did not look   8 made
9 were not   10 has improved

Ex 3: 2 New trains have **resulted in/led to** more reliable service.
3 The number of delays increased **because of/due to** track problems.
4 We can't raise prices. **That's why/Therefore**, we have to increase volumes.
5 Customer satisfaction has improved **due to/because of** better facilities.
6 Reduced ticket prices have **resulted in/led to** an increase in passenger volumes.

Ex 4: 1 D 2 A 3 G 4 H 5 E

Unit 6: Exam focus

Part One:	1 C	2 A	3 B	4 B	5 A
Part Two:	6 G	7 D	8 C	9 H	10 F
Part Three:	11 G	12 C	13 E	14 A	15 D
Part Five:	16 C	17 C	18 B	19 C	
	20 A	21 A			
Part Six:	22 A	23 B	24 B	25 B	26 B
	27 C	28 B	29 C	30 A	31 B
	32 A	33 C			

Unit 7a: Product description

Ex 1: 2 short   How long is the board?
3 cheap   How much does the game cost?
4 size   How big is Collect?
5 easy   How difficult are the instructions?

Ex 2: *Suggested answer:*
2 The Extra is 2 kilos **heavier than the Super**.
3 The Extra is more **expensive than the other display panels**.
4 The Super is not as **heavy/big/expensive as the Extra**.
5 The Standard is the least **expensive of the display panels**.
6 The Standard is the **lightest /cheapest/ smallest of the display panels**.

Ex 4:
1 B	2 C	3 A	4 B	5 C
6 B	7 A	8 B	9 B	10 A
11 B	12 B			

Unit 7b: Product development

Ex 1:
2 After that/Then   3 then/ after that
4 When   5 while

Ex 2:
2 are you going to do/are you doing
3 are starting
4 are using
5 Are you going to use/Are you using

Ex 3: 1 A   2 C   3 B   4 A   5 B

Ex 4: 1 B   2 C   3 A   4 B   5 C

Unit 8a: Business equipment

Ex 1:

Fax machine	Printer	Photocopier	Shredder
dial	jam	jam	jam
jam	press	enlarge	press
press	print	reduce	insert
print	insert	press	shred
insert	switch on	insert	switch on
switch on	overheat	switch on	overheat
overheat		overheat	send
send		copy	
copy		print	

Ex 2:

Noun	Verb
insertion	insert
operation	operate
reduction	reduce
copy	copy
printer	print
removal	remove

Ex 3: *Suggested answer:*
2 Open the paper tray and insert more paper.
3 Press the red button. Remove the excess paper. Start again with less paper.
4 Open the door of the machine. Remove any jammed paper.
5 Switch it off. Leave it to cool. Try again.
6 Check there are staples in the machine. If there aren't, insert some.

Ex 5: 1 C   2 A   3 C
        4 C   5 C   6 B

Ex 6: 1 C   2 E   3 D
        4 A   5 G

Unit 8b: Correspondence

Ex 1:
2 enclosed   3 department
4 note well *(from the Latin: nota bene)*
5 regarding   6 week   7 excluding
8 including   9 extension

Ex 2:
1 Dear Ms Garcia   Yours sincerely
2 Dear Paul   Regards
3 Dear Sir /Madam   Yours faithfully
4 Gentlemen   Yours truly*

* Gentlemen is the USA equivalent of Dear Sirs (UK). Yours truly is used in the USA but rarely in the UK.

Ex 3:
1 A spoken   B written or spoken
2 A spoken   B written
3 A spoken   B written
4 A written or spoken   B spoken
5 A written   B written or spoken
6 A spoken   B written or spoken

Ex 4: *Suggested answer:* (66 words)
Dear Ms Daley
I am writing to enquire about your latest photocopiers. We are currently renting a model from you however we would now like to purchase one.
I would be very grateful if you could send us a copy of your brochure and any relevant product literature. Would it also be possible for you to send us a current price list?
I look forward to hearing from you.
Yours sincerely

Ex 5: *Suggested answer:* (76 words)
Thank you for your letter of 5 April.
As requested, I am sending you a copy of our brochure and some additional literature about our range of photocopiers. I am also enclosing an up to date copy of our price list which includes details of discounts available for customers who currently rent machines from us.
If you have any questions please do not hesitate to contact me.

Ex 6: *Suggested answer:* (38 words)
Party
As you all know, Friday 23rd will be Simon's final day with us at Sonitech. In order to wish him well in his new job there will be a farewell party in Reception at 5.30. Everyone is invited.

Unit 9: Exam focus

Left Column
Part One
Suggested answer: *(38 words)*
I'm in a meeting with one of the suppliers. I'll be back at about 12.30. If Mr Jablonski calls for me, could you explain where I am and ask him when I can call him back?
Thanks

Part Two
Suggested answer: *(78 words)*
With reference to your letter of 24 September I am writing to confirm your travel and accommodation arrangements. I have reserved you a hotel room from the 24 to the 28 of October; however the company can only pay for the first four nights. If you let us have your flight details we can arrange for someone to meet you at the airport and take you to your hotel.
I look forward to hearing from you.
Yours sincerely

Right Column
Part One
Suggested answer: *(33 words)*
I am currently out of the office. I will be back on Thursday 23rd. If you have any urgent questions or problems before then please contact my colleague Andrea Humpert in our Frankfurt office.

Part Two
Suggested answer: *(77 words)*
As you know we have been having a lot of problems with our current photocopier (paper jamming etc.). I've seen an advert for a newer version, the TX200 Officepro which can also print excellent quality colour pictures and scan A4 colour documents. It's smaller than the present machine too so we would have more space in the corridor.
I think we should consider buying one, it costs €1,200 plus VAT and they can deliver in two weeks.

Unit 10a: Business hotels

Ex 1:
1 *rooms: informal, well-equipped, comfortable*
2 *service: efficient, friendly*
3 *hotel: elegant, centrally-located, quiet*

Ex 2:
2 *Wi-Fi, internet access* 3 *fitness centre*
4 *courtesy bus* 5 *single supplement*
6 *express check-in* 7 *rush hour*
8 *health club*

Ex 3:
1 *parts of a hotel: lounge, health club, fitness centre, restaurant, swimming pool, dining-room, bar*
2 *facilities in the rooms: desk, communication facilities*

Ex 4: ***Suggested answer:*** *(78 words)*
Further to your letter of 18 June I am writing to confirm the availability of four double rooms for 9–11 July. All our rooms are equipped with telephones and Wi-Fi access, the cost is $400 a night. Our business centre is open twenty-four hours a day and offers a range of facilities including presentation equipment. Please find enclosed a copy of our brochure for more details.
If you require any further information, please do not hesitate to contact me.

Unit 10b: Commuting

Ex 1:

1 C	O	2 M	M	U	T	E	3 R
		O					O
4 L	A	T	E				A
		O			5 A		D
6 P	A	R	K		C		
E		W			C		
7 T	R	A	F	F	I	C	
R		Y			D		
O					E		
8 L	A	N	E		N		
					9 T	A	X

Ex 2:
2 *Public* ***transport*** *is very good in the city where I live.*
3 *The Government's new* ***transport*** *policy won't change anything.*
4 *Sorry I'm late. I was stuck in* ***traffic*** *for hours.*
5 *There's always a* ***traffic*** *jam on the motorway in the morning.*
6 *City centre* ***traffic*** *was reduced by the park and ride scheme.*
7 *There isn't any alternative* ***transport*** *where I live.*
8 *With* ***traffic*** *growth of over 2% a year we need more roads.*

Ex 4: 1 *C* 2 *A* 3 *B* 4 *B* 5 *A*

Unit 11a: Arranging a conference

Ex 1:
2 *decide on a budget/details/a proposal*
3 *ask for a quotation/details*
4 *make a proposal*
5 *invite delegates*
6 *finalise details /a budget/ a proposal*

Ex 2:
1 *proposal* 2 *location*
3 *arranging* 4 *requirements*
5 *quotation* 6 *confirmation*

Ex 3: ***Suggested answers:***
2 *Do you have a preferred location?*
3 *Could you tell me what your budget is, please?*
4 *When do you want to hold the conference?*
5 *How long would you like it to last?*
6 *How many rooms will you need?*

Ex 4: ***Suggested answers:***
to organise *a conference* — *conference* ***organiser***
to hold *a conference* — *conference* ***programme***
conference ***package***
conference ***centre***
conference ***booking***

Ex 5: *Suggested answer: (77 words excluding salutation and closing phrase)*
Further to our telephone conversation, I am writing to confirm the Amtech marketing conference arrangements. The conference will be held at the The Central Hotel, Hong Kong. The 37 delegates will arrive for Friday dinner on 25 September and depart after Sunday lunch on 27 September. We will provide a conference room and a seminar room. I enclose a copy of the conference programme and will confirm the name of the Europa Events contact person as soon as possible.

Ex 6: *Suggested answer: (22 words)*
The marketing conference is from 25 to 27 September at The Central Hotel, Hong Kong. You should arrive in time for dinner on the Friday evening. Please confirm if you will be able to attend or not.

Unit 11b: At a conference

Ex 1: *Suggested answers:*
2 we know the number of delegates.
3 you arrive at the conference.
4 we have had the feedback session.
5 the guest speaker arrives.
6 I have finished it.

Ex 2:
2 badly-prepared   3 negative
4 useless   5 unproductive
6 boring / dull   7 unrewarding

Ex 3:
2 The conference was **easy** to organise.
3 She gave a brief (or **short**) sales presentation.
4 Some of the sessions were too **short**.
5 The hotel beds were very **soft**.
6 The journey to the restaurant was **short**.
7 The speaker was **easy** to understand.

Ex 4: 1 C   2 A   3 B   4 A   5 C

Unit 12: Exam focus

Part One:
1 B   2 A   3 A   4 C   5 A
6 C   7 C   8 B

Part Two:
9 HP420Y   10 15th
11 ten   12 17.5%
13 €176.13   14 KOSOR
15 688820

Part Three:
16 York
17 older, more mature women
18 Feel Good
19 young, modern and professional
20 price
21 14 September
22 Look Great

Part Four:
23 B   24 B   25 C   26 B
27 B   28 A   29 C   30 C

Unit 13a: Production

Ex 1:
2 The ingredients are fed into the mixers.
3 The baguettes are dropped onto a tray.
4 The baguettes are baked for ten minutes.
5 Cool air is blown over the baguettes.
6 The baguettes are packed into boxes.

Ex 2: *Suggested answer:*
First of all, the production line and sensors are checked before the line is started. If the line does not start, the sensors are re-set and the line is started again. After the line has started, the ingredients are fed into the mixers. If the mix is not correct, the mixer is cleaned out and the ingredients are fed in again. If the mix is correct, the dough is sent to the divider.

Ex 3: machines: cooler, oven, mixer
processes: mix, divide, form, bake, prove, cool, wrap, box, despatch
ingredients: water, yeast, additives

Ex 4: *Suggested answer: (21 words)*
We have experienced some problems in the packaging department. The 82K machines have not all been set correctly for the new packaging. Please ensure you check all settings before using the new packaging.

Unit 13b: Quality control

Ex 1: 2 inspection points   3 shelf-life
4 finished goods   5 goods in
6 chemical analysis

1 finished goods   2 inspection points
3 quality control   4 shelf-life
5 goods in   6 chemical analysis

Ex 2: 2 goods in   finished goods
3 rise   fall
4 reject   accept
5 reduce   increase

1 demand
2 goods in
3 finished goods
4 increase
5 suppliers
6 fall
7 rise
8 reject
9 reducing
10 accept

Answer key 155

Ex 3:   2   change   won't make/isn't going to make
        3   doesn't make   'll talk
        4   increases   'll have to/'re going to have to
        5   'll happen/'s going to happen   keep
        6   'll have to/'re going to have to   want
        7   don't arrive   'll look/'re going to look
        8   won't be/aren't/isn't going to be   increase

Ex 4:   1   H   2   A   3   E   4   B   5   C

Unit 14a: Direct service providers

Ex 1:   house, life, travel – **insurance**
        insurance – policy, line, company

Ex 2:
1   memorandum   (the others are all types of agreement)
2   claim   (the others are all something the customer pays)
3   location   (the others are all something you pay)
4   exciting   (the others are all to do with speed)
5   loan   (the others are all lines of insurance)
6   quality   (the others are all quantity)
7   provider   (others are all financial services)

Ex 3:   1   premium   2   loan
        3   broker   4   commission
        5   enquiry   6   monitor
        7   claim   8   policy
        9   supervisor

Ex 4:   1   A   2   C   3   B   4   B   5   C   6   A
        7   A   8   C   9   B   10   C   11   A

Unit 14b: The banking sector

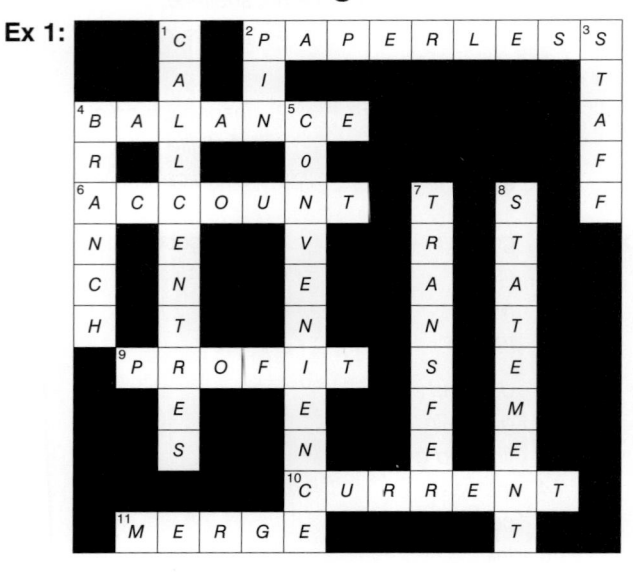

Ex 1: [crossword]
1 across: C... ; 2 across: PAPERLESS ; 3 down: ST...
4 across: BALANCE
6 across: ACCOUNT
9 across: PROFIT
10 across: CURRENT
11 across: MERGE

Ex 2:   2   transfer money   3   pay bills
        4   order a statement   5   sign a form
        6   follow instructions   7   key in a PIN number

Ex 3:   2   deal with problems
        3   invest in new technology
        4   pay for a service
        5   fill in a form
        6   note down some details

Ex 4:   1   consultant   2   two years
        3   six   4   512
        5   download

Unit 15: Exam focus

Reading
Questions 1–5
1   CLOSE & SONS
2   TIM NICHOLLS
3   10 DEC 2010
4   TEK 200
5   €3495

Writing Part One
Suggested answer: (32 words)
I'm working from home tomorrow so that I can finish preparing my presentation for the meeting on Friday. If anyone needs to contact me my home phone number is 020 8767 9289

Writing Part Two
Suggested answer: (73 words)
I think I have found a suitable hotel for the trade fair in Barcelona. It's called the Hotel Gaudi and it has special business traveller rooms with communication facilities. Moreover it is in a good location, in the city centre but only thirty-five minutes from the airport and twenty-five minutes from the exhibition centre.
If you agree, I think I should book rooms as soon as possible. Could you confirm the dates please?

Unit 16a: Delivery services

Ex: 1   2   in/within   3   on   4   in/within
        5   until   6   on   7   by   8   until

Ex: 2   1   documents   2   charge/rate
        3   vehicles   4   urgent
        5   rate/charge   6   destinations
        7   packages   8   weight

Ex: 3   1   B   2   A   3   C   4   C   5   A

Unit 16b: Trading

Ex: 1   1   enquiries, correspondence
        2   documents, specifications, a parts lists
        3   a sales network, a service, support

Ex: 2   2   C   3   H   4   B   5   A
        6   E   7   F   8   D

Ex: 3
1. Thank you for your enquiry.
2. We are pleased to quote as follows.
3. Our standard terms and conditions apply.
4. The price is quoted in euros.
5. The price does not include VAT.
6. We look forward to hearing from you.

Ex: 4 1 C 2 G 3 A 4 E 5 F

Unit 17a: Recruiting staff

Ex: 1
1. applicants
2. an application form
3. appointed
4. vacancy
5. recruit
6. candidates

Ex: 2
1. to fill, to advertise, to apply for
2. internal, external, to recruit
3. a candidate, internal applicants, workers
4. a vacancy, jobs, a position

Ex: 3 *Suggested answers:*
2. you would have to advertise.
3. I'd look for a different kind of work.
4. I'd miss my family.
5. the job was offered to you?

Ex: 4 1 D 2 E 3 F 4 B 5 C

Unit 17b: Applying for a job

Ex: 1
2. Could you tell me where you work at the moment?
3. Could you tell me if the position includes a pension?
4. Could you tell me how you heard about the vacancy?
5. Could you tell me if there is any training?
6. Could you tell me what your present salary is?

Ex: 2 personal qualities: flexibility, enthusiasm, motivation, communication skills
skills: word-processing, language, presentation, keyboard

Ex: 3
1. Please find enclosed a copy of my CV.
2. I am very interested in the position because ...
3. Since 2006 I have been working as ...
4. I am writing with reference to your advertisement ...

Ex: 4 1 B 2 B 3 A 4 C
5 A 6 C 7 B

Unit 18: Exam focus

Reading Questions 1–5
1 A 2 C 3 C 4 A 5 B

Reading Questions 6–10
6 D 7 F 8 C 9 H 10 G

Reading Questions 11–22
11 A 12 B 13 C 14 B 15 A 16 A
17 C 18 A 19 A 20 B 21 A 22 C

Reading Questions 23–27
23 Buddy Holly 24 Palace Theatre 25 3 July
26 20.00 27 6

Writing Question 28
Suggested answer: (36 words)
The company will be closed for the Christmas period from Wednesday 25 December to Thursday 2 January. If you want extra holiday please confirm the dates and fill in the holiday forms by Friday 15 November.

Writing Question 29
Suggested answer: (71 words)
I am very sorry that I have had to cancel our meeting on Friday at such short notice. This is due to the fact that my boss is off sick all week and so I am unable to leave the office.
I would like to suggest that we reschedule the meeting for next Tuesday at the same time, 10.45. Could you let me know if that would be convenient for you?

Listening Test 30–37
30 A 31 B 32 C 33 A 34 C
35 B 36 C 37 B

Listening Test 38–45
38 C 39 B 40 A 41 A 42 A
43 B 44 C 45 B

Answer key 157

Essential vocabulary

1a: Job descriptions

Jobs
- accountant
- consultant
- human resources (HR) manager
- marketing manager
- production manager
- sales executive

Work
- to work as (+ job)
- to work for (+ company)
- to work in (the food industry)

Duties
- to attend (a meeting)
- to deal with (a problem)
- to discuss (problems)
- to give (advice)
- to interview (applicants)
- to involve (+ -ing)
- to keep (a record)
- to organise (a conference)
- to provide (a service)
- to be responsible for (+ -ing)

General
- to advertise
- applicant
- to be based on
- department
- financial products
- head
- personnel

2a: Company history

Companies
- holding company
- joint venture
- parent company
- public limited company (plc)
- subsidiary

Activities
- to buy
- to expand
- to export
- to found
- to manufacture
- to merge
- to own
- to produce
- to register
- to set up
- to take over

General
- facilities
- partnership
- plant
- stake
- to survive
- turnover

4a: Telephoning

Telephone phrases
- Can I speak to ...?
- Can I have extension 204, please?
- Is Keith available?
- Who's calling?
- Hold the line, please.
- I'll put you through.
- I'm afraid the line's busy.
- I'm afraid he's not available.
- Do you know when he'll be free?
- Can I take a message?
- I'm calling about ...
- I'm returning his call.
- I'll call back later.
- I'll give him the message.
- Could you repeat that?
- Could you spell that?
- Did you say ...?
- We were cut off.
- Thank you for calling.

1b: Working conditions

Frequency
- annually
- daily
- monthly
- rarely
- weekly

Working conditions
- at (the current) rate
- bonus
- break
- day off
- employment
- equipment
- health and safety
- leave (holiday)
- line manager
- overalls
- overtime
- regulations
- salary
- shift
- supplies

General
- annoying
- to arrange
- to break down
- to consult
- efficient
- in operation
- instead of
- to review
- to run out of
- stationery

2b: Company activities

Addition
- also
- furthermore
- moreover
- not only ... but also

Contrast
- although
- however
- in spite of

Activities
- assembly
- to build
- to develop
- to distribute
- to grow
- to invest
- investment
- to modernise

General
- to attract
- attraction
- to climb
- costs
- to earn
- expertise
- flexible
- low
- model
- transport links
- to receive
- van
- wages

4b: Internal communication

Paperwork
- brochure
- diary
- memo
- note
- notice
- proposal
- receipt
- schedule

General
- appointment
- boardroom
- to cancel
- to claim
- essential
- expenses
- head office
- obligation
- prize
- quarter
- request
- requirements
- to take place

158

5a: Facts and figures

Describing trend
- to increase/increase
- to rise/rise
- to grow/growth
- to improve/improvement
- to recover/recovery
- to peak/peak
- to level off
- to remain steady
- to decrease/decrease
- to drop/drop
- to fall/fall
- sharp(ly)
- strong(ly)
- steady/steadily
- slow(ly)
- slight(ly)

General
- annual report
- brand
- income
- product launch
- range
- retail

7a: Product description

Describing products
- length (long/short)
- to be made of ...
- to measure
- size (big/small)
- to weigh
- weight (heavy/light)

General
- board game
- complicated
- difficult
- discount
- general knowledge
- instructions
- reasonable
- retailer
- to stock
- version

8a: Business equipment

Office equipment
- to copy
- to dial
- to enlarge/enlargement
- envelope
- eraser
- fax machine
- guarantee
- to jam
- operating instructions
- to overheat
- photocopier
- to print
- printer
- reduction
- to remove/removal
- scissors (pair of)
- shredder
- stapler
- to switch on/off
- video-conferencing equipment
- warranty

General
- to be careful
- convenient
- feature
- special offer
- to rent

5b: Performance

Giving reasons
- because of
- due to
- to lead to
- to result in
- that's why
- therefore

Presentations
- as you can see
- bar chart
- to draw attention to
- figure (Fig 3)
- graph
- the graph clearly shows
- to make a presentation

General
- customer satisfaction
- customer service
- delay
- to lease
- penalty
- performance
- privatisation
- to promote
- punctuality
- to reduce
- reliability
- revenue
- track
- to upgrade
- volume

7b: Product development

Product development
- to approve
- authorities
- average (on average)
- development
- to monitor
- to reach (the market)
- research & development (R & D)
- stage
- to take (+ time)
- to test

Drugs
- chemist
- disease
- healthy
- over-the-counter
- patient
- prescription
- safe
- safety
- side-effects

General
- advertising campaign
- information pack
- leaflet
- poster

8b: Correspondence

Formal letter phrases
- Thank you for your letter of ...
- With reference to ...
- I am writing to ...
- I am pleased to ...
- I am afraid that ...
- I would be grateful if you could ...
- I enclose ...
- If you require any further information, please do not hesitate to contact us.
- I look forward to hearing from you.
- Yours sincerely
- Yours faithfully
- Best wishes/regards

Abbreviations
- ASAP (as soon as possible)
- Dept (department)
- enc (enclosed)
- excl (excluding)
- incl (including)
- ext (extension number)
- NB (note well)
- re (regarding)
- wk (week)

General
- enquiry
- quotation
- seminar

Essential vocabulary 159

10a: Business hotels

Hotel
- business centre
- catering
- check-in
- communication facilities
- courtesy bus
- fitness centre
- guest
- health club
- room service
- supplement
- swimming pool

Directions
- along
- to cross
- near
- next to
- opposite
- past
- straight on

General
- centrally located
- comfortable
- desk
- lighting
- rush hour
- well-equipped
- Wi-Fi access

11a: Arranging a conference

Conference
- to arrange (a conference)
- to hold (a conference)
- to ask for (a quotation)
- to decide on (a budget)
- to finalise (details)
- to invite (delegates)
- to make a (proposal)
- conference booking
- conference centre
- conference organiser
- conference package
- conference programme
- conference room

General
- access
- accommodation
- to confirm
- duration
- location
- projector
- suitable
- workshop

13a: Production

Process
- to bake
- to box
- to check
- to collect
- to cool
- to despatch
- to divide
- to feed
- to form
- to mix
- to weigh
- to wrap

General
- circuit
- to damage
- dough
- electronic
- human
- production line
- ingredients
- mechanical
- oven
- sensor
- shape
- tray

10b: Commuting

Transport
- accident
- commuter
- fuel
- lane
- motorway
- pay-as-you-drive
- park and ride
- pedestrian zone
- petrol
- public transport
- stuck in traffic
- traffic jam
- traffic lights

General
- to affect
- effect
- affordable
- government
- note
- change
- pavement
- policy
- to share
- smart card
- tax

11b: At a conference

Conference
- delegate
- feedback
- guest speaker
- report
- session
- venue

Activities
- brief
- busy
- exciting
- hard
- heated
- helpful
- intelligent
- interesting
- positive
- productive
- professional
- rewarding
- serious
- useful
- well-prepared

General
- to last
- to perform
- target

13b: Quality control

Quality control
- to analyse
- analysis
- to inspect
- to reject
- to sample

Factory
- capacity
- finished goods
- goods in
- packaging
- shelf-life
- supplier
- warehouse

General
- demand
- flavouring
- hygiene
- quality
- quantity
- soft
- taste
- workforce

14a: Direct service providers

Insurance
- broker
- claim
- commission
- policy
- premium

General
- call centre
- competitor
- competition
- direct provider
- loan
- mortgage
- outsource
- offshore
- response
- supervisor

16a: Delivery services

Delivery service
- aircraft
- carrier
- charge
- delivery
- document
- electronic tracking
- express
- network
- package
- parcel
- shipment
- vehicle

General
- commitment
- to rely on
- urgent
- worldwide

17a: Recruiting staff

Recruitment
- application (form)
- to apply (for)
- to appoint
- blue-collar worker
- white-collar staff
- clerical job
- curriculum vitae (CV)
- employment agency
- external
- internal
- to fill (a vacancy)
- to place (an advertisement)
- position
- to promote
- to recruit
- recruitment
- to get rid of
- to take on
- vacancy

14b: The banking sector

Banking
- balance
- bank account
- bank statement
- branch
- current account
- PIN number
- sort code
- to transfer money

General
- to compete (with)
- date of birth
- to fill in (a form)
- to follow (instructions)
- to finance
- IT (information technology)
- merger
- PC (personal computer)
- postcode
- redundancy
- sector
- to warn

16b: Trading

Import agent
- ex works
- invoice
- packing
- to quote
- parts list
- spare parts
- specifications

General
- availability
- fair
- receipt
- skill
- technically advanced
- to translate

17b: Applying for a job

Applying for a job
- degree
- experience
- graduate
- to graduate
- higher education
- marital status
- nationality
- permanent
- temporary
- qualifications

Skills & qualities
- bilingual
- communication skills
- enthusiastic
- keyboard skills
- motivated

General
- honest
- to lie
- software package
- weakness
- words per minute (wpm)

Essential vocabulary

Irregular verbs

become	became	become	know	knew	known
begin	began	begun	leave	left	left
break	broke	broken	lend	lent	lent
bring	brought	brought	lose	lost	lost
build	built	built	make	made	made
buy	bought	bought	mean	meant	meant
catch	caught	caught	meet	met	met
come	came	come	pay	paid	paid
cost	cost	cost	read	read	read
cut	cut	cut	rise	rose	risen
drink	drank	drunk	say	said	said
drive	drove	driven	see	saw	seen
eat	ate	eaten	sell	sold	sold
fall	fell	fallen	send	sent	sent
feel	felt	felt	show	showed	shown
find	found	found	shut	shut	shut
fly	flew	flown	sleep	slept	slept
forget	forgot	forgotten	speak	spoke	spoken
get	got	got	stand	stood	stood
give	gave	given	take	took	taken
go	went	gone	tell	told	told
grow	grew	grown	think	thought	thought
hear	heard	heard	understand	understood	understood
hold	held	held	win	won	won
keep	kept	kept	write	wrote	written